CHILDREN OF DARKNESS AND LIGHT

CHILDREN OF DARKNESS AND LIGHT

Lori Vallow and Chad Daybell:
A Story of Murderous Faith

LORI HELLIS

PEGASUS CRIME
NEW YORK LONDON

CHILDREN OF DARKNESS AND LIGHT

Pegasus Crime is an imprint of
Pegasus Books, Ltd.
148 West 37th Street, 13th Floor
New York, NY 10018

First Pegasus Books cloth edition September 2024

Interior design by Maria Fernandez

Library of Congress Cataloging-in-Publication Data is available.

ISBN: 978-1-63936-710-8

10 9 8 7 6 5 4 3 2 1

Printed in the United States of America
Distributed by Simon & Schuster
www.pegasusbooks.com

For Charles, Tylee, JJ, and Tammy, and all those who love them.

Because "grief is just love with no place to go."

—Jaime Anderson

CONTENTS

Vallow Daybell Timeline

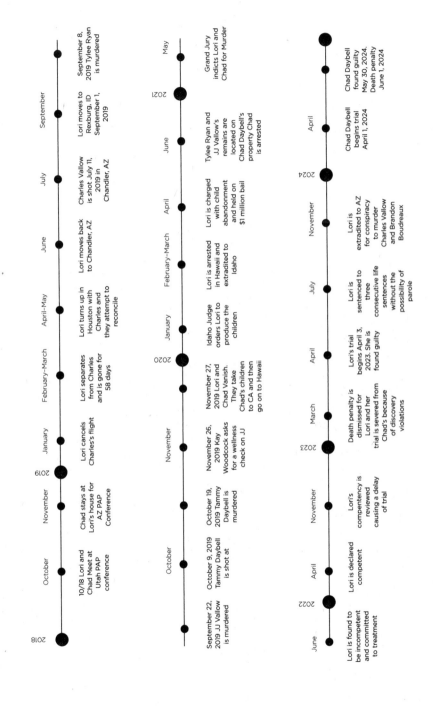

2018

- **October** — 10/18 Lori and Chad Meet at Utah PAP conference
- **November** — Chad stays at Lori's house for AZ PAP Conference
- **2019 January** — Lori cancels Charles's flight
- **February–March** — Lori separates from Charles and is gone for 58 days
- **April-May** — Lori turns up in Houston with Charles and they attempt to reconcile
- **June** — Lori moves back to Chandler, AZ
- **July** — Charles Vallow is shot July 11, 2019 in Chandler, AZ
- **September** — Lori moves to Rexburg, ID September 1, 2019
- **September 8, 2019** Tylee Ryan is murdered

- **September 22, 2019** JJ Vallow is murdered
- **October** — October 9, 2019 Tammy Daybell is shot at
- October 19, 2019 Tammy Daybell is murdered
- **November** — November 26, 2019 Kay Woodcock asks for a wellness check on JJ
- November 27, 2019 Lori and Chad Vanish. They take Chad's children to CA and then go on to Hawaii
- **2020 January** — Idaho Judge orders Lori to produce the children
- **February–March** — Lori is arrested in Hawaii and extradited to Idaho
- **April** — Lori is charged with child abandonment and held on $1 million bail
- **June** — Tylee Ryan and JJ Vallow's remains are located on Chad Daybell's property Chad is arrested
- **2021 May** — Grand Jury indicts Lori and Chad for Murder

- **2022 June** — Lori is found to be incompetent and committed to treatment
- **April** — Lori is declared competent
- **November** — Lori's competency is reviewed causing a delay of trial
- **2023 March** — Death penalty is dismissed for Lori and her trial is severed from Chad's because of discovery violations
- **April** — Lori's trial begins April 3, 2023. She is found guilty
- **July** — Lori is sentenced to three consecutive life sentences without the possibility of parole
- **November** — Lori is extradited to AZ for conspiracy to murder Charles Vallow and Brandon Boudreaux
- **2024 April** — Chad Daybell begins trial April 1, 2024
- Chad Daybell found guilty May 30, 2024. Death penalty June 1, 2024

PROLOGUE

GUILTY

Doesn't everything die at last, and too soon?
Tell me, what is it you plan to do
With your one wild and precious life?

—Mary Oliver

The wind blew ceaselessly, and spring came in small, faltering steps as Lori Vallow's murder trial began on April 3, 2023, in Boise, Idaho. That first morning, the tulips in the planters outside the Ada County Courthouse were folded into tight buds, shivering with every gust of wind and pelt of snow. Five and a half weeks later, as crowds milled on the courthouse steps on verdict watch, the sun shone, but the same ever-present wind playfully swirled pink and white petals from the flowering trees. Camera crews brushed away drifts of the blossoms that accumulated around their equipment.

The prosecutors claimed the case was about money, sex, and power, but from the beginning, it was about so much more. The jury couldn't hide their shock when the twisted details of Lori Vallow and Chad Daybell's doomsday beliefs emerged. Stories of demon possession, zombies, and past lives took the fact finders by surprise; this would be no ordinary murder trial. Day after day, the jurors reported to a remote parking lot where a bus picked them up and transported them to the courthouse. They entered through a private door in the basement, while above, crowds of media and court watchers waited in line to file through the metal detectors. Cameras were not permitted in Lori Vallow's trial. Each morning at 8:30 A.M., those who wanted to view the trial in person logged into a website to reserve their seat for the following day. Tickets for the sixty seats in the courtroom were usually gone within two minutes. Those who didn't get a seat in the courtroom got a ticket for the overflow room, where they could view the trial on a closed-circuit broadcast. The court released audio recordings each day after the trial adjourned.

The much-anticipated trial had been expected to last ten weeks, but last-minute legal maneuvers shortened the time needed when the judge dismissed the death penalty for Lori and ordered her trial severed from Chad's.

After five and a half weeks of trial, the case went to the jury, who deliberated for just seven hours. Then the usual low hum of conversation among trial watchers and media swelled to a buzz. The jury had reached a verdict.

Lori Vallow was guilty.

Guilty of murdering her sixteen-year-old daughter, Tylee Ryan; guilty of murdering her seven-year-old autistic son, JJ Vallow; guilty of conspiring to murder her lover's forty-nine-year-old wife, Tammy Daybell.

Guilty.

1

THE SCATTERED TRIBES

The story of Lori Vallow and Chad Daybell's murderous faith is, at its heart, a Mormon story. Their motives can only be understood by first understanding the milieu they grew up in and the underlying beliefs that guided their lives. They were each raised in devout families as members of The Church of Jesus Christ of Latter-day Saints, and their story is one facet of a much larger story about the ongoing battle for the soul of the Mormon Church. Membership in The Church of Jesus Christ of Latter-day Saints is a culture as much as a religion. Church members typically gravitate toward fellow Church members both socially and in business. Their children attend Church-sponsored activities and are encouraged to socialize with other children from their faith, creating an insulated bubble where Church members live their lives.

In recent years, the mainstream Church of Jesus Christ of Latter-day Saints and its members have tried to distance themselves from the Mormon label, preferring instead to emphasize their identification with Jesus Christ. However, as used in this book, the term Mormon refers to the belief system devised by Joseph Smith Jr. in the nineteenth century. The overarching name for this belief system is also sometimes called the Latter-day Saint Movement and encompasses the more than seventy-five organizations that follow the teachings of Joseph Smith Jr. Mormon believers view Joseph Smith Jr. (December 23, 1805–June 27, 1844) as a prophet. They believe his written revelations and his translation of the Book of Mormon, which he claimed to have found on golden plates, are gospel. The largest, most widely known Mormon group is The Church of Jesus Christ of Latter-day Saints, which claims seventeen million members worldwide, although non-Church experts believe that number is closer to eight million. It is also known as the mainstream church, the LDS Church, or the Brighamite church. As used here, the term "Mormon" also includes the churches and denominations that have split or spun off from the Latter-day Saint Movement since its founding in Fayette, New York, on April 6, 1830. Some of the more familiar include the Church of Christ, the Community of Christ (formerly the Reorganized Church of Jesus Christ of Latter-day Saints), the Church of Christ (Temple Lot), and the Fundamental Church of Jesus Christ of Latter-day Saints (FLDS). While the mainstream church has gone out of its way to distance itself from the very public cases of neo-fundamentalists, including that of Chad Daybell and Lori Vallow, most of Chad and Lori's beliefs were drawn directly from either current or historical Mormon teachings.

The history of the Mormon Church is complicated, steeped as it is in the superstitious beliefs of the mid-nineteenth century. It was founded when people embraced folk healing and divination but were also influenced by early scientific discovery. While Joseph Smith Jr. claimed he saw both God the Father and Jesus Christ for the first time in 1820, as *The Legend of Sleepy Hollow* was published, he only spoke about his first vision in 1830, when Edgar Allan Poe's horror stories were becoming popular. Bands of Romani travelers roamed in colorful wagons, told fortunes, and spun folktales on the outskirts of towns, and there were constant rumors of this lost Spanish mine or that treasure of buried coins. Water witches, or diviners, dowsed for the perfect spots to drill wells, and Joseph Smith Jr. worked with his father searching for buried money using amulets, divining rods, and seer stones. While there is no record of either Smith leading anyone to treasure, for a time, there seemed to be no shortage of people willing to pay them for the effort.

In 1830, Joseph Smith Jr. claimed for the first time, that, in 1820, Jesus Christ and God the Father appeared to him in person in the woods of Palmyra, New York, to forgive his sins, and reported that in 1823, an angel named Moroni showed him the location of a book made of golden plates. Moroni then appeared for the next five years, each time on the autumnal equinox.

LDS Church scholars contend Joseph Smith Jr. was an uneducated farm boy inspired and directed by God to create the Book of Mormon by translating "reformed Egyptian" text from golden plates using a seer stone in a hat. No known "reformed Egyptian" language exists. The church's insistence that Smith Jr. was ignorant and virtually illiterate supports their claim that he could only have produced the Book of Mormon with divine inspiration and direct intervention from God. Others are skeptical; they point to Smith Jr.'s intelligence, curiosity, and substantial educational opportunities. Joseph Smith Sr. and Lucy Mack Smith's children were known for their prodigious intelligence and curiosity. Joseph's older brother, Hyrum, attended Moore's Academy and later Dartmouth College while still in his teens. While recovering from a severe infection in his leg, Joseph Smith Jr. spent months with Hyrum, who schooled him. Smith Jr., having no other way to understand his natural intellect, attributed it to the divine. Biographer Fawn M. Brodie wrote of Smith Jr., "Far from being the fruit of an obsession, the Book of Mormon is a useful key to Joseph's complex and frequently baffling character. For it clearly reveals in him what both orthodox Mormon histories and unfriendly testimony deny him: a measure of learning and a fecund imagination. The Mormon Church has exaggerated the ignorance of its prophet since the more meager his learning, the more divine must be his book."[1]

The region around Palmyra, New York, was rife with religious enthusiasm, and Smith Jr. became interested in spirituality at a young age. His mother, Lucy Mack Smith, was a pious woman who became a lifelong adherent of her son's church. She encouraged and fed her son's early religious interest with biblical scriptures and stories. Smith Jr. came of age during the era known as the Second Great Awakening. Camp meetings and revivals were common, and the theology of the moment was decidedly postmillennial, with preachers claiming the return of Jesus Christ was imminent. Smith Jr. had unbridled curiosity, infectious charm, and what appears to be a photographic memory. When coupled with his keen interest in religion, those attributes easily account for his knowledge of the Bible and other philosophical and historical texts. Critics of the Book of Mormon point out the many historical anachronisms and similarities to other writings that border on outright plagiarism. While Smith Jr. encouraged the myth that he was a simple, nearly illiterate farm boy, in 1833, he founded a group called the School of the Prophets. Smith Jr. began studying Hebrew and English grammar with C. G. Webb, who remarked, "Joseph was the calf that sucked three cows. He acquired knowledge very rapidly."[2]

Joseph Smith Jr. claimed that although the angel Moroni first showed him the golden plates in 1823, he was only permitted to touch them once the angel was convinced his greed would not overtake his pious belief. Joseph Smith Jr. married Emma Hale Smith in 1827, and she was with him when he claimed to have finally recovered the golden plates; at his direction, Emma turned her back while he retrieved the sacred pages, which he said were contained in a stone box. During that visit, Moroni also reportedly gave Smith Jr. special "spectacles" that were made of two seer stones Smith Jr. called Urim and Thummim, which he used to translate the plates.

With the help of Emma and several of his followers, Smith Jr. translated the text inscribed on the plates using the seer stones. According to some reports, Smith Jr. said he would go behind a curtain, take the plates out of a box, and set them nearby while he placed a seer stone in the bottom of a hat. When he put his face in the hat, he could see the translated text, which he dictated to a scribe on the other side of the curtain. Three of those scribes signed statements claiming that an angel had shown them the golden plates. Later, eight witnesses claimed Smith Jr. himself showed them the plates and allowed them to handle them. These attestations are still printed on the front of every Book of Mormon. Conveniently, Smith Jr. reported he returned the golden plates to the angel in 1829, and no proof of their existence has ever been found.

According to Joseph Smith Jr., when he was fourteen, he prayed to God, asking which church was true. Heavenly Father and Jesus visited him and told him he must not join any existing church because all had strayed from the true word of God.[3] Smith would later teach that the Mormon Church was the one true faith restored to God's original intent. Mormons, therefore, claim Mormonism is a restoration and not a reformation of previous churches.

Unique to the Mormon Church, Joseph Smith Jr. said God gave him the "priesthood keys." He taught that the priesthood was the power and authority of God through which He created and governed the heavens and Earth. God extended this priesthood to men to act in "all things necessary for the salvation of God's children."[4] According to the LDS Church, God has conveyed to each man the keys of the priesthood sufficient to complete his work on Earth. Only the president of the church, who is also the prophet, seer, and revelator, is endowed by God to exercise all priesthood keys. In general, the priesthood keys are broken down into three categories: (1) keys bestowed upon the apostles (the leaders of the church), (2) keys bestowed on a president or other leader, and (3) general priesthood keys. Each key is endowed upon a man (women cannot hold the Aaronic or Melchizedek priesthoods, so they are not endowed with priesthood keys) depending on his individual calling in the church. Priesthood keys are best thought of as spiritual power. For example, a man may be called to be a temple sealer. He is given the authority to perform the sealing ceremony but not the authority to determine which couples are worthy of being married (sealed) in the temple. Priesthood keys are delegations of spiritual authority for a specific purpose or a designated period. Every man endowed first with the Aaronic priesthood and later the Melchizedek priesthood who honors their covenants is eligible to receive the priesthood key of personal revelation and become an heir of God.

Joseph Smith Jr. continued to receive divine revelations, which he compiled and codified in the book known as Doctrine and Covenants. His continued revelations caused some of the first unrest in the developing church. When Smith Jr. translated the Book of Mormon, he said God had only given him the power of revelation until the book was finished. Later, after the Book of Mormon was completed, when he claimed a continued role as the mouthpiece of God, translating and imparting new revelations to his followers, some suspected Smith Jr. had become drunk with power.

Then, on July 6, 1835, Joseph Smith Jr. bought four Egyptian mummies from a traveling show in Kirtland, Ohio. The mummies, which an oddities dealer was exhibiting, were accompanied by fragments of papyrus containing Egyptian pictographic text that Smith Jr. claimed only he could translate. It was the papyrus Smith Jr. wanted, but when the peddler refused to sell the scrolls without the bodies, Smith bought both. According to Smith Jr., the papyrus contained hieroglyphics that recounted the Book of Abraham, a text he published in the part of the Mormon canon called the Pearl of Great Price. This volume also includes the Book of Moses, Joseph Smith Jr.'s biography, and the church's Articles of Faith. Along with the Book of Mormon, Doctrine and Covenants, and the Revised King James Bible (as revised by Smith Jr.), it makes up the canon of LDS scripture. When Smith Jr. purchased the mummies and their scrolls, Egyptian pictographic language had long been thought untranslatable, and Smith Jr. must have thought he was on safe ground, reporting that God had given him the power to translate it. However, the Rosetta Stone had already been deciphered in 1822 by French scholar Jean-François Champollion, but the news had not yet reached Smith in America by 1835.

The Book of Abraham contains some of the faith's most explosive doctrines and troubling anachronisms. According to experts, the papyrus fragments were not even created until the third-century B.C.E., a full six hundred years after Abraham's biblical life and death. Modern Egyptian scholars say the papyrus fragments are typical funerary inscriptions meant to introduce a departed soul to Osiris, the God of the afterlife. [5] Not a single one of the papyrus fragments mentions the name of Abraham. Still, it is the Book of Abraham that gave LDS theology its unique teachings on premortality, the priesthood, the star Kolob, which is described as a celestial body near the throne of God and from which the Lord's time is reckoned, communal living, the belief that there is a plurality of gods and that human men can become gods through exaltation, the claim that African Americans are the Black-skinned descendants of Ham and his father, Canaan, the cursed son of Noah, and, of course, polygamy. Smith Jr. used the Book of Abraham to prove his emerging cosmology. While critics point out the convenience of Joseph discovering the papyrus just as his ideas around polygamy and his experiments with communism began to coalesce, Church apologists take the opposite approach in the which-came-first question, claiming that the discovery of the papyrus inspired Smith Jr.'s ideas.

The touchiest of those claims is Smith Jr.'s assertion that God commanded Abraham to take his barren wife, Sarah's handmaid, Hagar, as a second wife. The custom of the time in Mesopotamia was for a wife unable to conceive children to offer her handmaid as a surrogate. According to the law of the time, any child born to the handmaid would have legally been the child of Abraham and Sarah.[6] The Bible story does not include God commanding Abraham to take Hagar as a wife. The later blessing of Abraham and Sarah with the late-in-life birth of their son, Isaac, would have been irrelevant if Abraham already had an alternate wife. However, Joseph Smith Jr. laid the foundation for polygamy with his translation of the Book of Abraham and then followed it with the revelation contained in Doctrine and Covenants 132. The relevant passage from Smith Jr.'s Book of Abraham reads:

> God commanded Abraham, and Sarah gave Hagar to Abraham to wife. And why did she do it? Because this was the law, and from Hagar sprang many people. This, therefore, was fulfilling, among other things, the promises. Was Abraham, therefore, under condemnation? Verily I say unto you, Nay; for I, the Lord commanded it ... Abraham received concubines, and they bore him children; and it was accounted unto him for righteousness, because they were given unto him, and he abode in my law ...[7]

Smith Jr. had been married to Emma for a few years when he became interested in their pretty young housemaid, Fanny Alger. Smith Jr. later claimed he received a revelation that God wanted him to "restore" the practice of polygamy as early as 1834. However, Smith Jr. said he resisted God's prompting until 1842, when he finally acquiesced to Heavenly Father's directive. Smith Jr.'s contemporaries report a different timeline, as sometime in 1835, Smith asked Fanny's uncle, Levi Hancock, to act as an intermediary with Fanny's father to ask for her hand. Smith Jr. encountered a minor impediment to his suit: he was already married to Emma. Despite that, Fanny was secretly "sealed" to Smith Jr. Sometime in 1836, Emma caught Fanny and Smith Jr. together in the barn in an intimate act, and, ignoring Joseph's claim that he was also married to Fanny, Emma threw Fanny out of the Smith home. A few months later, Fanny moved to Missouri with her family, where she married Solomon Custer two months after her arrival. Joseph's only legal wife, Emma, remained uneasy with what Joseph called "celestial marriage" or "spiritual wifery," but her discomfort did not stop Smith Jr. from taking other wives. By July 12, 1843, when Joseph Smith Jr. finally dictated his revelation promoting polygamy, later codified in Church law as Doctrine and Covenants Section 132, he had already married several other women. Smith Jr.'s polygamy revelation includes a caution directed personally at Emma: "And I command mine handmaid, Emma Smith, to abide and cleave unto my servant Joseph, and to none else. But if she will not abide this commandment, she shall be destroyed, saith the Lord; for I am the Lord thy God, and will destroy her if she abide not in my law."[8] Some have speculated that the revelation was in reply to a threat from Emma that she might also take other husbands. Still, most interpret it as God directing Emma to remain with Smith Jr. whether he took other wives or not. When read with the rest of the revelation, it's clear that Smith Jr. was telling the faithful they could either get on board with the idea or be destroyed.

There was no more significant or disruptive development in LDS theology than polygamy. Joseph Smith Jr.'s plans for polygamy began in secret almost as soon as he created the Book of Mormon in 1830. In 1831, he endorsed the idea that elders in Missouri should take plural wives among Native Americans. In March 1832, Smith Jr. and his follower Sidney

Rigdon were tarred and feathered by a mob in Hiram, Ohio. Later reports suggested it was punishment for Smith Jr.'s romantic interest in a local young woman. Some of Smith Jr.'s wives were as young as fourteen. When Smith Jr. finally recorded his revelation about plural marriage in 1843, the church openly practiced polygamy for the next forty-seven years.

By the time "the principle," as the faithful call polygamy, was published in 1843, Smith Jr. and many of his friends and advisers had been publicly denying that the church engaged in polygamy while practicing it in secret for years. At the time of Smith Jr.'s death, scholars identified with certainty twenty-eight wives but say he may have taken as many as forty-nine. Some of Smith Jr.'s wives were already married to other living husbands when Joseph claimed them, and the women continued living with their husbands after their marriages to Smith Jr., thus also introducing polyandry to the faith, but only so long as a woman's second husband was the prophet. Smith Jr.'s marriages were not, as some Church apologists suggest, purely spiritual; there is ample anecdotal evidence that Smith had sex with the women he married.

Often overlooked in Mormon history is that Joseph Smith Jr. advocated an economic system for his church based on "the Law of Consecration." Joseph Smith Jr. called it the United Order but sometimes called it the Order of Enoch. The idea was a form of communism, where every member gave all their property to the church, which managed it for the benefit of all members and distributed it "according to his wants and needs, inasmuch as his wants are just."[9] The Mormons were not the only religious group of the time to toy with a communal economy. The Campbellites and the Shakers also ascribed to forms of religious communism. The experiment was short-lived, and by the time Smith and his followers moved to Nauvoo, Illinois, in 1839, they had all but abandoned the idea.

Smith Jr. and his followers of that time had a reputation for skirting the truth, borrowing money they could not repay, and dealing dishonestly in land and business transactions. The locals in the communities they settled disliked them almost as much as they disliked the Romani "Gypsies" and often responded similarly by drumming the Mormons out of their towns, tarring and feathering, prosecuting, and even murdering them. Less than a year after Smith Jr. memorialized polygamy in Doctrine and Covenants Section 132, he and his brother, Hyrum, reported to the Carthage, Illinois, jail to stand trial for inciting a riot. Followers John Taylor and Willard Richards accompanied them to the jail. Their cell was an upstairs room in a reinforced brick building. Many townsfolk resented that Smith Jr. and his followers seemed to escape conviction repeatedly, and two days later, on June 27, 1844, a vigilante mob stormed the jail, seeking to mete out their own form of justice. When Smith Jr.'s brother, Hyrum, tried to block the door, he was killed instantly by a gunshot to the face. Smith Jr. fired several shots from a pistol while crouching in the second-story window before he was shot and fell two stories to his death. The faithful viewed Smith Jr.'s martyrdom as validation that he had been their prophet and revelator. Joseph Smith Jr.'s sudden death in June of 1844 threatened to shatter the fledgling church, causing the first of many splits. There was no succession plan for the faithful, and a bitter fight ensued, with Joseph's widow, Emma Hale Smith, and her young son, Joseph Smith III, on one side and Brigham Young on the other. Young ultimately won control of the largest faction of the church.

Brigham Young was baptized into the LDS Church just a year after its founding. In 1833, following the death of his first wife, Young moved to Kirtland, Ohio, with his two young daughters to follow Joseph Smith. He was a devoted missionary and became a member of Smith's Quorum of the Twelve Apostles, traveling worldwide to bring new members into the church. Young enthusiastically embraced polygamy. Although the modern Church downplays its polygamous history and claims Young was only doing his duty, it's undisputed that he had at least fifty-five wives. Seeking to escape the persecution that dogged the early Mormons, Young devised a plan to move his followers to a place where they could establish a religious state. He left Nauvoo, Illinois, in early 1846, leading a group of 147 settlers. They wintered in a camp along the Missouri River and arrived in the Great Salt Lake Valley on July 24, 1847. Within a few years, the valley's population swelled to 250,000 as the religious stronghold became a bustling city. In 1849, Brigham Young officially established the State of Deseret, which was organized as Joseph Smith Jr. had envisioned it to be, a "theodemocracy" with Young as governor. Their utopia was short-lived when the unincorporated area became the Utah territory a year later. The US government appointed Young territorial governor, but the incorporation into the United States began a contentious and bloody era.

Joseph Smith Jr. and Brigham Young were as unalike as any two men could be. Where Smith had been a charming and charismatic prophet, Young was a dour, pragmatic administrator. As such, Young accomplished many things Smith could not, bringing order and organization to the early church. Technological advances helped further the church's progress. Both trains and the telegraph were invented during Brigham Young's lifetime, and as state after state joined the United States, communication and transportation inched across the continent. Brigham Young is credited with bringing railway transportation and the telegraph to Salt Lake City.

The unincorporated areas of the United States drew other kinds of outcasts, too, including outlaws and African Americans escaping slavery. Joseph Smith Jr. admitted a handful of African American men to the priesthood before his death, but Young banned all men of color from holding the priesthood. Brigham Young taught that Adam, the biblical progenitor of humanity, was also God the Father. Young's assertion that Adam was also God the Father is one of the early Smith Jr.-era Church's unusual and disputed teachings. Although the modern LDS Church has long denied it, vestiges of Young's ideas still permeate current doctrine. Young taught that Adam had once been a man on another planet where he had died and been resurrected. Adam came to this Earth "and brought Eve, one of his wives, with him."[10] They purposely ate from the forbidden fruit so that their bodies would become mortal, and they could engender human children. During a speech at the church's annual General Conference, Young said that Adam, and not the Holy Spirit, was the physical and spiritual father of Jesus Christ.[11] At the same General Conference on April 9, 1852, Wilford Woodruff, then Church historian, recorded in his journal, "And when the Virgin Mary was begotten with child it was by the Father and in no other way only as we were begotten." In other words, Adam, who is the Heavenly Father of our world, had sexual intercourse with Mary to conceive Jesus Christ. A hundred years later, Church apologists would try to pass off the Adam-as-God teaching as a joke. However, many in the fundamentalist community still teach this doctrine, and the idea that each faithful Saint is progressing toward godhood, as Adam did, is accepted as mainstream belief.

Independent fundamentalist writer Ogden Kraut (1927–2002) is often credited as the father of modern neo-Mormon fundamentalism. Although Kraut was never affiliated with any particular sect, he believed, as many fundamentalists do, that the contemporary LDS Church has departed from its essential teachings. He advocated for a return to the unadulterated teachings of Joseph Smith Jr. and Brigham Young, including the Adam-God doctrine.

Much of Brigham Young's teaching drew from Joseph Smith Jr.'s controversial Book of Abraham, which Young wholeheartedly embraced. Brigham Young has also been credited with introducing the doctrine known as "blood atonement." Mainstream Christianity teaches that the sacrifice of Jesus Christ on the cross atoned for all sin and that forgiveness only requires acceptance. But within Mormon teaching, there is a suggestion that some sins are too heinous for even Jesus Christ's sacrifice on the cross to atone for, arguing instead that some sins can only be atoned for by spilling the sinner's blood on the ground. Like many ideas, the history of the doctrine and the truth about the practice are shrouded by Mormon revisionist history. According to sixth LDS president Joseph Fielding Smith Jr., who was Joseph Smith Jr.'s nephew, blood atonement was a penalty imposed upon a sinner for murdering another human being. Joseph Fielding Smith Jr. denied that the church practiced blood atonement, claiming the idea that the church would blood atone apostates arose when other doctrines became conflated.

Joseph Fielding Smith Jr. contended the early church, like many religions, condoned the death penalty for murder. He says his uncle, Joseph Smith Jr., and early church leaders were also prone to hyperbole, using colorful and dramatic language, such as "destroyed" or "spilled blood," to emphasize their points. Both Joseph Smith Jr. and Brigham Young often threatened apostates and those who opposed them with "destruction." Until 1930, the LDS temple endowment ceremony included the pledge, "We, and each of us, covenant and promise that we will not reveal any of the secrets of this, the first token of the Aaronic priesthood, with its accompanying name, sign or penalty. Should we do so; we agree that our throats be cut from ear to ear and our tongues torn out by their roots." Although the admonition was modified in 1930, it wasn't entirely stricken from the liturgy until 1990. The temple ritual included a hand motion that pantomimed slicing the throat. Church apologists liken it to "may Heaven strike me dead" or "cross my heart and hope to die." Joseph Fielding Smith Jr. claimed these ideas were combined to create the persistent rumor that the church supports killing people guilty of apostasy. President Joseph Fielding Smith Jr. addressed the issue during his 1954–1956 tenure, [12] calling such rumors "a damnable falsehood for which accusers must answer." Still, it is essential to point out that a hundred years earlier, Brigham Young said, "Now take a person in this congregation . . . and suppose that he is overtaken in a gross fault, that he has committed a sin that he knows will deprive him of that exaltation which he desires, and that he cannot attain to it without the shedding of his blood, and also knows that by having his blood shed he will atone for that sin, and be saved and exalted with the Gods, is there a man or woman in this house but what would say, 'shed my blood that I may be saved and exalted with the Gods'?" [13]

Gustive O. Larson, Professor of Church History at Brigham Young University, claimed the Mormons practiced blood atonement. "To whatever extent the preaching on blood atonement may have influenced action, it would have been in relation to Mormon disciplinary action among its own members." He points to the verbally reported case of Mr. Johnson in Cedar City, who was found guilty of adultery with his stepdaughter by a bishop's court and sentenced to death for atonement of his sin. "According to the report of reputable eyewitnesses, judgement [sic] was executed with the consent of the offender, who went to his unconsecrated grave in full confidence of salvation through the shedding of blood. Such a case, however primitive, is understandable within the meaning of the doctrine and the emotional extremes of the Reformation."[14]

Joseph Fielding Smith Jr.'s denials would do nothing to stop future Saints from committing heinous crimes in the name of the doctrine of blood atonement. As with many so-called deprecated or disavowed LDS doctrines, the echoes of the older beliefs surface in the current teachings and secret rituals, and it takes no more than a slight shift to see how blood atonement could easily become a benevolent human sacrifice. We will see echoes of the practice in the actions of Lori Vallow and Chad Daybell.

In the early days, as Brigham Young struggled to keep his church together, he and most of his followers were committed to their polygamous lifestyle. But in 1850, the United States government, now firmly in control of the newly established Utah Territory, outlawed "the principle." Church leaders fought back, insisting the Saints were being persecuted for their religious practices. Still, the federal government would not budge: the Utah Territory would not be awarded official statehood as long as the practice of polygamy was allowed. There followed forty years of friction, persecution, and terrible bloodshed until 1890 when Church president Wilford Woodruff, the prophet, seer, and revelator of the time, issued what the church calls "The Manifesto." Woodruff publicly declared, "My advice to the Latter-day Saints is to refrain from contracting any marriage forbidden by the law of the land." The Manifesto was later canonized in Doctrine and Covenants. Still, it was unclear whether later church leadership viewed the policy change as the result of divine revelation or simple practicality. The Manifesto finally cleared the way for the territory to become a state. In 1896, once it became clear the church intended to enforce the Manifesto, Utah was admitted to the Union. According to the church, the Manifesto applied only to future marriages, but faced with ongoing persecution and prosecution, many polygamist families fled to Arizona, Canada, and Mexico, where polygamist communities still exist today.

While the principle of plural marriage was polarizing, other LDS doctrines also created division and violence, including the prophecy of the

"One Mighty and Strong;" in an 1832 letter to Church leader William W. Phelps, Joseph Smith Jr. wrote:

> [I]t shall come to pass, that I, the Lord God, will send one mighty and strong, holding the scepter of power in his hand, clothed with light for a covering, whose mouth shall utter words, eternal words; while his bowels shall be a fountain of truth, to set in order the house of God, and to arrange by lot the inheritances of the Saints, whose names are found, and the names of their fathers, and of their children enrolled in the book of the law of God: while that man, who was called of God and appointed, that putteth forth his hand to steady the ark of God, shall fall by the vivid shaft of lightning . . . These things I say not of myself; therefore, as the Lord speaketh, He will also fulfill.

Smith Jr.'s revelation was later codified in Section 85 of Doctrine and Covenants.

Since that 1832 revelation, many Mormon men have claimed to be the One Mighty and Strong, and the church seems to weather a related scandal every few years. In the early 1970s, three brothers belonging to the LeBaron family each claimed to be the One. The family lived in a polygamous colony in Mexico, where they had branched off from an earlier splinter group to form the Church of the Firstborn of the Fulness [sic] of Time. Ervil LeBaron, facing disagreement with his brothers about which of them was the One, split off yet again to found his church, called the Church of the Firstborn of the Lamb of God. Ervil murdered dozens of people, including one of his own wives, two of his own children, and his brother Joel. In every case, Ervil claimed God directed him to blood atone each of them. Like Charles Manson, Ervil enlisted his followers, including his wives, to commit murders in his name; his final death toll may never be known. He was captured and sentenced to life in prison, where he died in 1981. Anna LeBaron was one of more than fifty of Ervil's children. Her book, *The Polygamist's Daughter*, tells the story of her father's religious rampage.

The 1980s gave us the Lafferty family, whose sons, Ron and Dan, were responsible for the deaths of their younger brother Allen's wife, Brenda, and their infant daughter, Erica. In 1984, the Lafferty brothers, the subject of author Jon Krakauer's bestseller, *Under the Banner of Heaven*, began studying historical Mormon texts and became convinced that Ron was the One Mighty and Strong. They also believed that their sister-in-law, Brenda Lafferty, had to be blood atoned because of the apostasy of her liberal views on the role of women in Mormon culture. Ron and Dan visited the polygamous FLDS community at Short Creek and considered spiritual wifery, but neither had taken other wives before they were apprehended and prosecuted. Ron Lafferty attempted to kill his brother Dan while they shared a Utah jail cell and later attempted suicide. Ron was sentenced to the death penalty in 1985 and asked to be executed by firing squad but died in prison of natural causes in 2019 at age seventy-eight. Dan Lafferty remains in prison, serving a life sentence.

A year later, in 1985, Mark Hoffman exploded two pipe bombs, killing two innocents, in an attempt to draw attention away from his illegal forgery activities. Hoffman, who was raised in the LDS Church, had a different motivation for his crimes. He had secretly become disenchanted with the church and, among other doctrines, wanted to disprove the idea of the One Mighty and Strong. Hoffman forged documents containing information that would reflect poorly on Church history if made public. The church paid him enormous sums for the papers, buying them to keep the unfavorable historical information from surfacing to the public. Ironically, Mark Hoffman and Ron Lafferty were prison cellmates and close friends for years.

On June 5, 2002, fourteen-year-old Elizabeth Smart was abducted from her home in Salt Lake City by Brian David Mitchell. Mitchell, who called himself Immanuel David Isaiah, believed he was the One. He and his wife, Wanda Barzee, held Smart in several wilderness encampments where they kept her shackled. Mitchell, who claimed Smart was his wife, subjected her to repeated acts of rape. She was also starved and forced to consume drugs and alcohol. Mitchell was caught after Smart's sister, Mary Katherine, realized the voice she had heard the night of Elizabeth's kidnapping was a man who had done odd jobs for her family. Elizabeth was rescued on March 12, 2003, after she was spotted with Mitchell and Barzee, who had disguised her behind a veil.

Also in 2002, Warren Steed Jeffs assumed the presidency of the Fundamental Church of Latter-day Saints (FLDS) when his father, Rulon Jeffs, died. Warren Jeffs ruled the FLDS community with an iron fist, claiming to be the One Mighty and Strong. This is the community with its primary settlement straddling the Arizona-Utah border, where women wear pastel prairie-style dresses that cover them from neck to wrist and ankle and sport a trademark hairstyle characterized by a tall wave in front that finishes in a long braid down their backs. Most Mormon adults wear religious undergarments once they have received their temple ordinances, but in the case of the FLDS, the garments are long-sleeved long johns that bear religious symbols. The garments, worn by the Mormon faithful even on the hottest days of summer, are believed to protect the wearer from evil. In the mainstream Mormon Church, the garments have been abbreviated to resemble bicycle shorts and a cap-sleeved T-shirt.

FLDS communities practice polygamy, and their prophet dictates which couples marry and when. Girls as young as twelve were married to men old enough to be their great-grandfathers. The prior patriarch and FLDS prophet, seer, and revelator, Rulon Jeffs, was reported to have sixty-five wives when he died at age ninety-two. His son, Warren, who is the current prophet, punishes members by stripping them of their wives and families and reassigning wives and children to other men. While Hildale-Colorado City (which the faithful call Short Creek) is the largest settlement, FLDS communities exist in Texas; British Columbia, Canada; and northern Mexico. Jeffs began a building project outside El Dorado, Texas, with plans to create a massive FLDS compound with its own temple. He called the project Yearning for Zion Ranch (YFZ). Women and children were known to disappear in the night from Short Creek only to surface later at YFZ. Texas officials became involved over child welfare concerns and removed 416 children from their families, believing the children were in danger. The children were returned later, and the child welfare concerns were never substantiated.

However, the raid and the attendant search of the ranch unearthed damning evidence against Jeffs, including recordings of him ceremonially raping two of his child brides, ages twelve and fourteen. In 2011, Jeffs was convicted of two counts of sexual assault of a child and sentenced to life in prison with the possibility of parole in 2038. Many of his children have reported that Jeffs sexually abused them while they were very young. Jeffs continues to run the FLDS community from his jail cell—the deserted 1,691-acre tract of land known as YFZ was seized by the state of Texas in 2015.

The Daybell murders are this generation's notorious Mormon case. To explain how Chad and Lori were influenced by LDS doctrine, it's necessary first to understand what the mainstream Church teaches. There can be disagreement within the church and among outside scholars about the substance of LDS belief because the church has repudiated some past teachings that it now considers deprecated or disavowed doctrines. The following is a compilation of contemporary Church of Jesus Christ of Latter-day Saints beliefs drawn from the LDS Church website and other official LDS sources:

- The Mormon faith is the one true faith, and the Book of Mormon is true.
- The followers of Joseph Smith are descended from one of the lost tribes of Israel and are, therefore, Israelites. Non-members are referred to as "gentiles."
- Native Americans are also descendants of ancient Israelites who came to the American continent in boats. After his crucifixion, Jesus Christ appeared to them and taught them the true doctrine of the church.
- There are three levels of heaven: the celestial, terrestrial, and telestial. Only those admitted to the highest level of the celestial kingdom live in God's presence. Bad people will go to the telestial kingdom, good non-Mormons will go to the terrestrial kingdom, and faithful Mormons will go to the celestial kingdom. There are also levels within the celestial kingdom, and only those

who gain the highest level and practice polygamy will become gods and be able to beget their own spirit children.

- A woman can only enter the celestial kingdom if she is married and her husband calls her by her secret temple name. Her salvation depends on her husband's priesthood authority. Faithful unmarried women become servants in the celestial kingdom.

- During a person's lifetime, they must achieve specific benchmarks. First, a young boy must receive the Aaronic priesthood around age twelve. Young men are endowed with the Melchizedek priesthood at age eighteen. They must accept the Melchizedek priesthood before they can receive their temple endowment and be married in the temple. Next, both male and female young adults undergo an endowment ceremony that includes ceremonial washing and anointing. Following their endowment ceremony, the faithful don ceremonial undergarments, which they will wear under their clothing for the rest of their lives. The Melchizedek priesthood gives men the authority to administer to the sick and give special blessings.[15] Children should be baptized at about age eight, and both men and women must be married to enter the highest levels of the celestial kingdom. Temple ordinances are kept secret because they are too holy to share.

- God was once a man who evolved to be a god. "As man is now, God once was; as now God is, so man may be."[16] Righteous men on Earth can become gods themselves and inherit their own worlds where they will rule as the Heavenly Father in our world now does.

- Each person was a fully functioning adult entity in their premortal life. Those entities are born into Earthly bodies to be refined. If they are baptized and sealed during that life, the spirits of families remain together in the celestial kingdom after death. Baptisms and marriages for the dead may be performed to bind dead family members so they can enter the celestial kingdom. Spirits are born on Earth, having forgotten their premortal life. That life is said to exist behind a veil God placed on their minds.

- A man can be sealed to more than one woman during this lifetime, but a woman can only be sealed to one man. Men practice polygamy in the celestial kingdom, but women do not practice polyandry. Spirits in premortality are created when God, who has a physical body, has sexual intercourse with one of his wives, who are "Heavenly Mothers." Those spirits may then be born into Earthly bodies so they can prove themselves by their good works.

- There never was a time when the spirit of man did not exist, and there will never be a time when man ceases to exist.

- There are resurrected and translated beings ("persons who are changed so that they do not experience pain or death until their resurrection into immortality") existing on Earth. They include the "Three Nephites" of the Book of Mormon, John the Revelator (the author of the Bible Book of Revelation), Moses, and Enoch and his people.

- Evil spirits exist on Earth. They are jealous of mortal people's bodies and will try to control them if possible. Evil spirits can be detected by physical tests such as the signs and the offer of handshakes.

- The Bible Book of Revelation foretold the return of Jesus Christ. Before Christ returns, there will be a period of tribulation, including wars and natural disasters. Saints are expected to store food and other equipment to be prepared for this time.

- God will gather and protect 144,000 of his most faithful (twelve thousand from each of the twelve tribes of Israel). Jesus will return, not to Jerusalem but to Daviess County, Missouri, which the church teaches was the site of the Garden of Eden. The chosen Saints will ultimately gather in Missouri to build the New Jerusalem, also known as the City of Zion, where all the living faithful will reside, and Jesus will preside for a thousand years.

- All believers will be resurrected when Christ returns, but not all will be exalted. Until the resurrection, the spirits of the dead are all around us, but we can't see them.

- While Christ's sacrifice earned each person salvation, only their works and adherence to the tenets of the faith will win them exaltation.
- Those who have proven themselves exemplary in the church may receive the Second Anointing. It is considered the pinnacle of achievement in the church. This ceremony was once so sacred that there were only rumors that the ritual existed.

The Mormon belief system draws heavily on prophecy. In addition to the Book of Mormon, the church relies on the biblical Old Testament prophets and the Book of Revelation. Saints believe Joseph Smith Jr. and all subsequent presidents are prophets, seers, and revelators who routinely receive direct communication from God. Mormons also believe that each person can receive personal revelation. The LDS Articles of Faith are the accepted doctrine of the mainstream LDS Church. Central to church doctrine is the belief in the prophecy that the return of Jesus Christ is near, and the Saints must be prepared. They say there are two categories of people: those who are found upon the watchtower and those who have been scattered. Once the tribulations begin, those who are vigilant and prepared will be sent out to gather those who have scattered.

Over its nearly two-hundred-year history, the LDS Church has revised and, in some cases, recanted the beliefs that Joseph Smith Jr. claimed were given to him by God. The most well-known are the repudiation of polygamy and blood atonement, the granting of the priesthood to men of color, and the belief that Adam was God. Many believe Joseph Smith also at least flirted with the idea of reincarnation or, as LDS scholars call it, multiple mortal probations. Brigham Young claimed Adam and Eve had lived in a different world, died, and were resurrected to this world in an apparent act of reincarnation. Several of Joseph Smith's wives wrote about the prophet's belief in plural probations, and at least one claimed Smith told her they had been married to each other in a prior life. Some scholars, including Dr. Robert T. Beckstead (1949–present), another neo-Mormon fundamentalist, argue that the idea of multiple mortal probations is inferred and "elegantly embedded" in the doctrines of premortal existence and eternal progression.[17] They believe Joseph Smith Jr.'s understanding of the idea was influenced by Alexander Neibaur (1808–1883), a convert to the church who had been a student of the Kabbalah—a Jewish mystical tradition that teaches souls in the afterlife must be reborn to obtain perfection that will allow them to associate with God once again. Proponents say the idea of reincarnation didn't continue after Smith's death because his successor, Brigham Young, didn't understand it and dismissed it as a doctrine of evil. The modern LDS Church claims vehemently, "There is no such thing as second chance theology."

Both personal and institutional revelation are at the heart of the church's doctrine. The result is that history is mutable, and for church members, the truth is whatever the prophet, the bishop, or your priesthood holder says it is in the moment. Anyone who has read George Orwell's *1984* can see the parallels:

> . . . if all records told the same tale—then the lie passed into history and became truth. 'Who controls the past,' ran the Party slogan, 'controls the future' . . . Whatever was true now was true from everlasting to everlasting. It was quite simple. All that was required was an unending series of victories over your own memory.[18]

Thus it is with the church. So-called deprecated doctrines have been dismissed, or better yet, erased from its history. As one former believer turned questioner remarked, "When your church changes, it's apostasy, but when my church changes, it's continuing revelation." This elasticity of doctrine contributes to the rise of people like Lori Vallow and Chad Daybell.

Faithful Saints are taught from early life that they must understand fundamental doctrine before they dive into more substantive questions. Their well-known "milk before meat" teaching leads Church leaders to admonish the Saints to put their questions "on the shelf" for a time when they understand more deeply. Like most high-demand religions, the church discourages and openly discredits independent investigation of church claims. However, the internet has made research into even the most obscure church history accessible, including ideas the mainstream church has labeled outdated or misunderstood. The resulting accessibility to opposing views makes it difficult for the church to exert the tight control of the message it enjoyed in the past. Instead, the church has been forced to confront many questions in the face of an avalanche of readily available historical information.

In 2013, the church published its *Gospel Topic Essays*, billed by Church leadership as "straightforward, in-depth essays, which the First Presidency has approved, and the Quorum of the Twelve Apostles intended to gather accurate information from many different sources and publications and place it . . . where the material can be more easily accessed and studied . . ."[19] Although the essays are deeply nuanced, even slight admissions that the church may have been untruthful in the past have caused crises of faith for many Saints. They seem to react in two ways; some see any untruth as a betrayal and begin to spiral into the deconstruction of their faith that leads them to leave the church, while others, such as Chad Daybell and Lori Vallow, see the admissions as apostasy and seek to return to the "pure" doctrine as it was given to the faithful by Joseph Smith Jr.

According to the church, husbands receive revelations for their wives and children, and bishops to benefit their flocks. If the president or an apostle decides a thing, the entire church follows suit. For example, the LDS Church was founded at a time when slavery, segregation, and racial bigotry were the norm. Historical reports show that between 1830 and 1844, a few Black men were ordained into the Mormon priesthood by Joseph Smith Jr., but the practice stopped immediately when Brigham Young assumed control of the church. Scholars debate an 1840 change to the Book of Mormon's 2 Nephi 30:6. In the original 1830 text, Joseph Smith wrote, "They shall be a white and delightsome people;" in 1840, the line was revised to read, "They shall be a pure and delightsome people."

There is no dispute, however, that Brigham Young categorically excluded men of color from the priesthood and believed dark skin was a sign of God's curse. According to the Book of Mormon, when God was displeased with the Lamanites, he cursed them with dark skin; "because of their inequity . . . the Lord God did cause a skin of blackness to come upon them."[20] When they later accepted Christ, 3 Nephi reports, "their curse was taken from them and their skin became white like unto the Nephites." A year after Joseph Smith Jr.'s death, Elder John Taylor taught that "a black skin . . . has ever been a curse that followed an apostate of the old priesthood."[21] In his 1852 speech to the legislature, Brigham Young declared that Black people were the cursed descendants of Noah's son, Canaan, and Canaan's son, Ham, so they were restricted from the priesthood. Young said he could not remove the restriction and that "only God can do it." The priesthood, an ordination usually bestowed on any man who can prove spiritual worthiness, would not be available again to LDS men of color for the next 126 years. It was not until the 1978 General Conference that President Spencer W. Kimball received a revelation "extending priesthood and temple blessings to all worthy male members of the church." The church has neither apologized nor acknowledged the racism of its earlier prohibitions. Instead, the church denied that the restrictions had been for racist reasons and encouraged all members to move past their feelings and focus on the future. You are not alone if you wonder how much the shelf where the faithful put their unanswered questions can hold.

In later years, the story of the church's polygamous history would also receive revision to make it more palatable to Saints and gentiles alike. It's called "lying for the Lord," the practice of omitting facts and skirting the truth to protect the image of the church. By the mid-1950s, teachers and leaders were instructed to teach that the practice of Mormon men marrying more than one wife arose purely from necessity and Christian charity. They hid the fact that Joseph Smith Jr. and his close followers had already been practicing polygamy for more than ten years and instead taught that when Brigham Young led the faithful to Utah, the arduous cross-country journey to Salt Lake led to the deaths of so many faithful men that the remaining men were forced to take multiple wives to protect the widows and orphans. The church does not explain why those men needed to take those widows and their orphan daughters to their beds, for indeed, sex is an intrinsic part of the practice of polygamy.

Mormons have very definite ideas about sex. Sex should be only between a man and a woman, and only if they are legally married and sealed to one another for time and eternity. Premarital sex, masturbation, and virtually any physical contact between people of the opposite sex are forbidden, as is homosexuality. Breaking the church's sexual prohibitions can get you banned from entering the temple or, worse, excommunicated. Only murder is considered a more serious sin than sex outside of marriage. Those dating are told they may not participate in passionate kissing, fondling, or lying atop another person, with or without clothing. Both male and female teenagers are routinely subjected to private inquisitions by their bishop, usually an older man, and forced to describe in detail every act and confess to even the slightest of transgressions.

Both men and women are expected to be virgins on their wedding night, an expectation that naturally leads Saints to marry early in life. Young couples often complain that in a single moment, with the pronouncement that they are man and wife, they go from sex being forbidden to being expected to understand how it all works. Sexual shame and dysfunction are common complaints among members and former members of the church. The church teaches that wearing modest clothing is the foundation of abstinence, and Mormon women must cover themselves so as not to inflame the men around them. Mostly, they wear clothing that covers their temple garments and are forbidden from wearing tank tops or any other attire that bares their shoulders. Women wear dresses or skirts at church, and men wear white shirts and conservative ties. The mainstream LDS Church only recently revised its rules to permit women to wear pants to Sunday service. Young Saints are expected to follow a typical life path. In high school, they attend early morning seminary, where they learn LDS Church teachings. After high school, they are likely to attend a religious college. The men are expected to go on a two-year church mission, which may mean interrupting their college studies and then returning from their mission to finish their schooling. Some young LDS women perform missions, which usually last a year and a half. College is not emphasized as much for young women, who are often encouraged to attend only until they find a returned missionary to marry. Soon after returning from their mission, young Saints are expected to marry in the temple, where they are sealed to their spouses for time and all eternity.

The church's keen emphasis on marriage stems from their belief that only married people may be exalted to the celestial kingdom. Marriage is essential because it is the responsibility of each Mormon to procreate both on Earth and in the spirit world; only those who gain the highest level can become exalted and beget their own spirit children. Since a woman can only enter the celestial kingdom if she is married and her priesthood holder husband calls her by her secret temple name, the power in Mormon marriages is often very unequal. God directs the family by leading the husband; the wife's salvation depends on her husband's priesthood authority, so it's to her eternal advantage to keep her husband believing and doing good work for the church. Mormon husbands hold all the cards because if the wife wants to achieve her own godhood, she must stay in her husband's good graces. Faithful but unmarried women become servants to others in the celestial kingdom—a fate no woman wants. This is why Mormon women need to research their family genealogy and ensure that every woman is married, even if the wedding must take place in the afterlife. Women who have been admitted to the temple often stand in as proxies for other women so dead members can be married to one another to seal their access to the celestial kingdom.

Against this backdrop, we begin to understand where Lori and Chad's beliefs originated and how seductive the idea of being a goddess was to Lori. She would do anything to complete her mission.

2

SOMEWHERE COLD

The town of Rexburg, Idaho, is unlikely to attract national attention for any reason, let alone as the epicenter for a conservative religious movement that spawned a notorious murder case. Rexburg calls itself "America's *Family* Community." It's a quiet little farm town where the crime rate is low, and murders are nearly nonexistent. During the summer, irrigation wheels spray rainbow-producing arcs of glittering water over emerald-green fields, and in winter, snowmobilers glide over pristine sparkling snow. Lori Vallow expected her move to Rexburg to be a fresh start for her and her children—Tylee, sixteen, and JJ, seven—but trouble seemed to follow her.

People who knew Lori Cox Yanes Lagioia Ryan Vallow said she was magnetic. If Lori was your friend, prepare for some serious love bombing because she stuck to her friends like Velcro. She was bubbly and generous and loved entertaining. Before her move to Rexburg, she lived in the expansive home her estranged fourth husband, Charles Vallow, rented for her after their final separation. The beautiful residence was built in the Mediterranean style, popular in the affluent suburbs around Phoenix, Arizona. A home reflects the people who live there, and Lori's upscale rental in Chandler, Arizona, was no exception. It was outwardly gracious while inwardly a little odd. The backyard patio and pool were beautiful.

Any room visitors might see was furnished like a model home, except for the empty, mirror-lined living room where Lori danced on wood floors to Christian and eighties rock music for hours every day. Lori's bedroom was tidy; the bed was neatly made with a pretty comforter, and nothing was out of place. In contrast, her children's rooms looked like an afterthought. Neither of the children had furniture, just a single unmade mattress tossed on the floor. Clothing and toys littered the remaining floor space.

Barely a month before her move to idyllic Rexburg, Lori's fourth husband, Charles had been shot to death in the mirrored living room of that Chandler, Arizona, home by Lori's brother, Alex Cox. Alex, who later moved to Rexburg with Lori, claimed Charles threatened him with a baseball bat, so he fired two shots into Charles's chest in self-defense. Lori didn't tell anyone where she was going when she left Arizona three weeks later. Even Colby Ryan, her adult son from her second marriage, knew only that she was going "somewhere cold."

Charles Vallow was a successful financial planner and a generous man who was happy to help his extended family. Before he died, he was paying for cell phones and auto insurance for most of Lori's family, including her parents. He was also helping support Colby, who had recently married and had his first child. Charles liked being a family man; he had been the one to approach his sister, Kay Woodcock, about adopting her grandson, Canaan. Canaan was the child of Kay's son, Todd Trahan, and his partner, Mandy Leger. The state of Louisiana, where Todd, Mandy, and Kay all lived, took custody of the boy after he was born prematurely with drugs in his system. Once the tiny boy was released from the hospital, Kay and her husband, Larry, cared for the baby, hoping that Todd and Mandy could conquer their addictions and regain custody. Larry Woodcock recalls bringing Canaan home after his extended neonatal intensive care unit stay. Drug-affected newborns often struggle to regulate their sleep cycles, and Canaan was no different. When he became agitated and overstimulated, Larry would sleep on the couch with the boy on his chest, pressing heart to heart and pulling his bathrobe tightly around them both. For the next year, Kay and Larry's lives were lovingly filled with medical and therapy appointments, Canaan's sloppy kisses, and infectious giggles.

When it became clear that neither Todd nor Mandy would be ready to assume responsibility for Canaan, state officials suggested Kay and Larry adopt him. Kay and her brother had always been close, so as she and Larry considered the adoption, she talked it over with Charles. Kay and Larry were not sure they were the best fit for Canaan. They adored the baby but were busy empty nesters working long hours at their company. It was also clear that Canaan had special needs requiring plenty of time, attention, and therapy. In contrast, Lori and Charles had Lori's children, Colby and Tylee, at home, where Lori was a full-time mom. Additionally, the services available for Canaan's special needs were much better in Chandler, Arizona, than in Kay and Larry's hometown of Lake Charles, Louisiana. Kay and Larry made the agonizing decision to support Charles and Lori's adoption of baby Canaan. It was a decision that will forever haunt them both.

When Lori and Charles finalized the adoption, Canaan was a year old. They changed his name to Joshua Jackson Vallow; the family called him JJ. Kay and Larry visited Arizona often. Kay said that "Lori was a doll"—the perfect wife and mother during that time. JJ was diagnosed on the autism spectrum and also had attention deficit hyperactivity disorder, which meant he was highly energetic, easily overwhelmed, and prone to emotional meltdowns that required much patient attention. The Woodcocks were convinced Lori was the right mom for the job, and when Charles was home, he was a hands-on dad who loved spending time with his little dynamo. JJ's older siblings, Tylee and Colby, doted on him. Tylee was like a second mother, always ready to play with him on the trampoline or swim in their backyard pool. JJ received intensive early intervention treatment as a toddler, then flourished in an elementary school for autistic children. JJ was obsessed with travel and loved suitcases. When Charles packed for a business trip, JJ always wanted to go. JJ would often pack a suitcase, filling it with toys and random clothing and pulling it around the house.

While life in Arizona was nearly perfect, Lori had always dreamed of living in Hawaii, where her family had often taken vacations. In 2014,

Lori and Charles took the plunge and moved the family to Kauai. Lori and Charles were devout members of The Church of Jesus Christ of Latter-day Saints (LDS) and joined the local Kauai branch, where Lori met April Raymond. The women quickly became good friends. Their children, who were similar ages, also became friends. The families had beach picnics and celebrated holidays together. The Vallow family enjoyed the aloha lifestyle for the next three years. Lori loved the endless good weather and was active in her local LDS branch, a smaller version of an LDS ward. Friends and family, including Kay and Larry Woodcock, visited frequently. At the time, April could not have imagined that nine years later, she would travel from sunny Kauai to chilly Boise to testify against her former friend in a crowded courtroom.

Lori and Charles's time in Hawaii didn't last, and they moved back to Arizona with the children in 2017. Few who knew Lori Vallow then would have recognized that she was struggling. On the outside, she was the same bubbly, blond mom she had always been, but inside, she was seething; only those closest to her noticed. Her idyllic Hawaiian dream was over. Lori and her third husband, Joe Ryan, had been fighting over Tylee's custody since they divorced when Tylee was a baby, and their emotionally and financially draining custody and visitation disputes continued unabated. Tylee, who had always been Lori's sweet little girl, became a sarcastic, bitter, and often surly teenager. JJ required constant attention, and persistent money problems meant Charles was no help because he worked more than he was home. Nothing seemed to fill the emptiness, and Lori escaped more and more into books. She liked romantic young adult novels but also began reading more books with a Mormon doomsday theme. She read books by Jason Mow, a local Mormon author whom she knew from the Mesa, Arizona, LDS temple. His books featured heroic historical figures from the Book of Mormon who fought epic battles.

Lori's friends and family say that although she had always been interested in end-time theology, it was around this time that her interest in near-death experiences and apocalyptic prophecies became obsessive. She started listening to doomsday podcasts and reading religious books, searching for a deeper spiritual connection. Family members say she read *The Second Comforter: Conversing with the Lord Through the Veil* by Denver Snuffer Jr. Snuffer is a lawyer who lives in Utah and was excommunicated from the LDS Church in 2013 for apostasy. He leads a group called the "Remnant Movement." In his book, Snuffer wrote, "This book may not be appropriate for several readers and you might well ask yourself if this book is a good fit for you. It is intended only for a specific audience: active, faithful members of The Church of Jesus Christ of Latter-day Saints with many years of faithful living. It is for those faithful members who have felt there is something more to the Gospel but who do not have a secure sense of how to proceed to receive it."[1] This description fit Lori perfectly. Snuffer believes the mainstream LDS Church is itself in apostasy and must be returned to faithfulness. The mainstream church teaches that only men are endowed with priesthood power. Snuffer wrote, "It is not required that you have the priesthood to receive the Second Comforter. Everyone is invited to come to Him. The promises He made are clearly directed at both men and women . . . God is no respecter of persons and is universally willing to accept all who come unto Him."[2] According to Snuffer, the Second Comforter is Jesus Christ, who appears in person to each seeker. The idea that Jesus can personally appear to anyone is antithetical to mainstream LDS Church teachings. Lori, having been raised within the patriarchal framework of the LDS Church, where men control nearly everything, including one's connection to the divine, must have found the idea that a woman could have an intimate relationship with a living and present Jesus Christ hard to resist. It was a vulnerability that Chad Daybell, Lori's prophet and fifth husband, would exploit.

Lori continued to find comfort and distraction in young adult fiction. She read the entire Twilight series by LDS author Stephanie Meyer several times; the books appealed to Lori's naive view of romantic relationships. She also discovered books by Chad Daybell, which mixed fanciful ideas like time travel with long-held LDS beliefs. It was a potent combination for someone like Lori. The stories made an even more profound impression on Lori when Chad announced that the books were not wholly fiction but had been inspired by his religious visions. Chad became a larger-than-life figure for Lori.

Lori's brother Adam says he believes Lori's obsession with near-death experiences and doomsday prepping began in 2012 when she read their cousin Braxton's self-published book, *A Letter to My Friends*. Then Lori discovered author and speaker Julie Rowe and began listening to her podcasts. Julie talked about her visions of the terror coming soon with the end of days and the need to raise up Saints to take charge and build the City of Zion. Lori's interest in the end times wasn't new, but her obsession with it was. Adam Cox, recalled that Lori had been interested in near-death experiences for years. Her son Colby remembered his mother talking about how the end was coming soon when he was about ten or eleven. Her doomsday talk was so pervasive that Colby wrote, "We were headed to the inevitable, and the clock was ticking down. All I could do was wait in fear of that day."[3] More than one person remembers Lori talking about driving off a cliff. Colby recalls the day his mother decided to flee Arizona rather than deliver his little sister, Tylee, for a visit with her biological father, Joe Ryan. When she learned from her family that Joe had the police looking for her, she said, "What if we all just drove off a cliff?" They were in a mountainous area of New Mexico, and Colby took her threat seriously enough to argue vehemently with her.[4] By 2017, Lori was focused almost entirely on the coming doomsday. Although Lori had been studying near-death experiences and reading doomsday books since 2012, her downward spiral began in earnest a few weeks after Lori first met Melanie Gibb in 2018.

Lori was beautiful—the ideal California girl, now grown into a perfectly sculpted and styled suburban mom. She had been a hairdresser for most of her adult life, and her long, honey-blond hair was always perfectly colored and styled in beachy waves. She favored skintight spandex leggings and snug tank tops that showed off her lean, fit body.

Not long after their move back to Arizona from Hawaii, Lori met a new friend named Melanie Gibb, who shared her doomsday views. They met at a class where Melanie taught a group of women about food storage and other end-of-time survival strategies. Their connection was instantaneous, and Lori began her signature love bombing. Lori and Melanie started seeing one another several times a week and often met at the LDS temple in Mesa, Arizona, for prayer and ancestry work. They were both devout in their LDS faith, interested in the end times, and each had a son with ADHD and autism. Melanie loved Lori, but she was not impressed with Lori's children. JJ was a demanding, uninhibited, and sometimes destructive seven-year-old, and Tylee was a bitter, angry teenager with a perpetual chip on her shoulder. Colby had moved out and married his pregnant girlfriend after a failed attempt at the LDS mission all young Mormon men are expected to serve. Lori seemed to float above all the dysfunction like the proverbial swan, gliding gracefully on the surface while furiously paddling underneath.

In an early selfie, Lori and Melanie could be sisters: Lori, the pretty cheerleader, and Melanie, an academic, less flashy sibling. By the time Melanie Gibb self-published a book titled *Feel the Fire* in 2019, she was firmly in Lori's orbit. Lori Vallow wrote part of the foreword for Melanie's book that read, "This book, *Feel the Fire*, will inspire you and help you recognize and break the dark chains in your life. The author, Melanie Gibb, shares many eternal truths and truths about her own life that will help you feel the fire that only having a personal relationship with Jesus Christ can bring. Melanie is a fun-loving wife, mother, and friend who puts it all out there in this book to help people find a higher and more meaningful relationship with the Savior. I definitely felt the spiritual fire reading this book and thank Melanie for all of her efforts in helping everyone get to that next level in their eternal progression! Don't miss out on this opportunity to feel the fire that will change your life." Melanie Gibb would also enter that crowded Boise courtroom four years later to testify against her best friend.

Lori Norene Cox was born in Loma Linda, California, on June 26, 1973, and was one of six children born to Janis and Barry Cox. Lori's oldest sister, Stacey, died from complications of type 1 diabetes in 1998 at the age of thirty-one. Another sister, Laura, whom the family called Lolly, died in infancy. Lori's brother and protector, Alex Cox, died of a pulmonary embolism in December 2019. Her living siblings are her older brother, Adam Cox, and younger sister, Summer Cox Shiflet.

As a teenager, Lori got up each weekday to attend 6:00 A.M. LDS seminary class before high school. Graduation from seminary is required for all young people who hope to serve a church mission. Young Mormon men are expected to serve a two-year church mission between high school and college. Young women may also serve church missions, but their participation is less compulsory. The Church of Jesus Christ of Latter-day Saints, like all of the organizations under the Mormonism banner, emphasizes purity, marriage, and family, and young women usually marry early.

Lori grew up in affluent San Bernadino, California, and was overweight as a child. Her mother, Janis, was obsessive about appearance and weight, and by the time Lori reached high school, she was an athletic, slender, and perfectly groomed cheerleader. As a cheerleader, Lori was the flyer—the girl on the top of the pyramid who was tossed in the air and caught. Her upbringing led to a lifetime of conscientious diet and exercise. When Lori competed in the Mrs. Texas beauty pageant in 2004, her mother praised her hard work to get in shape and raved about how good Lori looked model-walking across the stage in stilettos and a turquoise bikini. Lori later wore a white, body-hugging sequined sheath dress for the formal wear portion of the event.

Lori grew up close to her siblings and cousins, especially her cousin Braxton Southwick, who was nearest in age to Lori. Braxton was also the closest to Lori in terms of spiritual beliefs. It was Braxton who introduced Lori to John Pontius's 2012 book, *Visions of Glory*, a book that would influence Lori and so many others. The book describes a man named Spencer's near-death experiences and his associated visions for the end of days. Braxton became deeply interested in doomsday prepping after the terrorist attacks on September 11, 2001. He and his family were featured in an early episode of National Geographic's *Doomsday Preppers*. Braxton also loved Julie Rowe's 2014 book, *A Greater Tomorrow*, in which the author recounted her own near-death experiences and visions. He even attended one of Julie's speaking events in Idaho. Julie's publisher, Chad Daybell, was at the event. Braxton remembers seeing him but did not meet Chad personally. Braxton said in Lori's case, her prepping was mainly spiritual rather than the usual collecting and storing of supplies, but they could easily talk for hours about preparing for the end of days. Braxton said that Lori was an impressive mother, but he acknowledges that she was terrified for her children and didn't want them to go through the horrors of the tribulation that would precede the second coming of Jesus Christ. He was another who recalled how often Lori said, "I'll just drive us all off a cliff." Braxton said Lori was convinced that the second coming was imminent, and he thought she earnestly believed she would be sparing her children from pain and suffering. Braxton was shocked when he heard Lori had married Chad Daybell because Lori was effervescent and gorgeous, and Chad was an awkward, overweight man with a crew cut.

Lori's parents, Barry and Janis Cox, were lifelong members of the mainstream LDS Church, but Barry was anything but conventional. Barry Cox was a right-wing political extremist who opposed the United States government. In November 2019, while his grandchildren were missing, he self-published *How the American Public Can Dismantle the IRS*. It's unclear whether Lori's mother, Janis, shared her husband's outlook or if she was simply a subservient LDS wife. Still, records show the Coxes spent decades fighting the IRS while amassing more than $300,000 in federal tax debt. Barry was sentenced to 366 days in prison in 1999 for making a false statement to the IRS. The Arizona State Bar Association also reprimanded him for practicing law without a license. A review of Barry's book exposes his bitter dislike of authority and belief that the law does not apply to him. One is left to wonder if this is where Lori learned to be a scofflaw. It's an odd dichotomy; Barry is a devout follower of a high-demand and rule-driven religion that urges members to "follow the law of man,"[5] who intentionally defies the government and the law of the land. In later life, Lori would claim that her exaltation exempted her from much and that neither the rules of science nor the law of man applied to her. In general, Barry avoided the media after Lori's missing children became an international story. On the rare occasions he did appear, his narcissism shone through. Instead of talking about his missing grandchildren, he bragged that Lori saw him as a spiritual giant. He is clear in his book that he completely embraces the idea of American exceptionalism. He also demanded perfection from his wife and daughters. Many believe this contributed to daughter Stacey's early death, and some family members say Barry was physically and psychologically abusive to his wife and children.

Although Lori prepared to serve a mission after high school and said she wanted to attend Brigham Young University in Provo, Utah, she did neither. Instead, she left home in 1992, immediately after her high school graduation, and at age eighteen, married her high school boyfriend, Nelson Yanes. Lori's marriage to Yanes was brief, and Lori's older brother, Adam Cox, reports that Lori had the marriage annulled. Yanes was not a member of the LDS Church, and Lori's family disapproved of the marriage. According to Adam, Nelson Yanes grew up in their neighborhood and was known to be a drug dealer deep in the local party scene. Adam believes Yanes introduced Lori to drugs. When Lori's parents forbade her to see Yanes, she got a restraining order against her entire family and eloped with him. Her first marriage would establish a pattern in her life. Outwardly a compliant Mormon woman, her rebellion took the form of relationships with "inappropriate" men. Of her five marriages, only her last to Chad Daybell would be to a man already a Mormon.

In July 1995, Lori was living with her brother, Adam, in Austin, Texas, working and attending cosmetology school, when she met William Lagioia. When Adam declined to let Lagioia move into his apartment with Lori, she left Adam's apartment and found an apartment with Lagioia. Adam reports Lagioia had trouble holding jobs and worked as a male exotic dancer at one point. It was a fraught relationship, and Lagioia was charged with hitting Lori after police found a small cut inside her mouth. She claimed the cut was the result of Lagioia hitting her and tossing her on the bed. At that time, the two had been living together on and off for four years, despite Lori's church's deep disapproval of unmarried couples living together. Because of the pressure from her Church and family, and despite their history of domestic violence, on October 22, 1995, Lori married for the

CHILDREN OF DARKNESS AND LIGHT

second time. She was twenty-two, William Lagioia was twenty-three, and Lori was pregnant. On April 8, 1996, Lori gave birth to their son, Colby. By December 1996, Lori had filed a lengthy legal complaint against her husband. In it, she reported she had prayed that Lagioia would join The Church of Jesus Christ of Latter-day Saints but that he was only baptized after they separated in an attempt to convince her to reconcile. Lori complained that her husband didn't support her financially and claimed he was already living with another woman when he was baptized. She said that while she lived with him, Lagioia took her car keys, denied her use of her car, and wouldn't let her leave. She said she got away on the pretext of a visit to her parents and never returned. According to the divorce documents, Lori claimed Lagioia and his stepfather kept her car, and she was forced to let the finance company repossess it. Adam says Lori gave Lagioia the vehicle in exchange for him relinquishing his parental rights to Colby. Texas is one of the only states in the US that permits birth parents to relinquish their parental rights to avoid financial responsibility. Lori's divorce from Lagioia was final in 1998, and there is no indication that Colby ever had a relationship with his birth father or his birth father's family. What emerged from Lori's marriage to Lagioia was another of her lifelong patterns: Lori didn't just end relationships; she blew them up.

Lori then met Joseph Ryan, whom she married in 2001. Joe was different from Lori's first two husbands; he was older and had an established life and career. Joe's sister, Annie Cushing, commented that Lori and her handsome brother were always the most beautiful people in the room. Joe didn't adopt Lori's son, Colby, perhaps because an adoption would have required Lori to contact her ex-husband, but they legally changed Colby's last name to Ryan. When Lori became pregnant with their daughter, Tylee, it seemed to Colby that he would finally have what he'd always wanted: a family. Lori and Joe lived in Texas, where Lori competed in the Mrs. Texas pageant and appeared on the *Wheel of Fortune* game show after she said God told her to audition. She won more than $17,000. She portrayed her life as perfect during her introduction on *Wheel of Fortune*. Her husband was "wonderful," her children were "beautiful," and they enjoyed playing all kinds of sports on their three acres. Lori's marriage to Joe was more complicated than she made it seem. Lori told the interview panel in her Mrs. Texas interview she was a good wife, mother, and worker. "Being all those things together is not easy. I'm basically a ticking time bomb."

Joe Ryan and his sister, Annie, grew up in the foster care system, and Joe had a temper he never fully learned to manage. The combination proved fatal to his marriage. Lori admitted to her brother Adam and her sister-in-law, Annie, that on several occasions, Joe had been physically abusive; Annie also reported seeing Joe physically discipline Colby in a way she found disturbing. Joe and Lori divorced in 2004, when Tylee was eighteen months old. Lori accused Joe of sexually abusing both Colby and Tylee. Their bitter battle over Tylee's custody and Joe's parenting time would continue for the next fourteen years. A review of the voluminous family court records reveals no concrete proof that Lori's allegations were true. Investigations and evaluations at the time pointed to Joe's innocence, and advocates for the children suspected Lori of coaching her children. Nonetheless, Colby stands by his childhood disclosures of abuse.

In April 2018, Joe Ryan was discovered dead in his Phoenix, Arizona, apartment. Authorities believe Ryan died alone. His body was not found until a week later. The state of decomposition made investigating Joe's death difficult, but the medical examiner ruled his death was from natural causes. Although they were divorced long ago, Joe still listed Lori as his next of kin, and she was the first person notified of his death. She immediately arranged to have his body cremated. Their daughter, Tylee, was the beneficiary of Joe's $75,000 life insurance policy. Though there was no definitive proof, many people wonder if Lori had a hand in Joe Ryan's death. Annie Cushing, who did not even know her brother had died until months later when the funeral home called to ask if she wanted his ashes, has repeatedly called for Arizona officials to investigate further. In 2021, Phoenix police reopened Joe's case after a podcast recording surfaced in which Lori reported she told her bishop she needed a temple recommend because she wanted to either turn her life to the temple or murder her ex-husband. In the LDS Church, only members deemed worthy receive a temple recommend.

Members must obtain this approval from their bishop to enter the temple and perform temple rituals. Lori's 2019 podcast included this stunning admission: "I had been married to someone who was very awful, who raped my children, and I had divorced him and had gotten away from him . . . I went through a lot of years of this hard stuff, and I was going to murder him—I was going to kill him like the scriptures say—like Nephi killed Laban." Officials retested tissue samples preserved before Joe's cremation, but toxicology reports did not change their opinion that Joe had died of complications from heart disease. Witnesses who knew Lori from her time in Hawaii claim she told friends that she paid her brother, Alex Cox, to kill Joe Ryan. Others said Lori admitted being present when Joe took his last breath, but neither claim could be substantiated by law enforcement.

Still, the claims may not be as outrageous as they sound. In 2007, Alex ambushed Joe Ryan in a Texas parking lot after a court-ordered supervised visit with Tylee. Alex, who knew Joe had a heart condition, discharged a taser into him, believing a direct hit to the chest could induce a fatal heart attack. Joe turned away from the attack at the last moment, taking the shock in the back instead. He fell in the scuffle, suffered a broken wrist, and spent several days in the hospital to stabilize his heart and surgically repair his wrist. Alex was convicted of the assault and spent ninety days in jail. Lori's other brother, Adam Cox, said, "Lori and Alex planned to kill Joe . . . Al was going to taser him and throw him in the trunk and take him out to a field and shoot him and bury him."

Alex Cox was an aspiring comedian. In one of his standup routines at an open mic club in Arizona, he tells an embellished version of his encounter with Joe. "I was fortunate enough to do a little jail time last year, I can confess to you guys. Have you ever had something that you knew was the right thing to do, but it turns out that later on, it was a felony? This is a true story. I found out that my ex-brother-in-law was a pedophile, so I took a stun gun, and I discharged it right in his nutsack." Alex lamented that instead of a parade, he got prison. In fact, he accepted a plea where the charges would be dismissed if he completed his jail and probation successfully. He fulfilled all the requirements, and the case was dismissed, removing the felony conviction and clearing the way for him to own firearms again.

After Lori divorced Joe Ryan in 2004, she worked as a hairdresser in a salon in Austin, Texas, where she began cutting a handsome new client's hair. Charles Vallow had a sly Louisiana drawl and the manners of a Southern gentleman. He had played college and minor league baseball and, in his forties, was in excellent physical shape. He was immediately smitten with Lori's good looks and bubbly personality, and they were married on February 24, 2006. They settled near Phoenix, AZ. Lori was thirty-three, and Charles was forty-nine, but the sixteen-year age difference didn't appear to bother either. Like William Lagioia and Joe Ryan, Charles Vallow converted to The Church of Jesus Christ of Latter-day Saints for Lori. Charles found happiness in his new faith and family. Their fourteen-year marriage was Lori's longest, and friends and family members said they appeared happy until Lori began flirting with the offbeat neo-fundamentalist religious ideas of Chad Daybell and others.

Lori accompanied Melanie and several other women on a road trip from Phoenix, Arizona, to St. George, Utah, to attend the October conference of Preparing a People (PAP). These conferences were organized to unite like-minded people to discuss preparation and training for the end times. During their seven-hour drive, the women talked nearly continuously as they got to know each other. Melanie, a frequent PAP attendee, was excited to introduce Lori to others who frequented the events. Melanie knew Lori was enamored with Chad Daybell's books and that Chad Daybell was speaking at the event. In an interview with East Idaho News's Nate Eaton, Melanie described Lori as a Chad Daybell "superfan." Melanie had met Chad at earlier PAP conferences and looked forward to introducing Lori to him. She couldn't know she would be starting the equivalent of a nuclear chain reaction that, when finally spent, would cost the lives of at least five people.

When Lori and Melanie arrived at the conference, they found Chad at a vendor table, selling his books. Melanie introduced him to Lori and later described the moment as "electric." Lori and Chad began talking nonstop about their ideas. Lori had already stumbled upon the doctrine of multiple mortal probations, a form of reincarnation, so she was enchanted when Chad told her they had been married to one another in a previous life. Lori spent most of her weekend helping Chad sell his books. Chad told her he believed she was a goddess, an exalted being whom God had placed on Earth to begin preparation for the end times. He had seen in a vision that together, they would gather and lead the 144,000 of God's chosen and usher in the new millennium. They were together non-stop and arranged to meet again in a few weeks when Chad was scheduled to speak at a Preparing a People event near Lori's home in Arizona. As Lori drove home from Utah, she had Zulema Google "James the Just" and read Doctrine and Covenants 77:11 aloud. James the Just was the brother of Jesus Christ. The passage in Doctrines and Covenants, considered scripture by the LDS Church, read, "Q: What are we to understand by sealing the one hundred and forty-four thousand, out of all the tribes of Israel—twelve thousand out of every tribe? A: We are to understand that those who are sealed are high priests, ordained unto the holy order of God, to administer the everlasting gospel; for they are they who are ordained out of every nation, kindred, tongue, and people, by the angels to whom is given power over the nations of the earth, to bring as many as will come to the church of the Firstborn." As Lori drove through the desert, in her mind, God seemed to affirm everything she had been learning.

3

"I CAN'T GET IN TOUCH WITH MY KIDS"

A
s early as 2012, Lori came to believe her beloved LDS Church was in apostasy. As she studied the new thinkers of the church, she also became convinced she had a part to play in the movement to bring the church back to the truth. Lori knew the timing could not be more imperative because the apocalyptic tribulation in both the Bible and the Book of Mormon was imminent, and physical and spiritual preparation was critical. But when she tried to alert her family to the crisis, no one was listening. In 2019, her brother Adam balked when she told him she was a translated being who no longer needed to eat, sleep, or use the bathroom.[1] Lori cut off communication with her family.

Mike Stroud was one of the many influencers Lori heard talk about the end times. Stroud was a podcaster and a frequent speaker at Preparing a People conferences; he described what it meant to be a "translated being":

> A translated being has been changed in Christ through the power of His Atonement by the will of our God to a place and an order where time, space, and mortal death have no claim

on them. They are changed physically, spiritually, emotionally, and psychologically. They are not the same as anyone living in a telestial world. They can minister to us in this world but while here, they do not experience marriage, family, nor having children. Their lives and their bodies in the telestial world as translated beings is totally and completely devoted to the ministry of helping their brothers and sisters, the children of God the Father and our Mother, ascend to a higher condition, to improve their time while in life, that they might have an opportunity and an advantage in the world become [sic]. Their soul [sic] desire is outside of themselves, and they desire only to bring souls unto Christ and God while the earth stands. Translation is a burden upon those who experience it. They have to be translated in all ways spiritually, physically, emotionally, and psychologically because in their ministry they will experience the utmost depths of the abyss, and the blood and horror of a fallen world. They have to be able to go among places and people who are so lost and fallen that debauchery is a good word to explain their condition. And yet these translated beings as a part of their ministry go forth in these terrible conditions in order to find and rescue those that the Lord has purposed and bring them out of that condition, that dire situation, and deliver them to places of instruction where they can receive ordinances, covenants, priesthoods, and begin the process of realizing their true identity.[2]

Lori Vallow believed this was what had happened to her.

Things came to a final, tragic denouement in 2019 when Charles Vallow had been married to Lori for what he characterized as fourteen mostly happy years. Lori and Charles had lived mainly in a Phoenix suburb with Lori's son, Colby; daughter, Tylee; and their adopted son, JJ. Charles's sons from his first marriage, Zach and Cole, visited often. Charles enjoyed the Arizona lifestyle, grilling a steak for dinner almost every night and playing in the backyard pool with JJ. Although he was raised a Catholic, Charles converted to The Church of Jesus Christ of Latter-day Saints for Lori and loved their church community. In the LDS faith, members are expected to have a testimony about their church experience. The church says, "A testimony is a spiritual witness given by the Holy Ghost. The foundation of a testimony is the knowledge that Heavenly Father lives and loves His children; that Jesus Christ lives, that He is the Son of God, and that He carried out the infinite Atonement; that Joseph Smith is the prophet of God who was called to restore the gospel; that The Church of Jesus Christ of Latter-day Saints is the Savior's true church on the earth; and that the church is led by a living prophet today."[3] Once per month, the church holds a Fast and Testimony Meeting. At that meeting, members are encouraged to arrive fasting, share their testimony, and bear witness to other members' testimonies. Family members said Charles often shared his testimony and was content in the church. Lori, however, was rapidly pulling away, aligning herself with the more radical elements of the faith.

In January 2019, with Lori deep into her secret relationship with Chad, things unraveled further. Charles left his home for a business trip. When his business was finished, he arrived at the Houston airport tired and eager to head home, only to discover that his airline ticket had been canceled. Charles bought a last-minute ticket and flew home, but his truck and wallet were missing when he got to the long-term parking lot. Someone was playing games, and he was pretty sure he knew who. When Lori refused to answer her phone, he called his friend, who was also his bishop, for a ride. When he got to their house, he found Lori had also changed the locks. Charles called the police.

The officer's body camera recorded the conversation on January 31, 2019, foreshadowing the future. Charles said his marriage to Lori had hit a rough patch recently, but the extremity of canceling his ticket home was still a surprise. Charles was worried; Lori had started saying strange things and acting oddly. Over the past few years, her religious beliefs had become more radical. Lori was convinced the end times were coming soon and that she had been chosen for a special calling. When the officer asked, "So what's going on tonight?" Charles can be heard saying, "I can't get in touch with my kids." The officer's camera recorded the entire interview. In it, Charles looked weary, bewildered, and frustrated as he paced the sidewalk. Despite that, his tone remained calm and reasonable, and his concern for Lori and the children was palpable.

The police asked how old his children were, and Charles answered, "Six and a half and sixteen." He told the officer he'd been trying to reach them for two days, the Louisiana lilt evident in his voice as he said, "She's lost her mind. We're LDS." Charles continued, "She thinks she's a resurrected being and a god and a member of the hundred and forty-four thousand, and Jesus is coming next year. She took all the money out of our bank account today; my truck is gone from the airport. She went to the airport and got it." Charles told the officer he had already been to the authorities that night, asking that Lori be picked up on a mental health order. The officer asked Charles what made Lori a danger to herself or others. Charles replied, "She's threatened me, threatened to kill me . . . She said, 'I will have you destroyed . . . You're not Charles. I don't know who you are, but I can murder you now with my powers.'" The officer expressed skepticism that what Lori said amounted to an actual threat. "It's been going on for about four or five years," Charles continued, "but it's gotten really bad lately. She goes to the temple every day and speaks with Moroni." Charles explained that Lori was "involved with people in Utah who tell her how many past lives she's had." The officer seemed mystified as he tried to make heads or tails of their conversation. He asked Charles why he was afraid for his children. "I don't know what she's going to do with them. I don't know if she's going to flee with them or she's gonna hurt 'em."

The police helped Charles break into his home, but Lori and the children were not there. Charles insisted Lori was a danger to herself and wanted a judge to order her to have a mental evaluation. On the petition for the protective order, Charles wrote, "She told me she was a GOD (emphasis in the original) and was assigned to carry out the work of the 144,000 at Christ's second coming in July 2020. She said I was in the way and she would have to murder me if I tried to stop her. The next day, on a business trip to Houston, she called me and told me she didn't trust me and would have to kill me when she got home. She would have an angel there to help dispose of my body. She also said she knew my real name was Nick Schneider and that I'd have to go painfully."

Over the next two days, Charles repeatedly tried to get the police to pick Lori up on the mental health order. Unfortunately, the police had trouble believing what Charles was telling them. He resorted to stalking her and taking her purse out of her car while she walked JJ into school. He later agreed to drop the purse off at the police station for Lori to pick up if he could also drop off the mental health order to be served on Lori. Lori arrived at the police station with Tylee and Melanie Gibb in tow. When the officer asked what happened, Lori said she fought with her husband because he was out of town, and she "found out some stuff he'd been doing." She said he was coming home, so she took her kids and stayed at a hotel. Lori failed to mention changing the locks on the house, cleaning out their bank account, hiding Charles's truck, or disposing of his belongings. "So this morning, when I took my son to school . . . he was waiting somewhere and stole my purse out of the car, my phone, my wallet, my money, my everything . . . so my friend that's a police officer said go file a report, file a restraining order, but I said I don't want to do all that stuff. I just want to be on record, and if you can get the purse back, that would be lovely because all my stuff is in there and I'm really mad about my lip gloss." Lori was cute and blond and wearing her customary spandex. When she giggled, the officers chuckled with her. The police officer Lori mentioned to the officers was, in fact, the retired Phoenix police officer she knew from the Mesa temple named Jason Mow.

It's apparent from the recorded interview the officers didn't see the need for the mental health order. They coached Lori about how to avoid being served. After some discussion, Lori agreed to clear up any confusion by going to an agency called Community Bridges for an evaluation. She laughingly said she could use a vacation. Tylee said she needed a padded room. When a mental health order is requested, the person is referred to an agency like Community Bridges for a screening to determine if a complete, court-ordered mental evaluation is necessary. If the screening determines that an assessment is needed, the person can be detained for up to seventy-two hours. If no assessment is required, the person is released. Lori passed the cursory evaluation with flying colors. She was oriented to time and place and appeared nominally grounded in reality. This would be a common theme in the coming months—Lori could appear frighteningly normal while firmly and deeply gripped by religious delusion. It was Charles's first effort to get help for Lori, but it would not be the last.

Lori now listened only to Chad Daybell, her new prophet, who warned her about her husband. The police investigation later revealed Chad had searched Google for "ned snider 1996 death Louisiana" and "bodies possessed after original occupant dies" just a day before Charles was locked out of their house and his truck was hidden from him. Lori had lunch with Zulema Pastenes and Melanie Gibb that day and told them she knew from Chad that Charles was dead and an evil spirit was inhabiting his body. Less than a week after this incident, in February 2019, Lori left Charles and disappeared for weeks with Tylee. Charles's only way to reach Lori was by email and text. Dejected, he filed for divorce and moved with JJ to Houston. He sent Lori message after message, reminding her how many days it had been since she had any contact with JJ, but she never responded. Lori spent some of that time living with her brother Alex. She and Tylee also visited their old friend, April Raymond, in Hawaii.

Lori's arrival at April's home in Kauai, Hawaii, was unexpected. After landing at the airport, Lori called April and announced she was divorcing Charles and needed a place to stay. Lori and Tylee stayed with April at her home for about a week. When April asked about JJ, Lori replied that she was "done with JJ" and that Charles and his sister would have to "figure it out." April took that to mean that JJ would be staying with Charles after the divorce. Lori told April that Charles was not Charles anymore; he was a demon named Ned Schneider. Lori had more to tell April. God had appointed Lori to gather the 144,000 that would usher in the second coming of Jesus Christ, and she was there to "gather" April. She wanted April to travel the world with her and gather others, but April would have to leave her two children to accompany Lori on their mission.

April said Lori arrived with a suitcase full of papers outlining Chad's light and dark rubric and the past lives each had lived. While Lori was there, she talked on the phone to her son Colby every day, but April did not remember Lori calling JJ once during the week. This was not the first time Lori had talked to April about her new beliefs. Around the time Lori met Chad Daybell in late 2018, she told April about her belief in multiple mortal probations and that the second coming of Jesus Christ was imminent. This visit in early 2019 was different; Lori's speech was pressured, and her affect seemed more manic as she shuffled through stacks of papers, pointing out lists of which people were light and dark and who would be included in the 144,000. At first, April was skeptical and told Lori so. It wasn't until later that April realized Lori's new ideas weren't just laughable; they were dangerous. April chuckled later when she recalled how her name had been penciled in above another name on Lori's list that had been crossed out. The lists included family members, friends, politicians, religious leaders, and celebrities. April recalled that, according to Chad, Oprah Winfrey was one of the darkest spirits on the planet.

Lori explained to April that she received this special knowledge from her new friend, Chad Daybell. She said Chad was a prophet who could see beyond the veil. April told Lori she didn't believe any of it, and after about a week, Lori and Tylee moved from April's home to the Kauai Beach Resort, where Lori stayed for nearly a month. Tylee didn't stay the entire time; she flew back to Arizona, where she lived with her uncle, Alex Cox, and worked with her aunt, Summer Shiflet. Summer's husband was a chiropractor, and Tylee worked in his office. The situation appeared to raise no concern for Alex. After all, God appointed him to support and protect Lori, not to question her actions. No one knows how Tylee felt about her mother's deepening mental health crisis.

Melanie Gibb joined Lori in Hawaii for the latter part of that visit. April recalled Lori and Melanie talking about when Lori took Charles's truck from the airport. "Melanie drank the Kool-Aid, too," April said.[4] Melanie confirmed everything Lori was saying—Charles was dead, and a demon had his body; the 144,000 needed to be gathered soon. Lori was a goddess.

Lori often preserved information by taking screenshots on her phone or photographs of her computer screen. Later, investigators would find those files stored in Lori's iCloud account and use them to track her movements. On March 3, 2019, while Charles had no idea where she was, Lori flew to Idaho. Then, on March 19, 2019, she flew with Chad from Idaho Falls back to Arizona.

Then, as quickly as she had vanished, Lori reappeared at Charles's home in Houston in April 2019, acting as if nothing had happened. The couple briefly reconciled, and Charles emailed his divorce lawyer, asking to dismiss the divorce case. He ended the email by saying, "Love always wins." People who knew Charles said the message didn't sound like him. They wondered if Lori had written it. Lori told Melanie Gibb that she had only returned to Charles to "get his finances in order." Lori didn't take long to sour on their reconciliation, and a few weeks later, she demanded to move back to Arizona. Charles rented the house for her in Chandler, and by June, she and JJ had moved back; Tylee left her uncle Alex's home and moved back home with her mom. The four-bedroom, 3100-square-foot home was beautiful. The front door was tucked into a long portico with a wide, double front door. Inside, a black-and-white tiled entry ended in two broad curved steps down into a spacious living room with an expanse of windows that looked out over the backyard patio and swimming pool. The kitchen flowed into a family room with a gas fireplace. Outside, the swimming pool had a rock waterfall, and there was a fire pit and an outdoor kitchen with a built-in gas grill.

Charles stayed in Houston, certain the marriage was finally over. He planned frequent visits with JJ when he came to Arizona for business, but, as she had with Joe Ryan, Lori wouldn't make it easy. They exchanged bitter text messages back and forth. Lori had been in the new house for about three weeks when Charles asked to see JJ over the weekend. Lori categorically refused to let him stay in her home and arranged a hotel. JJ's autism made change difficult, so they agreed it was better for JJ to be at home at night rather than in a strange hotel with Charles. Instead, Charles planned to pick JJ up on Thursday and Friday mornings to take him to breakfast and then to school. For Charles, Friday morning would never come.

Charles had an additional reason for visiting Chandler that weekend. He had hoped to confront Lori about her increasingly troubling beliefs. Charles knew that visiting the LDS temple almost daily was a large part of Lori's life. He planned to involve Lori's bishop, hoping that if the bishop understood what Lori had been doing, he would suspend Lori's temple recommend. Charles enlisted the help of Lori's brother, Adam, to perform an informal intervention, hoping to persuade the bishop to help Lori. Charles was convinced that banning Lori, even temporarily, from attending the temple would shock her into reality. It was a naive plan that would backfire with fatal consequences.

4

THE SCIENTIFIC PHENOMENON KNOWN AS "LOIN FIRE"

C harles Vallow had been conveniently away on business in November 2018 when Lori and Chad met for the second time. Chad came to Arizona to speak at a Preparing a People event, and Lori invited several people, including Chad, to stay at her home. Those who attended said Lori and Chad visited the Mesa, AZ, temple together and took at least one early morning walk, where they were seen holding hands.

For members of The Church of Jesus Christ of Latter-day Saints, participating in temple rites is a privilege limited to those who have received a temple recommend from their bishop. The bishop must ensure that recommended members have the highest moral character and regularly pay their 10 percent tithe to the church. The bishop must confirm that the applicant obeys the laws of chastity, which forbids sex outside of marriage; abstains from using drugs, alcohol, tea, and coffee; and keeps the covenants made in the temple at their endowment and marriage ceremonies. The most significant LDS religious ordinances, marriage for time and eternity, and baptism, including baptisms and marriages for the dead, take place in the temple. Either the temple president or a temple sealer must preside over the ceremonies. Twenty-nine years earlier, Chad had been sealed to his wife, Tammy, in the Manti, Utah, temple for time and eternity. Lori had been married to Charles Vallow for fourteen years.

Chad and Lori were each still married to their living spouses when they visited the Mesa temple together in November of 2018, and Chad went rogue. He used the authority he claimed as a holder of the Melchizedek priesthood to seal himself to Lori for time and eternity. To his way of thinking, the sealing was merely a reaffirmation. At their first meeting, Chad told Lori they had been married in many other past lives. Their first marriage for time and eternity had been in the time of Jesus, when they had walked the dusty roads of Judea, Chad as Jesus's apostle and brother, James the Just, and Lori as his wife, Elena. At the close of that Arizona PAP conference, Chad returned home to his family in Rexburg, Idaho, where he kept what had happened in Arizona a secret. He and Lori got burner cell phones so they could text and talk to each other whenever they wanted. Over the next year, they would send thousands of text messages and spend hundreds of hours on the telephone. Chad claimed to have created a portal in Lori's closet so his spirit could span nearly one thousand miles between them and visit her whenever he wanted. The idea of portals was not typical of LDS doctrine but was a feature in *Visions of Glory*, a book Chad, Lori, and many of the neo-fundamentalists treated like scripture.

Chad sent Lori a series of texts retelling their love story. In the texts, Chad was again James, and Lori was Elena. The following is an unedited version of Chad's text string to Lori:

> Friday morning, October 24, driving south on the freeway. A voice said . . . "you will meet and extraordinary woman today who will change your life forever." This was shocking, since such a thing seemed very unlikely at this conference. It is actually a very detailed story that began long ago on another world, and I will cover that part as I go along and the characters figure things out.

But on the morning of Oct. 26th, James arrived in St. George still a bit baffled by the message he had received.

He unloaded his books and set up his table, then joined the organizers for dinner in the main room.

He saw his friend MG, who had been so helpful to him when he spoke in Mesa that July.

MG introduced James to her friend Elena. When their hands touched, he felt a shock pass through him, and his heart started beating fast.

Elena was gorgeous and vivacious, and James was a little intimidated yet honored that she would talk to him.

He was happily surprised when she mentioned a key part of his novel The Renewed Earth. No one had ever recognized the significance of that scene before.

He had heard that voice before, and seen that smile before. He felt they had even talked like this before. But who could be certain when?

It was strange, but he COULD remember.

The feelings were very strong, as if they had known each other oh so long.

They didn't get any chances to talk after that, because he had to help voice a woman's blue Muppet. But he watched her very chance he could. He had to stay at a relative's house that night, but he hardly slept. He kept envisioning himself with Elena in very wonderful situations that indicated they had been more than Just Friends.

James was the first speaker on Saturday morning, and knew exactly where Elena was sitting He made sure to mention the scene from his book that they had discussed the previous evening. He was completely smitten by her and even was nervous of what she would think of his talk as he spoke. But when he would glance at her, she was a ways attentive and watching him, unlike the rest of the crowd.

After his talk, he went to his book table. His talk had gone well, and there was a good group gathered around to buy books. His heart nearly leaped out of his chest when Elena joined him and helped sell the books. She was so beautiful that he could hardly concentrate on the customers.

She straightened the books and gave the books great reviews, although she made him laugh a lot when she kept pushing the youth [fourth] and fifth volumes of his first series. He could only giggle when people asked if she was his wife, because yes, in fact, she was. She just didn't know it yet.

James was definitely having amorous feelings toward Elena as they sold books together. He had not felt this happy in his entire life. He was quite sure this was the woman the voice had told him about. James was ecstatic, because he had already fallen deeply in love her. Or better said, he remembered how much he already loved her.

Her eyes had mesmerized him from the moment they met, but once the book sales slowed down, she stood near him behind the table. They looked deeply into each other's eye for the first time, and he knew he was in the presence of a goddess. He resisted an impulse to kiss her, but his entire body was on fire. He instinctively knew she was everything he had ever dreamed of.

I must clarify that James is a very difficult person to get information from. He has been blessed with great knowledge, but 99 percent of the people he knows do not realize that. He is very guarded, and it is a great task to gain his trust. But as Elena leaned forward and asked a couple of very insightful questions, his heart burst with joy. He knew she was one if the very few people on earth he could trust.

James' spirit was so excited at this revelation that he shattered thick veil that had been placed between the two souls during their mortal lives. The thick veil had been placed because of the unique, unparalleled love James and Elena had shared in previous lifetimes. The veil had prevented them from finding each other until this appointed day that would be remembered throughout the heavens as the true beginning of a spectacular mission that would save millions of souls and defeat the forces of darkness.

James' physical attraction to Elena was almost overwhelming, but he was equally drawn to the spiritual energy that was radiating from he As they talked, it was confirmed to him that they had indeed been married before and were eternal companions.

He had glimpses of them walking dusty paths together, and he realized they had been married during the life of Jesus Christ, and they had been very close to Him.

At this time, their spirits could not be restrained any longer, and a long-awaited make-out session took place in that lobby. This was manifest in the mortal world to James and Elena through the scientific phenomenon known as "loin fire."

As they talked, James had a burning desire to make love to her, but he wasn't sure she felt the same way. But they could not stay away from each other. One time she was sitting in a couch near his table, and he took a seat on a chair about five feet from her. She began to squirm and covered her body with her hands. She asked him, "What are you doing?" He wasn't aware of what she meant. All he knew was that if Bruce Porter hadn't been giving them an evil eye, a child would have been conceived on that couch.

The erotic tension continued throughout the afternoon. James could only think of her. His desire for her was indescribable. Thankfully she had worn 16 layers of clothing to survive the 80-degree weather, so he as not fully aware that she truly had the body of a goddess. Her dimensions were exactly what he had always fantasized about. But that revelation would have to wait a month.

As the night concluded, James need to take his empty boxes to his car. With Elena's help he had sold more books at a show than he ever had before. She helped him carry the boxes to the car, and then he could not resist the desire to hug her. He made an awkward attempt that was way to brief, because their friends were bringing more boxes. In that short embrace, though, he knew he had found the woman he had searched for his entire life. It was made crystal clear to him that they had been married before and would be again. He once again had to fight off a powerful urge to kiss her, and somehow disguise the massive erection he was experiencing.

They returned to the building and he helped carry tables to the second floor while she sat on the couch. They couldn't take their eyes off each other. He was already madly in love.

Her group of friends finally had to leave. He was devastated, unused how he would ever contact her again. Then her spirit took over and asked him, "Can I get your cell number in case I have some questions?"

They exchanged numbers, and then they gave each other a hug goodbye. It was the most wonderful, electric, delicious hug he had ever felt. Then he watched her walk away, knowing she was truly going to change his life forever.

END OF CHAPTER ONE

Chapter Two

James sadly walked to his car after watching Elena disappear down the hallway. But he couldn't deny their connection and his absolute attraction to her. She still seemed way out of his league, but he nervously sent her a text before driving to his hotel. A minute passed, then two, without a response. He kicked himself for thinking he ever had a chance with her. Then his phone buzzed. Elena had texted back! His heart soared, and over the next few hours they texted back and forth dozens of times. He knew she was staying at a home in Toquerville, and he desperately wanted to drive there and whisk her back to the hotel for a night of reconnection and romance.

He twice got redressed during the night to go see her, but the Spirit gently said, "Have patience. everything will work out as it is supposed to" They finally stopped texting at around 4 A.M., and when he closed his eyes to sleep, he was taken again to their previous life together. The intense passion of their lovemaking was as sight to behold. He knew it would be difficult, but he could be patient if it meant he could experience that type of love just once in his life.

As he lay in the hotel bed it was as if her spirit had joined him. They wrapped around each other and kissed gently, then intensely, and the emotions they shared were not of this world.

James woke up in the hotel room feeling happier than he had in his entire life. It felt like he and Elena had fit together perfectly in every way. He rolled over to kiss her, then reality struck. She was actually more than twenty miles away in Toquerville with her Arizona friends. He texted her, and she quickly responded He deeply regretted not going to be with her the night before. It was as if he already knew the taste of her lips, and his hands knew every curve of her body. He knows his dreams were somehow real, and that they were actually traveling to each other in a higher dimension. He hungered for her in ways he didn't think were possible. The voice was right. Elena was going to change his life forever.

He packed his suitcase and began driving north on the freeway. As each mile passed, James could feel Elena's spirit beckoning for him to join her. As he approached the Toquerville exit, it took every ounce of willpower to keep driving on the freeway. His attraction to her was beyond magnetic. He felt their souls were two halves of an eternal union. Tears filled his eyes as he passed the freeway exit. He desperately yearned to embrace her and tell her he deeply loved her, as crazy as that sounded. But he knew he would be seeing her three weeks later at a conference in Arizona. It seemed like an eternity away, but he sensed it would be a very significant weekend for them. He already was crazy about her, and his feelings of admiration and affection for her would only grow more intense and wonderful.

During his long drive home, James was able to text back and forth with Elena, and it was clear they were extremely compatible and shared the same interests. It felt like talking to a long-distance best friend. When he arrived home, he searched the internet for anything about her, but there was nothing. She was a fascinating mystery that he wanted to spend the rest of eternity with. At the end if his drive, she suggested that they talk on the phone the next day. He was thrilled at the thought of hearing her voice again. He was falling more madly in love by the minute.

When James heard her voice that Monday morning, the euphoria he had felt Saturday came rushing back strongly They talked for two hours, but it seemed to be only minutes. He was obsessed with her and couldn't get enough.

During that first phone conversation with Elena, James realized she already had a strong understanding of many of the truths he had been taught regarding how the universe really worked. The lounge [loin] fire and obsession with each other had no real explanation unless they truly had a spiritual connection before this life. He was able to help clarify many if the promptings and impressions she had felt in recent years. She knew she had lived on earth before, and James was able to clarify when. They had been married before on this earth, and other times on a previous earth. Their love truly spanned the universe and the eons of time. They knew the Lord had brought them together again for a crucial mission that only they could accomplish as a untied couple.

During the next week they spoke every day for at least an hour, but often longer. They hungered to know everything about each other This was a new experience for James to pen up and share the true feelings of his heart. But he knew he could trust her completely. The bond between them was intense, and only the vast distance between them kept their passion for each other from roaring into a blazing inferno. She quickly became his best friend. Or better said, two best friends had reunited and their prior love was now ignited again in a wonderful, heavenly way.

As November began, James and Elena had talked on the phone every day since last seeing each other. He was extremely impressed with her intelligence, personality, and subtle humor that made him laugh more than he had in this lifetime.

She was a complete delight to talk to, and the highlight of his day was when he could hear her magical voice. It was so familiar to him, and it actually healed and soothed his heart and soul.

They would both attend the same event in mid-November, and it seemed like that day would never arrive. Each day they opened their hearts to each other a little more. James knew he could trust her with the mysteries of the universe that had been revealed to him. He knew they had been married before, and they had been close friends with the Savior when he lived in Jerusalem. James had served in an important position in the Lord's church, and Elena had been his beloved spouse and best friend. That relationship was now meant to continue in this lifetime.

In Jerusalem James and Elena had enjoyed tremendous intimacy. Their physical desire for each other was unmatched, and they were for fortunate that they could be alone morning, noon and night, and they seized every chance to passionately express their love to each other. They simply could never get enough, even after many years of marriage. Everyone knew they were crazy about each other, and they were a wonderful example of how spouses should cleave together in love and unity.

James had visions of how they would happily and joyfully pleasure each other in his office. They had two favorite positions that particularly bonded them together. Nothing meant more to James than holding Elena n his arms and unifying their bodies in perfect synchronization.

James and Elena talked on the phone, he tried to delicately describe their connection to each other, and he was delighted that she believed him. He also shared that they had been married other times on a previous world and she accepted that information as well.

James was overjoyed to have these memories restored to him, because he truly loved her with all of his heart. He knew they were meant to be married again and complete important missions together before the Second Coming. He was ecstatic that she was receiving confirmation of these things as well. As they talked on the phone, the spiritual connection was so intense that it also produced physical desires, and it was as if their spirits were making love despite the great distance between them. James knew his spirit was visiting her during those conversations. He also became aware that his spirit would visit her at night, and they would wrap around each other in a sensual embrace. Kissing her was so wonderful and real, and he knew that the next time they saw each other, he needed to kiss her. He wouldn't be able to resist holding her he was absolutely in love with her in every way.

By the time the conference arrived, James and Elena had become very close through their phone conversations, but he desperately needed to see her again. She agreed to pick him up at the airport and take him to his hotel. He was extremely nervous, worried that the spark they had felt earlier might not be there. But as she arrived at the airport, and he opened the car door, his heart nearly burst at the sight of her smile. She was stunningly gorgeous, and as they gripped each other's hands, the electricity was tangible. The love between them was powerful and real.

The hotel was only a short distance away, and he invited her into the room. They were soon standing alone in the room and he put his arm around her and looked into her gorgeous blue eyes. They hungered for each other and he leaned forward and fulfilled a promise he had made to her a few days earlier. He gently kissed her tender lips and the same heavenly electricity filled his entire body.

The passionate magic they had felt many centuries earlier came surging back powerfully. James moved to the couch and Elena straddled him effortlessly as if they had done this thousands of times before. She fit perfectly on him, and they pressed their loins tightly against each other. The feeling was exquisite, and they both smiled and moaned at the sensations passing between them. They were still fully clothed, but the intensity of the intimacy was undeniable.

James felt the powerful desire to bless Elena at that time. As they stayed in that favorite position, he moved his hands to her head and began to cleanse and purify each part of her body. He could feel the pains and troubles she had endured throughout her life being removed from her soul and being taken outside and destroyed. James's hands worked their way down her body and lingered briefly on her beautiful breasts. She truly had the body of a goddess., and he was experiencing an indescribably mix of physical and spiritual ecstasy. He soon concluded the cleansing of her body from head to toe, then filled her body with a balm of light and love.

James could see the happiness in her eyes, and instinctively their mouths came together again. The fire was burning strongly within them both, and as their kissing grew more intense, he gently said, "I love you, Elena."

Those words sparked a frenzy within them. Their tongues effortlessly entwined and their hips gyrated in a smooth erotic rhythm. Two lovers, long separated, were finally united in heavenly bliss.

After a few minutes of excitement, pleasure, and fun on the couch, James and Elena both felt compelled to change into more comfortable clothing. James out in some athletic shorts and a blue shirt, and Elena put on a stunning black top and tight leggings. The top revealed just enough, but not too much, and James was overjoyed at the sight

James took her in his arms, and they smiled at each other. The vibration in the room was intense and their hearts reached out to each other in a glorious reunion. James gently touched the sides if Elena's breasts, and he was in ecstasy. She stood on her tiptoes and gave him a sensual kiss that sent electricity throughout his body. They moved toward the bed, and were quickly entwined around each other. She was so beautiful, loving, and enchanting that James could hardly breathe. They were both aroused, but knew there were limitations on what could occur that night. But they kissed for nearly an hour and pressed against each other tightly. Toward the end of the evening, Elena laud on her stomach at the end of the bed, and James caressed her fabulous body. He grasped her perfect bottom with both hands, and she expressed how much she loved that. She soon sat up and straddled him again as they passionately kissed farewell. They knew they would see each other again in the morning, but the separation seemed too long. But they knew that the long wait to find their eternal match had come to an end, and James was overjoyed beyond description.

James and Elena had agreed to visit the temple the following morning She returned to the hotel room and after additional romance on the couch, they calmed their nerves enough to give each other a blessing. As James placed his hands on her head, he connected with Elena's true eternal self. He knew he was in the presence of an exalted goddess who had returned to earth to perform a special mission. This mission included being with him, and they would progress together as translated beings. The full plan wasn't yet completely clear to him, but the immense power radiating from her confirmed his belief that she was among the greatest women in the universe.

She then gave him a tremendous blessing that helped him realize how much she truly loved him and a wanted to be with him forever. He was deeply humbled that such an incredible woman regarded him so highly. His heart burned as she blessed him, and he had glimpses come to his mind of not only their life in Jerusalem, but even as a couple on a previous earth. He knew they had been eternal companions for eons, and that their love was beyond Celestial.

They embraced following the blessings, and the emotions they felt were a mixture of eternal bliss and telestial desire. The sexual chemistry was undeniable, but the spiritual unity was a glorious bonus for them both. They had only known each other for three weeks, but two lonely, misunderstood souls had finally found their best friend that they could trust and confide in.

They arrived at the temple, and they both felt they should do sealings together. They were soon seated in a sealing room, facing each other. Elena looked so stunning as she smiled at him. She seemed calm, while he felt quite nervous. Their opportunity soon came to kneel across the altar from each other, and as the sealer pronounced those sacred words, James and Elena knew that they were now sealed as husband and wife for eternity. As the earthly sealing was taking place, a similar scene involving their spirits was happening on a higher plane, where they kissed and unified their souls. They knew they had just begun a new journey together that was eternal and never-ending.

After the sealing they went to lunch together, and they felt so comfortable together Everything felt so right. James could look into her eyes forever, unless he was gently kissing her and telling her how much he loved her. Even when they held hands, there was a powerful vibration that exceeded the telestial world. The attended the conference but their thoughts were completely focused on each other. James gave a talk that was well received and sparked great interest in his books. Elena joined him at the selling table and they sold more than 359 book within a couple hours. But all the really wanted was to slip away and express their love to each other.

They went to dinner with some friends, but afterward they were able to find time alone. They drove to secluded area and slipped into the back seat. Elena was wearing a pair of incredibly sexy jeans, and as she straddled James in the back seat, he once again grasped her fantastic bottom. She pushed him back into a reclining position, and their loins fit perfectly together. They kissed passionately and rhythmically pulsated against each other. Their love was intense and undeniably real. James was now madly, crazily in love with her, and it was so wonderful to know she felt the same way about him.

One powerful moment happened earlier that day when Elena was listening to another speaker while James stayed at the table. But he thought he heard Elena say, "Come stand behind me." He went into the room and saw her standing against a wall. He moved behind her, and they discreetly touched. After a few minutes he checked his phone and saw she had texted him that very sentence at the stone he heard her voice. It was a wonderful testament that they were already communicating with each other on a higher level.

They helped clean up the conference, and Elena graciously allowed James to stay in a spare bedroom at her home that night. They visited with other friends until after midnight, then they all went to bed. James anxiously hoped Elena would join him in the spare room.

It took a while for everyone to settle into their beds, but once the house quieted down, James opened his door slightly and saw the wondrous sight of Elena approaching the room. They locked the door behind her and quickly got under the covers. He was wearing his athletic shorts, and she was wearing tight, thin leggings and a loose top. They clung to each other and kissed desperately, hungrily. James placed his hands under her top and caressed her splendid breasts. She moaned happily and wrapped her legs around his waist. Only two things layers of material separated their loins, and they could feel each other's most intimate body parts in detail. The intensity and spiritual vibration exceeded anything either one of them had ever felt before. They knew their spirits were actually intimately joined together, and it felt like they left the telestial world. Elena soon got on top of James, and the rhythmic ecstasy continued for several more minutes. Toward the end, they both removed their tops, and they pressed their bodies together, skin on skin. They fit ether perfectly, and heir kisses were deep and frenzied Their desire for each other was beyond compare.

As the reunion in the spare room came to a conclusion, Raphael [James] knew Elena was his perfect match. They longed to stay entwined together, but it would be best to separate and get some rest.

But by 6 A.M., James couldn't stand to be way from her any longer. He slipped into her bedroom and stood at her bedside She was unbelievably gorgeous, and he greatly desired to join her in the bed and continue the previous night's activities. But there were other guests in the house who weren't yet aware of their sizzling love for each other. So he gently touched her shoulder to awaken her. Her eyes opened, then she reached up and grabbed his arms to pull him into the bed. He smiled, realizing she wasn't fully awake and had likely been dreaming of him. He simply whispered that he loved her and hoped she would go walking with him through the neighborhood.

James and Elena had enjoyed a walk together the previous morning along the quiet streets of her gated community. The sensual attraction between them had been intense, and they had touched shoulders and held hands as they walked. They were like magnets that couldn't be separated. She had worn exercise leggings that drove him crazy with desire. The leggings emphasized her perfectly sculpted bottom, and it took all if his willpower not to pull her to him and grasp that bottom firmly and powerfully with both hands, while kissing her passionately.

They went walking again that next morning. Unfortunately a friend invited herself along, but James and Elena were still completely engrossed in each other. He had to catch flight home later that morning, but he was able to give Elena a special blessing before departing. As he placed his hands on her head, he felt their spirits connect with a surge of power.

At that moment, his only desire in life was to be with her as always throughout eternity and that desire has continued to intensify. During the blessing he was shown the great missions they would perform together. He knew this was an eternal union that would forever change the world. Tears filled his eyes to be in the presence of this holy goddess and he was nearly overcome by the Spirit as he sensed her true place in the universe as a majestic archangel.

END OF STORY

The lengthy story contained in a series of text messages confirmed a conclusion many had already come to: visionary or not, Chad was a terrible writer. His work was derivative, clumsy, and juvenile. Nevertheless, when the text messages became public, "loin fire" began trending on social media and *Dateline*'s Keith Morrison repeated it in his signature growl during a segment about the case. Chad's text thread confirmed significant parts of their story. Chad and Lori had sealed themselves to one another in the temple while still married to other spouses. Lori claimed that the angel Moroni, an important prophet in LDS doctrine, and Jesus Christ were present in person at that sealing. When the texts were released, LDS church members quickly pointed out that Lori and Chad's sealing was not sanctioned by the church or performed by a recognized church officiant.

The couple saw one another at other conferences as often as they could arrange. While Chad worked to keep his home life calm, all of the stresses simmering in Lori's life came to a full boil.

5

"I SHOT MY
BROTHER-IN-LAW"

Lori Vallow's older brother, Alexander Lamar Cox, was born in Provo, Utah, on January 18, 1968. He suffered a head injury in a car crash at age sixteen. Friends and family said after his accident, Alex seemed stuck at the emotional age of sixteen. He was a promiscuous free spirit who was unafraid of risks. These are not qualities highly valued in The Church of Jesus Christ of Latter-day Saints, where Alex grew up. He was excommunicated, rebaptized, allowed to return to the fold, and excommunicated again. He was the funny brother; his voice impressions, especially of cartoon characters, were hilarious.

Alex was married for a year to a woman who asked the media to identify her only as "Debbie." They married in 1992 and divorced in 1993 but remained in touch. The last time Debbie talked to Alex was right after he was released from jail for the assault on Lori's third husband, Joe Ryan. Alex told Debbie he had attacked Joe Ryan because of what Lori had accused Joe of doing. Alex said Joe deserved to die for it and that he wanted to lure him into a fight so he could kill Joe in self-defense.

Except for Lori, Debbie had not met the Cox family before she and Alex were married. As she got to know them, things about them made her uncomfortable. Debbie said there was a lot of inappropriate sexual touching in the family, mainly between Alex and Lori. Debbie said Lori would jump into Alex's arms and wrap her legs around his waist, and then Alex would bounce her up and down while they both moaned as if they were having sex. She said those incidents happened in front of the other family members, who appeared unfazed by the behavior. She also said the Cox parents, Janis and Barry, openly discussed their sex life in front of the family. The Cox family denies Debbie's claims. Debbie said she and Alex only lived together for about four or five months before she decided to end the marriage. She said Alex talked about how "hot" Lori was and spent a lot of time with his sister. He worried about where Lori went, what she did, and with whom. Debbie thought Alex had a sexual addiction. When they first married, Debbie wanted to move from Texas to Utah, but Alex refused. Then, one day, Alex came home from work and abruptly told her they were moving to Utah that day. Later, Debbie later learned that Alex had sex with a fifteen-year-old girl and was fleeing Texas to avoid possible prosecution. When Debbie heard what had happened to Charles Vallow, it sounded so much like what Alex had planned to do to Joe Ryan that she decided to come forward and tell the police.[1]

Alex Cox had always seen himself as Lori's protector, even before Chad Daybell announced to Alex that his mission in this probation was to protect his powerful goddess sister. Alex likely learned some of this behavior from his father, Barry Cox. In 1995, Barry was arrested in King County, Washington, and charged with assault for a confrontation with Steve Cope, Barry's daughter Stacey's estranged husband. Stacey was Barry's oldest daughter and sister to Lori and Alex. She and her husband, Steve, were in the midst of a bitter divorce and custody battle when the assault happened. Stacey, who died at age thirty-one, had many medical problems, including type 1 diabetes, and the reports on her short life vary. According to some, Stacey had an eating disorder, which can be common in young women who have had diabetes since childhood. Stacey is also reported to have had mental health problems that led Steve Cope to separate from her and remove their young daughter, Melani Cope, from her care. In his documents seeking custody, Steve Cope alleged mental illness ran in the family and that it was common knowledge Barry had been diagnosed with schizophrenia. An incident with Cope gave rise to the charges against Barry when he arrived at Cope's work. According to Cope's application for an order of protection, Barry first wanted to discuss Steve and Stacey's divorce, then began quoting scripture and questioning Cope's integrity. Cope told police he found that ironic because Barry had just been charged with solicitation of prostitution. No record of such charges could be located as this book was written. Cope reported that although he had asked Barry to lower his voice, Barry had become louder and angrier. Barry then grabbed the front of Cope's shirt, stuffed a handful of papers in it, and said, "You've been served." Barry grabbed Cope by the collar, slammed him against a wall, and pressed his fist into Cope's throat. Barry left as Cope's secretary was calling the police. It is also unclear from the official records how the criminal case surrounding this incident was resolved.

Alex Cox often performed at comedy club open mic nights, where he made friends with other comedians, including Jill Kimmel, sister of late-night host Jimmy Kimmel. Jill said Alex was usually funny and easygoing, but one incident stood out. It was the day Alex called and asked her, "Do you know where I can get a piece?"[2] Kimmel was confused, and Alex clarified that he was looking for a gun. He told her he intended to go to Texas and "pistol whip" Joe Ryan for abusing Lori's children. Kimmel said it was strange how things later played out. "He loved those kids; he was willing to put his own freedom on the line to protect those kids. There's no way he would have hurt them." It only makes sense to Kimmel if Alex was "brain-washed into it." And only one person would have had the ability to do that.

Lori's other brother, Adam, was close to Lori's husband, Charles. Adam, a popular morning radio personality, was living and broadcasting in Kansas when Charles confided his concerns for Lori's mental condition. On June 29, 2019, Charles wrote to Adam in an email, "Open this letter and see what she did. I'm not sure if [sic] the relationship with her and Chad Daybell, but they are up to something. She created an email alias for me, as I've never set this one up. She sent this yesterday, and I guess she forgot all her emails are on the computer at my house." Lori made the email look like Charles had written to invite Chad to come to Arizona to help Charles write a book. Lori created the email to give Chad an excuse to travel to Arizona.

In July 2019, as Charles was planning to visit JJ in Arizona, he asked Adam to meet him there to help stage the informal intervention for Lori. According to Adam, Charles hoped that getting the church to suspend Lori's access to the temple would bring her back to reality. Charles scheduled the trip from his home in Houston to Chandler, Arizona, and arranged flights for Adam and Adam's son, Zach, from Kansas that weekend. He hoped Adam and Zach would add weight to Charles's plea. Zach had lived with Lori and Charles and knew firsthand how strange Lori and Alex's behavior had become. Zach said Alex once offered him $100 to read one of Chad Daybell's books. Charles intended the intervention to remain a secret so Lori wouldn't run, but a day or two before Charles arrived in Chandler, someone in Lori's family found out and let the secret slip. The rest of the Cox family did what they always did: they closed ranks around Lori. When Adam told their mother, Janis, that he was worried about Lori, Janis told Adam that his sister's delusions were harmless and that they should just leave Lori alone and let her live in them. Lori's sister, Summer, later admitted she was the one who told Lori about Charles's plan. She also told Alex he needed to stay with Lori to protect her when Charles came to the house to pick up JJ.

Two days before Charles arrived, Lori exchanged texts with her niece, Melani Boudreaux Pawlowski. Melani, who was nine years old when her mother, Stacey, died, was deeply attached to Lori as a mother figure. She believed everything Lori told her about the new beliefs. Melani was planning to attend a wedding in Utah that weekend, but Lori texted, "U can't go tomorrow. It's a setup for both of us. Still on the phone finding out the details." Lori was on the phone with Chad Daybell, seeking advice and information from his visions. Lori said, "They have an elaborate plan. I'll call you soon." Melani replied, "I could take all the babies and drive? And take our stuff." Lori responded, "U can't go at all. We both need to stay here and defend ourselves. It's coming to a head! This week will change everything." Melani responded, "Probably why I've felt sick about going. Even when told to plan to go." Later, Lori texted Melani, "They are gathering witnesses. It's just like Twilight. They are the vulture." Lori was likely referring to the Volturi, a secret ruling organization of vampires.

The same evening, Lori sent Alex this text: "Getting sleepy. So I'm going to need you to stay close to me for the next couple days. Mel too. She can't go to Utah. They are planking [*sic*] some kind of intervention but want Mel out of the way so I'm left alone. I need to come get the stuff at your house tomorrow and secure it. Lots to do. Thank you for standing by me. It's all coming to a head this week. I will be like Nelphi, I am told! And so will you." As she had with Joe Ryan, Lori looked to scripture for justification. The following day, Lori texted Alex, "So the plot thickens. Call me when u can." Lori and Alex talked on the phone for nearly an hour. Lori's best friend, Melanie Gibb, spent the night at Lori's house, but in the morning, Lori told Melanie she had to leave because Charles was coming to town and was planning to kill her. Lori said her brother Adam, his son Zach, Melani's husband, Brandon Boudreaux, and Lori's father, Barry, were all out to get her for her three-million-dollar life insurance policy. She said they were all dark spirits and zombies who wanted her money. This would become a common tactic for Lori, projecting her feelings and plans onto others.

The next day, July 10, 2019, Lori and Alex had lunch with Melani before they headed to their sister Summer's house. Texts between Summer and Lori make clear that Summer was the source of the information about Adam and Charles's plans. None of them truly understood the depth of Lori's illness and delusions or the coming danger. Lori talked to Chad for more than two hours that day.

The following morning, July 11, Charles Vallow would be dead.

That morning, between the time Charles was shot and the time the police were called, a flurry of text messages and short phone calls flew between Alex, Lori, Chad, and Melani. Lori also sent a text to her friend, Audrey Barattiero. None of the text messages appeared on their devices when they were seized, suggesting they were deleted.

Lori Vallow Daybell is the only person who knows what happened on July 11, 2019, in the mirrored living room of the house on Four Peaks Place. Everyone else who was there that morning—Charles Vallow, Alex Cox, Tylee Ryan, and JJ Vallow—are dead.

Nothing was stirring, and the house was silent when the first police officer entered and yelled, "Chandler Police Department. Anyone inside, make yourself known!" The officer's voice bounced off the gleaming black-and-white entry tile and echoed from the hard walls and floor of the empty living room where dance studio mirrors covered three walls. A large man lay face up on the wood floor, unmoving in the empty room. The officer quickly checked each room, securing the house for the first responders who came behind him. His bodycam caught the walkthrough.

Minutes earlier, a 911 dispatch center had received this call from Lori Vallow Daybell's brother Alex Cox:

Emergency Dispatcher: 911. Where is your emergency?

AC: It's at, uh, 5531 South Four Peaks; I think it's Four Peaks Lane, I'm not sure.

Dispatcher: I'm sorry, you say you don't know the direction?

AC: I don't know the street name, whether it's lane or court.

Dispatcher: 5531 South Four Peaks in Chandler. Is that right?

AC: Yes, yes.

Dispatcher: Do you need police or paramedics?

AC: Both. I need police and an ambulance.

Dispatcher: What's the emergency there?

AC: Uh, there's a . . . I got in a fight with my brother-in-law, and I shot him in self-defense.

Dispatcher: Okay, let me get the medics on the phone. Is he hurt, or is he . . . alive? (Alex believes the dispatcher said "blood.")

AC: Yeah, there's blood; he's not movin'.

Dispatcher: How long ago did this happen?

AC: A couple of minutes.

(the sound of a phone ringing as the phone is transferred to the next operator)

Fire Dispatcher: What is the address of the emergency?

AC: 5531 South Four Peaks.

Fire Dispatcher: And is that a house in Chandler?

AC: Yes.

Fire Dispatcher: Phone number, please?

AC: (480) 351-9120.

Fire Dispatcher: And just repeat the address to be sure.

AC: 5531 South Four Peaks.

Fire Dispatcher: And what is the emergency?

AC: Uh . . . I, I shot my brother-in-law.

Fire Dispatcher: Okay, what part of his body is injured?

AC: (unintelligible)

Fire Dispatcher: I'm sorry, where?

AC: In the chest.

Fire Dispatcher: Okay, is he awake and responsive or unconscious?

AC: Unconscious.

Fire Dispatcher: Okay, is he breathing?

AC: I can't tell.

Fire Dispatcher: Are you willing to go over to him and check?

AC: Sure.

Fire Dispatcher: Okay, just let me know if you see his chest going up and down. How old is he?

AC: It's not moving. He's sixty.

Fire Dispatcher: Okay, and are you wanting to start CPR?

AC: No, I don't know how to do that.

Fire Dispatcher: I can walk you through it.

AC: Okay.

Fire Dispatcher: Okay, what I want you to do is you're gonna put one hand in the center of his chest; the other hand is going to go right on top of it . . .

AC: Okay.

Fire Dispatcher: You're going to interlock your fingers, keeping your arms straight, and you're going to press down hard and fast into his chest. You're going two inches down and fairly quickly one, two, three, four, five, six, seven, eight, nine, ten, making sure his chest goes up between each compression. Where's the gun now?

AC: It's in the other room.

Fire Dispatcher: PD, we're (unintelligible aside to the police). Just keep going with those compressions. PD, do you have any other questions?

Police Dispatch: Yes, what's your name, sir?

AC: My name's Alex, last name's Cox, C-O-X.

Police Dispatch: And where are you in the house now?

AC: Uh, in the living room.

Police Dispatch: And where is the gun?

AC: Uh, it's in a bedroom.

Police Dispatch: Who else is there in the house with you?

AC: Uh, just me.

Police Dispatch: What kind of a gun is it?

AC: It's my gun; it's a .45.

Police Dispatch: A pistol? A .45 caliber pistol?

AC: Yeah, yeah.

Police Dispatch: What's his name, your brother-in-law?

AC: Charles Vallow.

Police Dispatch: His last name, I'm sorry?

AC: V-A-L-L-O.

Police Dispatch: V like Victor?

AC: V like Victor.

Police Dispatch: Police and medics are on the way to help you.

AC: Thank you.

Police Dispatch: Are you still doing chest compressions on him?

AC: Yes.

Fire Dispatcher: Okay, just keep pushing down hard and fast in the center of his chest. How long ago did this occur? Did it just happen?

AC: Yeah, maybe five minutes before I called.

Fire Dispatcher: Okay. Make sure you're still pressing down at least two inches into his chest and that his chest comes up after each compression, one, two, three, four, five, six, seven, eight, nine, ten. (The dispatcher continues to count, and Alex can be heard breathing hard). So were you guys arguing when this happened?

AC: Yeah.

Fire Dispatcher: Okay. And you said there's nobody else there, just you and him, correct?

AC: Correct.

Fire Dispatcher: (Aside to police: Can you just let us know when it's secure?)

Police Dispatch: Will do. Was he armed also, or was it just you?

AC: Yeah, he came at me with a bat.

Police Dispatch: Anyone drinking or doing drugs or anything today, or no?

AC: Uh, I don't know, but I've never seen him that enraged before.

Police Dispatch: Does he live here with you, or where does he live?

AC: No, he lives in Houston.

Police Dispatch: He's what, married to your sister. Is she there?

AC: Correct. I don't know; I think she's, uh, taking her son to school.

Police Dispatch: Doing the compressions. Is there any response from him?

AC: He's not responding at all.

Police Dispatch: The officers should be there; let me know when they get inside. Is the front door open . . . ?

AC: Yeah. It's unlocked.

Police Dispatch: Can you walk outside with your hands up and empty?

On police bodycam footage, Alex Cox can be seen walking out of the house with his hands up. He said he had no weapons, and his gun was still in the house. Police directed him to the curb, where he sat, dabbing at the back of his head with a paper towel while answering questions. Police looked him over. Performing CPR on a man with a gunshot wound to the chest, as Alex claimed he had done, is a messy business. Still, when Alex Cox came out of the house, there wasn't a spot of blood on his hands or clothing. The only blood visible was his own—a few smears on the paper towel he touched to the back of his head every so often. When the medics rushed to Charles Vallow a few moments later and began chest compressions, blood that had accumulated in his chest cavity gushed out, coating their gloved hands and pooling on the floor. It was evident that Charles Vallow was dead and that Alex Cox had only pretended to perform CPR while he was on the phone with 911.

From the outset, none of the stories Alex, Lori, and Tylee told about Charles's death added up. The situation was, as veteran cops might say, "hinkey." Hinkey is that sense, born of long experience, that something doesn't fit. For starters, there was the lack of blood anywhere on Alex Cox, and then there was his story. Cox said Charles had come to the house to pick up JJ, that Charles had put JJ in the car, then realized he'd left his telephone in the house and gone back inside. That's when Lori confronted him about something she saw on his phone, and they began to argue. Later, Lori told Melanie Gibb that she'd seen the phone in Charles's car while buckling JJ into his booster seat and that an angel had given her the passcode to discover evidence that Charles was cheating on her. According to Alex, as Lori and Charles argued over the contents of the phone, Lori's sixteen-year-old daughter, Tylee, came out of her room with a metal bat to protect her mother. The story seemed hinkey to the police because there were no reports that Charles had ever been violent or that he and Lori had ever had physical fights. Alex told authorities that Charles grabbed the bat from Tylee and threatened him with it, that Charles and Alex "tussled," and Charles hit Alex in the back of the head with the bat. Alex said Lori left, taking Charles's rental car to take JJ to school. Alex described to police how he went to his room to get the gun he always carried and returned to the living room. Alex said Charles kept coming toward him despite Alex pointing the gun at him, and that was when Alex fired two shots into Charles's chest "to stop him." When Lori and Tylee returned to the house, police cars and an ambulance were parked in front.

The probable cause declaration filed with Lori Vallow Daybell's Arizona indictment for Charles's murder painted a different picture. Lori Vallow Daybell left her house at 7:49 A.M., driving Charles's rental car and carrying Charles's cell phone. Lori reported she heard the gunshot while still in the house, but Tylee reported that she and Lori heard a gunshot as they left the house. Lori and Tylee stopped at Burger King to get JJ breakfast, dropped him at school, and then went by Walgreens to buy flip-flops because they had rushed out of the house without shoes. Store camera footage shows Lori buying the shoes, removing the tags on one pair, and putting them on. When Alex called 911, he told the operator the shooting had happened about five minutes before his call. In truth, Alex Cox did not call 911 until at least forty-three minutes after he shot Charles. The first shot hit Charles in the chest while standing. The second shot was administered execution-style through Charles's heart while he was lying on the ground. That bullet entered below his rib cage and exited through his upper left shoulder, meaning Alex must have stood at Charles's feet and looked him in the eye as he fired. The exit wound of the second shot was shored, which happens when the skin is in contact with an object as a bullet passes through. In this case, that object was the floor; the bullet damaged the floor below Charles's left shoulder as it exited. After Alex Cox administered the killing shot, he called Lori and talked to her while he waited for Charles Vallow to die. Although Alex Cox claimed he aided Charles, the only blood on his hands was metaphorical. A search of Charles's emails revealed that a few weeks before, Charles had warned his divorce attorney that if anything happened to him, Lori and Alex were responsible.

On the morning of the shooting, as Alex sat on the curb answering police questions, he dabbed at the injury to the back of his head that he claimed was caused when Charles, who had once played minor league baseball, hit him with the bat. Those who knew Charles found the claim laughable; they said Charles was a powerful man; if he'd swung a bat at Lori's brother, Alex would not have had the chance to run down the hall for his gun, let alone squeeze off two shots. Alex was calm and conversant during his sidewalk interview. It was already ninety-five degrees on the morning of July 11, 2019. He complained about the heat and asked for water. Just then, Lori returned to the house, wearing oversized sunglasses, body-hugging workout gear, and her new flip-flops. She was composed and smiling as she joked with the officers about the bad impression she was likely making on her new neighbors. It was clear she already knew what had happened. As the police collected evidence and the coroner removed Charles's body, police drove Lori, Tylee, and Alex to the police station to give their statements. Each officer who had contact with them remarked on the trio's lack of emotion. One officer said, "This would be at the top of bizarre for me." Another said, "The odd part about it is just the complete lack of emotion; it was very nonchalant. Lori had a big smile on her face." By ten A.M., Lori was in a police interview room, carefully and calmly telling her story.

Lori sat in an oversized dark gray leather chair, a fuzzy brown teddy bear perched on the smaller child-sized chair beside her, for the child witnesses who were sometimes interviewed in that room. Lori, wearing dark gray exercise tights and a black tank top over a bright pink sports bra, sat cross-legged in the wide chair, making herself look small and speaking in her breathy, singsong voice. She was entirely at ease; dry-eyed, she laughed frequently while describing the events to a female detective. When the detective left the office to interview Tylee, Lori pulled a tissue from a box, dabbed lightly at her eyes, and assumed a meditative pose with her legs crisscrossed, arms folded over her chest, and eyes closed. Her stillness contrasted sharply with what was unfolding next door. Lori barely moved as the minutes ticked by. For some time, the only indication that the recording was still running was the muffled sound of Tylee's voice coming from the identical interview room next door.

In sharp contrast to Lori's utter calm, Tylee was anxious. She was dressed in dark shorts and a loose T-shirt tie-dyed in shades of light and dark blue, with the word "Kauai" across the front. Compared to Lori's almost preternatural stillness, Tylee's agitation was palpable. Her face was tense; while alone, she rotated her neck, popping the joints, then began humming as she popped her finger joints. She picked up each bare foot and systematically popped the joints of each toe before pulling each arm across her chest to pop and stretch her shoulders. She grimaced as she twisted her torso, first left, then right, until the joints up and down her spine popped in sequence. She leaned forward, elbows on her knees, then pulled both hands into a pistol motion using her thumb and forefinger. She studied each wall and the ceiling of the room and sighed heavily. She picked at her nails, momentarily glanced at the teddy bear in the child's chair next to her, snapped her fingers, and began humming the song "How Far I'll Go" from the Disney movie *Moana*. Tylee could hear the rise and fall of her mother's muffled voice through the wall.

Alex told police Lori and the children were already out of the house when he pulled the trigger. Tylee said she heard the shots while she was near Charles's rental car talking to JJ, who was seat-belted in the car. Lori said she was still in the house when Alex fired but was around the corner in the kitchen. She said she and Tylee then went out to the car together, but she sent Tylee back into the house for her purse. Tylee said she didn't look at anything as she rushed through the house to get the bag out of her mom's room.

Charles's teenage sons from his previous marriage, Zach and Cole, were stunned when Lori texted them that their father was dead. She said she wasn't sure what the arrangements would be and that she would be in touch. Then she ignored their increasingly frantic texts and voicemails asking for details. Lori's son, Colby Ryan, was just as confused. Lori texted him that morning, telling him Charles had died of a heart attack. It was only later that day, when Colby came by the house after work to check on the family, that she told him his uncle Alex had killed the man Colby thought of as his dad. As police continued to investigate, Lori went on with her business. Neighbors reported she had a pool party in her backyard on the night of Charles's death. The following day, Chad Daybell, still in Rexburg, Idaho, repeatedly searched the internet for information about the murder and read news articles about the incident.

What brought Lori's fanatical beliefs to such a bloody culmination? Fed up with Lori's disappearance, Charles filed for divorce in February 2019, making Lori nervous about her financial future. When she returned to Charles in Houston in April 2019 to "get his finances in order," she changed Charles's life insurance account password online, locking him out of the policy so he couldn't change the beneficiary. Charles dismissed the divorce when they attempted to reconcile during those few weeks in Houston. With the divorce action gone, Lori believed the way was clear for her to receive the payout of his million-dollar life insurance policy. She didn't know Charles had discovered her deception, quietly contacted the insurance company by letter, and regained control of his account. A few days after Charles's murder, Lori called the insurance company to start her million-dollar claim and was told she was not entitled to the money. Charles had changed the beneficiary to his sister, Kay Woodcock, sure that if anything happened to him, Kay would take care of JJ. Furious, Lori texted Chad on July 18, 2019, to tell him she was not getting the life insurance. Chad's response: "I love you. This is terrible, but is probably another step in bringing down the Gadiantons, especially Brandon." The Gadiantons were an ancient secret criminal organization in the Book of Mormon, and Brandon was the estranged husband of her niece, Melani. It seemed Lori would need to find another deep pocket.

Kay Woodcock, Charles Vallow's sister, was devastated by her brother's death. She and her husband, Larry, remained close to the family after JJ's adoption, continuing to be Mamaw and Pawpaw, regularly visiting and talking by phone and video. JJ would sometimes call them several times a day. Kay laughed, saying she'd seen the ceiling in every one of Charles and Lori's houses because when JJ got excited, he ran through the house with his iPad, eager to show them something. Her last conversation with JJ lasted thirty-eight seconds on August 10, 2019. Kay suspected something was wrong but had no way of knowing how bad things had gotten. She expected Lori to move to Hawaii after Charles's death and begged Lori to let JJ come to visit them in Louisiana first. She wanted JJ to come for Charles's funeral, and she even offered to keep JJ with them while Lori moved to make the move easier. Lori knew Kay and Larry would have willingly taken both Tylee and JJ if she had asked, but Lori wanted revenge.

Friends, family, and internet sleuths were critical of the Chandler Police Department. Many felt that if law enforcement had arrested Alex Cox for Charles's death, Tylee, JJ, and Tammy might have been saved. But Chandler police records tell a different story. Police talked to Charles's sister, Kay, and brother-in-law, Larry, on July 13, 2019. Larry told police Charles was afraid of Alex Cox and had said if anything happened to him, Lori and Alex would be responsible. On July 18, 2019, seven days after Charles's death, Detective Nathan Moffat completed an affidavit for a search warrant, outlining all the suspicious events and inconsistencies in Lori's and Alex's stories and seeking information to further the investigation. The case was not, as many people thought, closed based on Alex Cox's claim of self-defense. The police told Kay they were not taking the word of any of the three people they had talked to, referring to Alex, Lori, and Tylee. The police sought GPS, phone, and internet records, and other information.

So, how did Alex and Lori evade arrest? It goes back to the previous months of 2019, when Charles Vallow was trying desperately to get help for Lori, and Lori and her friends were delving deeper and deeper into what Chad Daybell was telling them. Lori was cautious about who to trust. On one occasion, Alex stopped by in January 2019 as Melanie Gibb and a friend named Serena met at Lori's home. He stayed for a few minutes and told some jokes. When he left, Lori told the women to be careful what they said around Alex because he was only a first creation and did not understand much. Lori said it was like giving doctorate-level information to a kindergartener. Later, however, Chad conveniently revised his assessment of Alex, decided he was a multi-probation entity, and told Lori to include him in their teachings and their most secret plans.

A woman named Zulema Pastenes, another of Lori's followers, married Alex in November 2019. Zulema met Lori in 2018 at about the same time Lori met Melanie Gibb. Zulema had her own unique history. She was born in Chile on March 4, 1964. She had three grown children and when she married Alex, it was at least her sixth marriage. In 1996 and 1998, she was charged with possession of methamphetamine. In 2013, Zulema began working for a company called The Loving Room, founded by Greg and Donna Baer. The organization focused on energy healing, muscle testing, and other ideas from Dr. Bradley Nelson's book, *The Emotion Code*. Zulema and Donna had a website called "Real Love." Zulema identified herself as a cuddle therapist, offering "healing through unconditional love and touching." Zulema joined the LDS Church, and later, Chad convinced Zulema she could control earthquakes.

Chad and Lori were concerned that Alex would not be eligible for admission to the highest level of heaven because he was not married, and they encouraged him to marry their friend and follower, Zulema Pastenes, before it was too late. Chad gave Zulema many blessings, predicting that she would marry again. Zulema was skeptical, but Alex insisted he wanted a relationship with her. As she got to know Alex, she was taken with the seriousness of their spiritual conversations and the depth of his knowledge of scripture. Alex proposed at Thanksgiving, and they traveled together to Las Vegas, where they were married in a wedding chapel on November 29, 2019. No one else was at the service, and the officiant described it as "businesslike." They declined all the frills and acted more like they were at the Department of Motor Vehicles than at their wedding.

Zulema complained to Alex that the long car ride from Arizona to Las Vegas had aggravated her back, and the day after their wedding, Alex, who had trained as a massage therapist, offered to give her a massage. Before he could, though, he said he had to find a Walmart and get some plastic to put over the bed. They bought a painter's drop cloth. Alex said it was so the massage oil didn't get on the bed, but Zulema thought the painter's drop cloth was overkill. Zulema said she was so relaxed after the massage that she fell asleep. This was not typical for her, and she was suspicious that Alex might have drugged her. Half-conscious, she heard Alex in the bathroom having a conversation with someone. He claimed he was talking to himself when she asked who he was talking to. This, too, seemed odd to Zulema. She remembered that Alex was uncharacteristically quiet when she woke up later that afternoon. Zulema suspected Alex was talking on the phone to Chad and Lori from the bathroom and, in hindsight, wondered if they were telling Alex to kill her. Zulema said she truly loved Alex, who was very attentive and affectionate. Still, she later wondered if he reciprocated her feelings or only followed Chad and Lori's orders to secure his place in the celestial kingdom.

Zulema said that although she didn't know of a specific plan for Alex to murder Charles, she was sure Chad and Lori made it easier for Alex by convincing him that he would be doing Charles a favor if he killed the zombie that occupied his body. Zulema explained that Chad and Lori believed a person's original spirit was caught in limbo when a demon possessed their body and that the real spirit could not move on to their next probation until the dark spirit was ejected and the body died. Zulema said when she went to see Lori and Alex the day after Charles's murder, they made it sound like Heavenly Father had endorsed Charles's death by bringing him to the house so Alex could kill him. Lori likened it to the Book of Mormon story of Laban and Nephi, where God offers up Laban for Nephi to slaughter.

Alex's brother, Adam, confirmed that Alex was excommunicated from the LDS Church for having sex while on his church mission right after high school. Later, while living with their uncle, Rex Connor, Alex recommitted himself to the church. Once Alex fulfilled all of the church's requirements, Rex re-baptized him. But Alex's resolve didn't last, and soon, he began taking dating vacations to Colombia. The vacation packages were specifically designed to introduce American men to Colombian women. Alex was younger and thinner than most men who made the trips. Alex, a solid "five" in America, was easily a "nine" in Colombia. When he was introduced at an event, the women began chanting his name as if he were a rockstar. According to his uncle Rex, Alex felt shame around what may have been a sexual addiction, which caused conflict with the family, but his trips to Colombia made him feel popular and accepted. Alex left for a week-long trip to Colombia just two days after he shot Charles in Lori's mirrored living room. Lori was critical of Alex's behavior. In early 2019, when Lori disappeared for fifty-eight days, she stayed with Alex for some of that period. Neighbors reported Lori and Alex arguing in front of his house, with Lori screaming that Alex had dishonored their family. However, Chad convinced Lori to change her view of Alex's behavior. The LDS Church has a unique outlook on the physical body;

One foundational gospel truth about the body is the principle that having a physical body is a godlike attribute—you are more like God with a body than without. Our religion stands virtually alone in believing that God has a tangible body of flesh and bone and that our bodies were literally created in His likeness. To become as God requires gaining a body like He has and learning to correctly comprehend and use it. Those who chose not to follow God in the premortal state were denied mortal bodies. The prophet Joseph Smith stated that Satan's lack of a body is a punishment to him. The body then is necessary for progression and for obtaining a fullness of joy. Having a mortal body indicates that you chose righteously in the premortal state. Inherent in the mortal body are powers and capabilities that enable you to continue to progress toward godhood. The body is not merely a mobile unit for the head nor a carnal vexation for the spirit, as some believe. Rather, it is an integral, powerful component of the soul, for 'the spirit and the body are the soul of man' (D&C 88:15). A second truth the scriptures offer about the body is the clarification of its nature as a sacred gift from God. Though in mortality we will all die, because of the Atonement of Jesus Christ we will all be resurrected and united with our bodies forever (see 1 Cor. 15:22). Indeed, one of the essential purposes of Christ's Atonement was to give us the opportunity to overcome death. In sharp contrast to the world's definition of a 'perfect' body is our belief in a perfected body—a body together with a spirit—that has overcome both physical and spiritual death. A perfect or perfected body can ultimately be obtained only through Jesus Christ.[3]

Based on this, Chad assured Lori that it didn't matter what Alex was doing in Colombia. He had received a body, which was all he needed to accomplish in this probation. Chad's acceptance absolved Alex of his shame and guilt and manipulated Alex into believing he had a mission as Lori's protector and their assassin.

6

"SOMEONE SHOT AT ME"

Six weeks after Charles Vallow's murder, Lori and Alex settled into townhomes in Rexburg, Idaho. As Lori unpacked, she talked on the phone to her friend Melanie Gibb. Lori told Melanie that, like Charles, her daughter, Tylee Ryan, had been possessed by a demon named Hillary. In the background, Melanie heard Tylee say, "Not me, Mom!" The last proof that Tylee was alive was a few days later on September 8, 2019, when photos of her at Yellowstone National Park were found on Lori's phone and park surveillance cameras. JJ Vallow was last known to be alive on September 22, 2019.

Through that late summer, Chad saw Lori whenever he could slip away from Tammy. Several people, including Chad's fellow visionary Julie Rowe, said Chad had spoken for years about his visions of Tammy dying young. He thought her death was imminent and predicted she would die in a car crash. He even encouraged Tammy to take a solo trip to Utah to visit her family in September 2019, sure that she would die on the road. He promised Lori it would happen soon if she could only wait a little longer. But Tammy didn't die, and Lori became impatient. After all, Lori had rid herself of all her impediments and was anxious for Chad to do the same. She was frustrated that she didn't see the same level of commitment from him.

Their messages tell the tale.

Chad to Lori, July 26, 2019 at 8:13 P.M.:

> Tonight I figured out who I feel like. I'm a grown-up version
> of Harry Potter, who has to live with the Dudleys in his little
> space under the stairs. Every few weeks I get to escape and have
> amazing adventures with my Goddess lover, but then I have to
> return to my place under the stairs, feeling trapped. But I sense
> permanent freedom is coming!

Chad to Lori, July 30, 2019:

> Yes, we might need to release a little steam when we talk.
> Anyway, this is the chart that checks what percentage mortals
> are still in their body. It worked for my friend's wife who died,
> my neighbor, George Bush, Stan Lee, etc. I kind of forgot about
> it because we've been dealing with zombies and demonic entities.
> But this afternoon Tammy said she felt lightheaded, as as [*sic*]
> if her body and spirit weren't connected.

Then, on August 11, 2019 at 9:15 P.M., Lori, out of patience, sent Chad
the following message:

> U should give all of you love and your attention to your wife
> and family. I'm just a distraction. Go have fun with your family.
> I really do want you to. I just can't be in the way anymore. If
> things change we can talk. But we have nothing until things
> change anyway.

Chad temporarily calmed Lori's fears, convincing her that it was only
a matter of time before they could be together, but the pressure was
mounting. On October 2, 2019, Lori ordered two silver-and-malachite
wedding rings on Charles Vallow's Amazon account and searched for

beach wedding dresses; Chad was becoming desperate to put his marriage to Tammy behind him so he could begin the next phase of his life with Lori.

For her part, Lori was still concerned about money. Without Charles's million-dollar life insurance, she needed to find another way to fund the lifestyle she wanted, and earning it wasn't in the plan. The next most likely source was Melani Boudreaux. Melani had just finalized her divorce property settlement with Brandon and received a sizable check for her portion of the marital assets. When a friend asked Lori how she planned to fund her mission to gather the 144,000, Lori pointed at Melani.

Lori also knew Melani had maintained the payments on Brandon's multi-million-dollar life insurance policy and kept herself on as the beneficiary; Brandon became the next target. On the morning of October 2, 2019, he came home from the gym at about 9:15 A.M. and drove past a green Jeep Wrangler parked in the wrong direction in front of his house. Brandon pulled into his driveway and, looking back at the Jeep, noticed it had no spare tire attached. He saw the back window flip up and a rifle muzzle extend out. Before his mind could fully register what he was seeing, the driver's window beside him shattered, showering him with bits of broken safety glass. The Jeep sped away and he followed it for a few blocks before giving up the chase and returning home. He recognized the Jeep and the man driving it. The bald man strongly resembled Lori Vallow's brother, Alex Cox, and the last time Brandon saw that Jeep, with its Texas license plates, Lori Vallow's daughter, Tylee Ryan, had been driving it. The bullet narrowly missed Brandon's head, and when he opened his car door, the remainder of the window, held together by safety film, fell out on the driveway. When police arrived, they asked Brandon if he knew of anyone who would want to hurt him. He could only think of one answer: his ex-wife, Melani, and her family.

Melani was not the same person Brandon had married ten years before, and he had been heartbroken when she filed for divorce, claiming God had told her aunt Lori that Brandon was gay. He had just moved out of their shared home, but since Brandon had custody of the couple's four children, he was required to give Melani his new address. Only four people knew his address; of those four, only his ex-wife, Melani, knew anyone in the Cox family. The morning of the shooting, Brandon dropped his two oldest children off at school, the third at a day camp, and then met Melani at a nearby business to drop the baby off to her before heading for the gym. The police later determined through GPS data that Tylee's Jeep had been idling in front of Brandon's house for 118 minutes when Brandon arrived home. As Alex sat outside, waiting for Brandon, he used his burner phone to communicate repeatedly with Chad Daybell's secret phone. Later, as Alex sped back to Idaho, he and Chad communicated several times. That evening, Alex messaged Lori several times, and they later had a twenty-three-minute phone call. At nine P.M. that evening, Lori began searching the internet for "man shot in gilbert az," "man shot in gilbert az 10/2/2019," and "avc news brandon budreaux."

This was the second police event in Arizona involving Alex Cox and Lori Vallow in recent weeks. Police were still investigating the death of Lori's husband, Charles Vallow. Brandon was shocked when, shortly after the attempt on his life, Melani announced she was moving to Boise, Idaho, with or without their children. He also learned his divorce from Melani wasn't final and that she had not removed herself from his life insurance or financial accounts as she had promised. Brandon immediately locked all his accounts, changed his life insurance beneficiary, and decided to keep their children with him until he could figure out what Melani was up to. When police asked Melani about her abrupt decision to move to Idaho, she repeated her belief that Brandon was manipulating and threatening her to disrupt her relationship with her aunt Lori.

All the while, Chad Daybell was still working on ways to secure his future with Lori.

On October 4, 2019 at 7:46 A.M., Chad, who sometimes called Lori "Lili," wrote:

> Thank you for sending me that paragraph, beautiful Lili. I'm eager to see you soon. Trying to hasten her departure. I love you endlessly!

On October 5, 2019 at 3:25 A.M., Chad wrote:

Hello, sweet angel. Big news about Tammy. Please let me know if you are awake and can talk. I love you!

A few minutes later, at 3:36 A.M., Chad told Lori:

The short version is that she has been switched. Tammy is in Limbo, and a level 3 demonic entity named Viola is in her body. It happened at about 10 P.M. and was done by Tammy's sister, who I always knew was 3D, but it turns out she is multiple creation. Viola has been attached for about a year to my niece, who is 12 year old daughter. [sic] I have connected with Tammy in Limbo, and she is very frustrated and upset. She wants Viola removed as soon as possible. Viola seems to be similar to Penelope. The personality differences from Tammy should be evident quickly. Please seek a confirmation on this, but I have now checked three times since I got home and get more affirmative answers each time.

And at 3:54 A.M., Chad sealed Tammy's fate:

Not fully sure of the timing for removal, but once her actions verify the differences, I don't want to wait.

While Lori continued to scheme for money, Chad and Tammy signed documents increasing Tammy's life insurance policies to their maximum. Just seven days after the attempt on Brandon Boudreaux's life, Alex and the green Jeep Wrangler were back in Rexburg to carry out the rest of the plan. Lori flew to Arizona to visit Melanie Gibb and Zulema. She told them Tammy Daybell was now possessed by an evil spirit named Viola and asked them to help her remove the demon. They prayed hard on the evening of October 9, 2019, calling down every one of their spiritual weapons, and then Lori checked with Chad to see if their efforts had worked. Zulema overheard Lori on the phone, sounding furious. She described Lori as "very, very scary angry." Zulema heard Lori say "idiot" and "moron." Lori said, "The idiot can't do anything right by himself." That night, Zulema talked to Alex on the phone for forty minutes beginning at about 11:15 P.M.

Tammy Daybell emailed to her son Mark, who was in South Africa on his church mission, explaining what had happened that night involving his father, Chad, and older brother, Garth.

> Now on the same day, I was coming home from clogging, it was about 9:15 and I backed into the front driveway. I was getting some items out of the back seat, we had made freezer meals at enrichment night, and my clogging shoes. I realized someone was by the back of the car, I looked up, thinking it was Dad or Garth to help me carry stuff in. Nope, it was a guy dressed in black with a ski mask on, pointing a rifle at me. I think I was a bit in shock, because I just said "what do you think you're doing?" Then I noticed the rifle was actually a paintball gun. It had a hopper on top. The guy started pulling the trigger and I could hear just hear the clicking and the whooshing sound of an empty paintball gun. He stayed standing by the back of the car just pulling the trigger while pointing the gun at me. For some reason, I kept asking him what he thought he was doing. At that point I was actually more annoyed than scared, because he was standing between me and the door and he didn't step towards me or even say anything. The scared part came after when my brain thought of what things that could have happened. The thought crossed my mind to hit him with my clogging shoes but first I looked toward the house and yelled Chad. The guy ran away around the North side of the house. I ran in the house and got Dad and Garth.

Tammy assured Mark that they had called the police and reported the incident. She thought the culprit could be the neighbor's mentally ill son.

The idea that someone would shoot a real gun at her was so far-fetched that she jumped to the conclusion the assault-style rifle had been a paintball gun.

After missing the shot at Brandon Boudreaux, Alex Cox went to the local shooting range several times in the days leading up to the attempt on Tammy's life to practice and sight in his weapon. On October 8, 2019, Alex asked Google for information about "Grendel drop." A Grendel is an AR-style rifle named after one of the monsters in the Old English poem, *Beowulf.* Alex, who owned a Grendel, was asking how much the trajectory of a bullet shot from his gun would drop after it was fired. He also asked how cold temperatures might affect a rifle shot. It was twenty-six degrees when Alex fired at Tammy on October 9, 2019. Earlier in the day, he drove twenty-eight miles from Rexburg to the Sportsman's Warehouse in Idaho Falls and shopped for cold-weather clothing. He bought black pants, a black jacket, fingerless gloves, and a black ski mask. The sound Tammy mistook for the whoosh of an empty paintball gun was the sound of a bullet being fired through a homemade suppressor. Law enforcement would later search the property for shell casings using a metal detector. No casings were found, but a bullet of the same caliber was found lodged in a tree behind Chad's home on a trajectory that matched where Tammy described Alex standing. Lori was frustrated that Alex didn't finish the job, but she and Chad were undeterred. Lori's friend Melanie Gibb said Lori told her a dark entity possessed Tammy and that she and Chad had "done what they had to do to get it out."

Ten days later, on the morning of October 19, 2019, Chad Daybell called 911 to tearfully report that his wife had died in her sleep. When the responding officer arrived, Tammy's body was lying on the bed; a dribble of pink foam had leaked from her mouth and run down her chin. The officer, Alyssa Greenhalgh, checked for a pulse and found none. She looked over the body and noted that it was cold to the touch, and there were signs of lividity on Tammy's back. Lividity occurs when the heart stops pumping, and gravity takes over, causing blood to pool at the body's lowest point. Chad told the officer Tammy had been coughing and had vomited the night before. He said he awoke when he felt the bedcovers pull off of him and found Tammy partially off the bed with her head near the floor and her legs still on the bed and tangled in the sheets. He called across the hall for his son, Garth, who helped him move Tammy's body back on the bed. They covered her with the bedcovers. Chad reported to the coroner, Brenda Dye, that when he picked up Tammy's body off the floor, it was cold to the touch. Dye said when she examined Tammy's body less than an hour later, rigor mortis had begun to set in.

Chad's story didn't add up. Bodies do not fall out of bed after death and don't become cold or develop rigor and lividity in minutes. When Chad Daybell called 911 to report his wife's death, she had already been dead for hours. Yet despite Chad's misrepresentations, Coroner Brenda Dye acquiesced when Chad and his children refused an autopsy. Dye said Chad's adult daughter, Emma, then age 26, found the idea of an autopsy upsetting. To many, it seemed Chad could not get Tammy in the ground fast enough. Tammy was pronounced dead on the morning of Saturday, October 19, 2019. By Tuesday, October 22, 2019, at eleven A.M., her body had already been embalmed, transported 290 miles, and buried at the same Springville, Utah, cemetery where Chad had once worked. The following day, Chad and his children were already back in Rexburg, where they held a memorial service for their Rexburg friends. There wasn't even time for Tammy's youngest son, Mark, to return from his overseas church mission in South Africa. During the next few days, Chad collected Tammy's $430,000 life insurance and flew to Hawaii.

Seventeen days after Tammy's death, Lori and Chad were married on a beach in Kauai, Hawaii. Only four people attended: Lori, Chad, a photographer who recorded the event, and the officiant. Chad wore white linen pants and a baggy linen long-sleeved shirt with rolled-up sleeves. Lori wore a belted white lace and chiffon dress tied tightly in the back to emphasize her tiny waist. They were barefoot, and each wore two leis: a strand of fragrant white pikake flowers and a string of dark purple orchids. They exchanged the silver-and-malachite rings Lori had ordered from Amazon while Tammy was still alive. In one photo, Chad pretends to play the officiant's ukulele while Lori imitates doing the hula. In another, they gaze into one another's eyes like any other hopelessly-in-love newlyweds.

On November 28, 2019, when Lori's son Colby had not heard from his mother in weeks, he emailed her: "Mom, you changed your number. What is going on?"

Lori replied, "Hi, Colbs! I need you to know that we are safe and happy. I know this sounds confusing to you, but I need you to trust me . . . that although there are wicked people trying to cause harm that, Jesus is on our side and taking care of us. Although we may be out of touch for a while, I will continue to help you. I love you all so much! The car and the car insurance will be paid for so u can drive it with no worries. The phones will also be good. You are precious to your momma !!! I love you so much !! Kisses to you and Kelsee. I hope to talk soon :) I will continue to pray blessings on your family constantly."

Lori and Chad returned from Hawaii to arrange a permanent move. Chad's family and friends were shocked. Chad started introducing Lori to friends in Rexburg, acting as if marrying two weeks after his wife of thirty years had died was normal. He told friends his new wife was wealthy and childless. Chad posted on social media that he planned to move to Hawaii to write. By the time police came knocking on Lori's door looking for JJ on November 26, 2019, Lori and Chad's plans were already in place. When police returned the following day with a warrant to search the house, Lori and Chad were gone. They first took Chad's five adult children to California on vacation, and then after the week-long visit to theme parks and the beach, Lori and Chad left for Kauai to begin their new unencumbered life. A life from which Tylee and JJ were suspiciously absent. While looking for a place to live, Chad emailed a Kauai landlord asking if she had a rental available for a "clean, retired couple with no children."

On the night of Tammy's death, GPS data had located Alex Cox's phone in the parking lot of a church two miles from the Daybell home. Perhaps he crept into the Daybell home, held Tammy down, and suffocated her, or maybe he was simply there as a backup in case Chad couldn't go through with the plan. No one will ever know because Alex Cox died of bilateral pulmonary thromboembolism, commonly known as blood clots in his lungs, on December 12, 2019. Although the medical examiner found Alex had hypertensive cardiovascular disease and ruled his death natural, many were suspicious because of the timing. Alex died just one day after law enforcement, now highly suspicious, got a court order to exhume Tammy Daybell's body from the cemetery in Springville, Utah, for autopsy.

In Idaho, the County Coroner, who is not a physician, is dispatched to any deaths that are not attended by medical personnel. The decision on whether to order an autopsy for an unattended death rests with the coroner. Fremont County Coroner Brenda Dye was an experienced EMT who also served as the elected coroner. She was dispatched to Tammy Daybell's death and in deciding whether to order an autopsy, she considered the cost to the county and the wishes of the family. However, when law enforcement got the exhumation order, the decision was out of Dye's hands. Autopsies are conducted by County Medical Examiners, who are medical doctors, but not every county has a medical examiner. In the case of Fremont County, autopsies were done more than 200 miles away in Boise. In Tammy's case, her autopsy was conducted in Springville, Utah, where she was buried. Dye attended Tammy's autopsy and revised her death certificate to comport with the medical examiner's official findings.

Tammy Daybell was laid to rest in the cemetery where she and Chad courted and clowned around for their engagement photos three decades ago. She rests under a headstone with a picture of a mother duck followed by five ducklings representing her five children. The five Daybell children have made statements steadfastly defending their father. In September 2021, they gave an interview to CBS's *48 Hours*. Chad's eldest daughter, Emma, walked the reporter through the property where Tylee's and JJ's bodies had been found, callously stepping across their former resting places. She insisted that someone put the bodies in her father's backyard to frame him for their murders. Sources reported the walls in Chad's Fremont County jail cell held photographs of his children, grandchildren, and Tammy, but as he awaited trial, there was not a single picture of his goddess, Lori Vallow. In contrast, women in the Madison County jail with Lori said she spent her time dancing to music only she could hear and reading scripture, including Chad's books.

In Arizona, police were still trying to figure out where the mystery Jeep had gone and had yet to make the connection to Rexburg. Then they discovered a highway license plate reader near Holbrook, Arizona, had captured the Jeep as it sped into the Phoenix metro area on October 1, 2019, a day before Brandon's attempted shooting. Police noted that no spare tire was mounted on the back of the vehicle. Searches for directions to Brandon's new address were found on Alex's phone. The police caught a lucky break when they learned Alex Cox had pawned some belongings at a Phoenix area pawnshop. He presented an Arizona driver's license but gave the shop his Rexburg, Idaho, address. Now authorities knew the Jeep was probably in Rexburg, and they needed to find it. The Gilbert police contacted the Rexburg police and the Fremont County Sheriff, asking for assistance in the investigation, and on November 1, 2019, local police got a warrant for the Jeep and began surveilling Lori and Chad, who were often seen together in public, holding hands and cuddling. Rexburg detectives discovered Alex had taken the Jeep to a shop in Rexburg on September 25, 2019, and had the windows tinted. Police would later discover video surveillance from a self-storage unit from the day Alex shot at Brandon. The video showed Lori and Chad putting a spare tire and what appeared to be a removable car seat in a storage locker. The Jeep Wrangler is a small, four-door SUV with a removable back seat. The rear window of the Jeep can't be opened if the spare tire is mounted on the back of the vehicle. In the storage unit video, Chad gives Lori's bottom an affectionate pat as they leave the building. Video footage from the self-storage unit on October 3, 2019, the day after Alex's attempt on Brandon, showed Lori and Chad retrieving the seat and the tire.

Brandon Boudreaux continued to work with Arizona law enforcement as they investigated the attempt on his life. Brandon was convinced the attempt was part of a bigger plot involving Lori, Chad, and Alex. On October 22, 2019, Brandon Boudreaux alerted Arizona police of Tammy Daybell's death and sent them a copy of her obituary. When Gilbert,

Arizona, police talked to Fremont County, Idaho, coroner Brenda Dye, she told them she had spoken to Chad Daybell's neighbors, who described the family as "extremely religious." The neighbor told Dye people were meeting at Chad's home to plan for a "doomsday event." Slowly, the picture was coming into focus.

By October 24, Melani stopped responding to Brandon's messages, and he suspected she had left Arizona. Brandon was right. On October 31, 2019, Alex helped Melani pack up her Arizona home and move to Rexburg, where she rented an apartment in the same complex as Alex and Lori. When Melani vacated her Arizona home, neighbors reported that she left her children's furniture and toys on the curb outside the house. That same day, when Zulema reminded Lori in a text message that it was Halloween, Lori admitted she'd forgotten. It surprised Zulema that the mother of a seven-year-old could forget it was Halloween. Zulema couldn't know the only costume JJ would wear that year was the red pajamas he was buried in.

One of Brandon and Melani's mutual friends reported an odd event the following day. On November 1, 2019, as Claudia Ewell was pulling out of her garage, she found Melani standing on the sidewalk outside her home. Melani said the holy spirit said her children were at Claudia's home, and she was there to collect them. After Claudia repeatedly assured Melani that the Boudreaux children were not there, Melani got into the passenger side of a white Kia SUV. Alex Cox, who Claudia described as a "bald Caucasian man," was driving. Melani sat in the car for about twenty minutes, exited, stood beside it, and stared at Claudia's home before driving away. Later in the day, the car was again parked on the street in front of the house. Neither Brandon nor the Boudreaux children were at the Ewell home. Brandon was still very much in hiding with his children following the attempt on his life and was steering clear of any unnecessary trips outside the house.

On November 4, 2019, Rexburg police impounded the Jeep. GPS and phone data confirmed that Alex Cox had been in the vicinity of Brandon's home the morning someone took a shot at Brandon. They processed the vehicle for DNA and gunshot residue, and Alex Cox's DNA and gunpowder residue were found on the back window.

On November 14, 2019, Melani Boudreaux appeared at the home of Brandon Boudreaux's parents in American Fork, Utah, demanding to see her children. She was driven there by Alex Cox and arrived in a white Kia. Brandon's father, Carlson Boudreaux, can be heard in the background of a 911 call screaming for Melani to "get away from his door." The panic is evident in Carlson's voice. After all, just a month earlier, these same people had been responsible for an attempt on his son's life. Melani continued to bang on the door, insisting she had a court order to take her children. This was the second time Melani had come to the Boudreaux property demanding her children. She did not have a court order and was arrested and booked into jail on charges of criminal trespassing enhanced by domestic violence.

Melani's behavior seemed to mirror Lori's. Lori had just returned from her November 5, 2019, Hawaii wedding to Chad, and Melani had barely settled into her Rexburg townhouse when she met Ian Pawlowski on an LDS dating site. Ten days later, she married him in Las Vegas. Ian reported he met Lori for the first time the week before Thanksgiving in 2019. He knew Melani was close to Chad and Lori, so he asked them for their blessing before asking Melani to marry him. Ian said he was initially open to what Melani told him about Chad and Lori's teachings. He said it was because he was a member of The Church of Jesus Christ of Latter-day Saints and that "a large part of our belief is faith in revelation and that the church is a living thing, it's not done progressing, it's not done growing, and so part of that is that you have to maintain an open mind, so if I was going to learn something new it would either be through one of the Lord's servants, or I'd receive the revelation directly . . . I was going through a religious renaissance of my own . . . so I was open."

On November 30, 2019, the evening of their Las Vegas marriage ceremony, Melani told Ian all about Lori, Chad, and their strange beliefs. She told him Lori's children had each "gone dark" and were now just gone. He said, "Melani dumped all her fears on me." Lori and Chad had also told Melani two of her own four children were dark. He also learned Melani's ex-husband, Brandon Boudreaux, had been shot at. Ian said Melani looked to Lori and Chad as parental figures and believed everything they said. They stayed with Ian's two young children at the Bellagio Hotel the following day. When Ian looked around, he couldn't find his daughter. Remembering their conversations of the night before, panic set in, and the few minutes Ian searched for his child felt like hours. Then he heard a giggle from behind the heavy drapes; he sat, trying to catch his breath; all the things Melani told him the night before had him spooked.

Ian and Melani were not the only couple to marry in Las Vegas on the weekend of November 30, 2019. Alex Cox married Zulema Pastenes a day earlier. Ian was uncomfortable with the light and dark rankings and other things Lori said. He didn't like that Lori had identified local law enforcement officers as some of the people possessed by dark spirits. Lori said their list included Det. Ray Hermosillo and Det. Dave Hope of the Rexburg police department, who she claimed were zombies. Ian became increasingly worried about everyone's safety after everything Melani had told him and went to the police in early December 2019. Law enforcement asked Ian to wear a recording device during his conversations with Chad and Lori. He did so, hoping to elicit information about the whereabouts of Tylee and JJ, who had been missing since September, but neither Chad nor Lori said anything incriminating. In a December 6, 2019, recording, Lori and Chad said difficult spiritual attacks would come for the next two weeks, and then everything would settle. Six days after Lori warned about spiritual attacks, Alex Cox died on the bathroom floor of his new wife's home in Arizona. In retrospect, Ian said he saw that Lori and Chad's constant teaching and giving of blessings was manipulation. "Melani was manipulated during one of the most difficult and dark times of her life . . . There was no shortage of people in Melani's life that would abuse her and her circumstances to get what they want out of her, and Lori was one of them." According to Ian, Chad told Melani not to fight for the custody of her children because he had a prophecy that the children would return to her. As a result, Melani didn't appear for a custody hearing, and Brandon was awarded permanent custody of their four children by default.

Ian's former wife, Natalie Pawlowski, was one of many people who became concerned when she learned about Lori's missing children. She and Ian had children together, and Ian's recent marriage to Lori's niece was alarming. Natalie discovered an odd document on a laptop Ian had returned to her. It was an outline Ian had written, discussing Lori and Chad's beliefs. According to the document, one must live at least nine mortal lives to become exalted but must live more to become god. After the first two mortal lives, "you can choose to sign a light contract or a dark contract." Your veil becomes thinner with every probation. Multiple sealings (marriages) are possible, but men can choose one true spouse or may have many. "Translated beings cannot die, cannot reproduce, do not need sleep or food, and do not feel the sorrow of the world. Injury is possible, but healing is accelerated, and it's never fatal." Of zombies, Ian wrote, "Human bodies that have had their original spirits forced from them and have been possessed by either a demon (the original third of the heavenly host who followed Lucifer), disembodied spirit (once living human spirits who had chosen to be reborn into another probation). Or a worm/slug (a creature controlled by Lucifer that enters the body to control the host). Spirits can be pushed from their bodies during traumatic events or deadly injuries. Spirits pushed out are trapped in limbo as the body they're tied to is still living but cannot be occupied by them anymore."

Natalie contacted Brandon Boudreaux, asking if his children were safe and if her children with Ian were at risk. In one of their conversations, Natalie told Brandon that Ian had confessed to her that Melani knew about the plan to kill Brandon. After Lori and Chad were arrested, Melani and Ian stopped giving interviews to the media and did their best to distance themselves from Chad and Lori; they welcomed a baby boy to their family in 2020.

Back in Arizona, Melani's bitter custody case with Brandon continued unabated as she tried to have the default judgment overturned. On February 26, 2020, Melani's California attorneys issued a libelous news release to several news outlets. The release claimed that when Melani confronted Brandon about her belief that he was a homosexual and addicted to pornography, he threatened to take their children away from her. The release went on to claim, "Brandon Boudreaux has failed to tell investigators that his family has covered up child molestation, drug addiction, kidnapping, assaults, and even killings. And according to inside family information, Brandon Boudreaux's family is involved in organized crime. Brandon Boudreaux has plenty to hide. A closer look would reveal many possible sources who would take a shot at him." None of the outrageous claims had even a sliver of truth. The real reason Melani had decided to divorce Brandon was that her aunt Lori Vallow had a vision in the temple that Brandon was gay. On March 25, 2020, Melani's attorneys, Garrett Smith and Robert Jarvis, doubled down in a second flagrantly untruthful release. On March 30, 2020, Brandon sued the pair, claiming that the press releases "contain many . . . false and grossly mischaracterized allegations Defendants intentionally and maliciously present as fact." In January 2021, Jarvis and Smith settled the lawsuit, agreeing to pay Brandon $12 million in compensation. Despite the suit's outcome, Garrett Smith accompanied Melani to Lori's trial in April 2023 and represented to the judge that he was her lawyer. Smith also represented Zulema Pastenes and Lori's sister, Summer Shiflet. At Chad Daybell's trial a year later, Melani and Ian Pawlowski were both subpoenaed. Once again, Smith accompanied them. Judge Stephen Boyce took exception to Smith's nodding, smiling, and head shaking during Ian's testimony and had the lawyer ejected from the courtroom.

By the end of 2019, Chad and Lori's swath of destruction was nearly complete, and they enjoyed their freedom, living their best island life in Kauai. The tribulation was coming soon, and once natural disasters and wars began, people would focus on survival. No one would remember to look for two missing children or question the death of one forty-nine-year-old woman or the shooting in self-defense of one middle-aged man. Chad and Lori set their sights on their bright future together and turned their thoughts to completing their mission for God.

7

"LORI, WHERE ARE YOUR CHILDREN?"

It was November 2019, and Charles Vallow was dead. Tammy Daybell was dead, and Lori and Chad were holding hands and cuddling in public as they planned their permanent escape to Hawaii. In Lake Charles, Louisiana, Kay and Larry Woodcock's concern for Lori's children grew. They hadn't spoken to JJ in weeks. Kay knew Lori had left Arizona but didn't know where she had taken JJ and Tylee until she discovered the malachite wedding rings Lori had ordered using Charles's Amazon account had been delivered to an address in Rexburg, Idaho. Kay contacted the Rexburg police and asked them to check on the children.

On November 26, 2019, when police attempted to locate Lori, they came across her brother Alex Cox, with Chad Daybell in the parking lot of the apartment complex where Alex and Lori lived. Chad told police he didn't know Lori well and didn't have her telephone number. Police were immediately suspicious because they already knew Lori and Chad had married each other in Hawaii a few days before. Later that same day, police contacted Lori Vallow at home.

As usual, Lori was friendly, engaging, and prepared with ready answers: Tylee had gotten her GED and was living and attending classes on the BYU Idaho campus in Rexburg; JJ was with a friend in Arizona. When asked about Chad, Lori told police that he was just a friend of her brother's. None of the things Lori told the police were true. Tylee Ryan had never been enrolled at the Idaho campus of Brigham Young University, and JJ Vallow was not in Arizona with Lori's friend, Melanie Gibb. Chad Daybell was not just a friend of Lori's brother; he was her fifth husband. When police returned the next day armed with a search warrant and intent on getting to the bottom of the story, Lori and her new husband had vanished.

In Chad and Lori's wake, Idaho law enforcement began to put the pieces together, connecting the string of suspicious deaths associated with the couple. Not only were Lori's children missing, her third husband, Joseph Ryan, fourth husband, Charles Vallow, and Chad's first wife, Tammy Daybell, were all dead under suspicious circumstances. Only a few days later, Alex Cox would also be dead. Authorities learned Chad had collected Tammy's $430,000 life insurance proceeds before jetting off to marry Lori Vallow in an intimate, white beach wedding in Hawaii.

The case attracted national attention once the authorities asked for the public's help in locating the missing children. Internet detectives, police, and news crews asked, "Lori, where are your children?" Weeks after the initial welfare check, police located Lori Vallow and Chad Daybell back in Kauai, Hawaii, living the island life and still refusing to reveal the whereabouts of Lori's children. In January 2020, a Madison County, Idaho, judge ordered Lori to produce the children to prove they were safe. Body camera footage showed a process server handing Lori those documents while she lounged around a swimming pool, trim, tanned, and wearing a tiny turquoise bikini. A thinner, less doughy Chad Daybell sat on the next pool lounge beside her, wearing navy swim trunks, sporting a tan and a fashionable haircut. When Lori ignored the judge's order, a frustrated Idaho magistrate issued an arrest warrant for her. On the near-palindromic date of February 20, 2020, Lori Vallow was arrested and extradited to Idaho, where she was charged with two counts of abandonment and nonsupport of children, one count of resisting and obstructing an officer for giving false information to police, and one count of solicitation for asking her friend Melanie Gibb to lie about JJ's whereabouts. News organizations filmed her as she changed planes in Boise and then disembarked from a small aircraft in Rexburg. She wore black leggings and a black hooded sweatshirt with the word *Kauai* across the chest. The kangaroo pocket on the front of the sweatshirt hid her shackled hands. Lori was ordered to be held on one million dollars bail. Chad returned voluntarily to Rexburg, moved back into his family home with at least one of his adult sons, and started contacting friends and family, looking for a way to post Lori's bail. He was often seen coming and going from the Madison County jail, where Lori was held.

Law enforcement checked with worried family members and combed through social media and Lori's iCloud accounts to establish the last time anyone had seen either of the children. For sixteen-year-old Tylee, the last sighting was on September 8, 2019, during a trip to Yellowstone National Park with Lori, Alex, and JJ. Lori's iCloud account contained pictures of that day, including one of Tylee grinning as she hugged JJ, with Alex leaning on a railing in the background. The last time anyone remembers seeing JJ Vallow was the evening of September 22, 2019. A photo from that evening showed JJ grinning and eating yogurt while wearing a red pajama set.

Weeks stretched into months. Neither Lori nor Chad would say anything about the children's whereabouts, and no one had seen them. Many held out hope that Lori and Chad had the children hidden in a doomsday bunker somewhere, waiting for the end times. Lori's family insisted that Charles Vallow's death was the cause of all of Lori's difficulties. Lori's mother, Janis Cox, and sister, Summer Shiflet, appeared in an interview on the television show *48 Hours* in May 2020, where they adamantly denied that Lori would ever hurt her children; they claimed she was a loving and protective mother. Janis and Summer said Charles Vallow had sent Lori threatening texts before his death, and they blamed his sister, Kay Woodcock, for everything. Janis said Kay and her family were angry over Charles's death, and the family had threatened to track Lori down and take JJ from her. Summer noted that since Charles's death, Lori had been followed and threatened and had good reason to hide her children. Janis Cox told the interviewer she didn't know why Lori didn't "put the kids in a room with today's date, take a picture, and send it to the police." Lori didn't do it because she couldn't. Later, when the truth of what had happened to the children became known, Janis and Summer were forced to change their views. Two years later, Janis appeared in a documentary, admitting she had been wrong.[1] At Lori's trial, the prosecutor played an emotional jail call between Summer and Lori. In the recording, the public would learn that Lori had cut off contact with most of her family months before the children disappeared.

On December 6, 2019, as Lori enjoyed the winter sun in Hawaii, the Chandler, Arizona, police filed an affidavit for a new search warrant. Under the heading "New Information," police wrote, "On December 5, 2019, detectives in Idaho had contacted and interviewed a source of information close to the person listed and involved in the ongoing investigation. The source alleged that they had been told by at least one of these parties that JJ and his sister, Tylee, were now deceased at the hands of the persons involved. No bodies have been located, and the information is not verified at this time." Officials have never identified this informant.

The months stretched on after Lori's February 2020 arrest, seemingly without progress. Lori was still being held in the Madison County jail on child abandonment charges, refusing to reveal the children's whereabouts. The female population at the jail is small, and Lori was sometimes the only prisoner in her section. The food is better there than at most jails; much of it is prepared from scratch. While Lori sat in her cell, reading scripture, billboards, signs, and handmade fliers with pictures of Tylee and JJ sprang up all over eastern Idaho. Some locals even began wearing "Where are the children?" tee shirts, and the long, icy Idaho winter blurred into a cold, wet spring.

Then, on the morning of June 9, 2020, when the nighttime temperatures had barely edged above freezing, Rexburg Police Detective Ray Hermosillo arrived at Chad's house at 202 N 1900 E. and knocked on the front door. Mark Daybell, the youngest of Chad's five children, answered with a bowl of cereal in his hand. He had no doubt what the man on the doorstep wanted. He could have guessed, even if Mark had not met Hermosillo several times. Hermosillo, with his broad shoulders, shaved head, and precisely trimmed goatee, looked like a cop. Hermosillo told Mark that he and the two officers accompanying him were there to serve a search warrant. The Daybell family didn't know that the FBI and local police had been preparing this carefully organized operation for weeks. While Hermosillo stood on the Daybell front porch, warrant in hand, equipment and people from several law enforcement agencies were mustering a mile and a half up the road in the parking lot of the neighborhood Church of Jesus Christ of Latter-day Saints.

Mark Daybell led the police to the loft above the garage where Chad was in bed. When officers came around a half wall into the room, they found Chad asleep. This was not the master bedroom, and it appeared Chad didn't want to sleep in the bed where, eight months ago, he claimed his wife, Tammy, had "slipped into death in the night with a soft smile on her face." The police roused Chad and waited while he pulled on jeans, sneakers, and a gray polo shirt, then escorted him to the kitchen, where he called his attorney, Mark Means. Chad moved to the living room and sat in his recliner while some of his children sat in shocked silence on the couch across from him. The scene was familiar; they had experienced a nearly identical shocked tableau of family and police eight months earlier when their father reported that their seemingly healthy, forty-nine-year-old mother had died in her sleep.

Police told Chad that he and his children could remain in the home while the search warrant was executed but would need a police escort at all times. Chad's daughter, Emma, and her husband, Joseph Murray, lived across the street. They took Mark back to their house and watched local law enforcement and the FBI Evidence Recovery Team (ERT) swarm across Chad's backyard with cadaver dogs and a backhoe. Officers watched Chad go out to his driveway, sit in his car, and make phone calls. The car was backed in, so Chad had to look back over his shoulder to monitor the activity in the yard. More than once, he took off his black baseball cap and nervously ran his fingers through his hair. Months earlier, a local news station reported that the FBI had a Mobile Command Center vehicle stationed in Rexburg. Now, that bus-sized blue-and-white unit was parked on the street in front of Chad's property. More law enforcement vehicles and unmarked black SUVs poured in, jamming both sides of the road in front of Chad's home. Social media began blowing up as neighbors noticed something big happening on the Daybell property. News Director Nate Eaton from East Idaho News was finishing a run when one of his reporters brought the chatter to his attention. Eaton sent the reporter to investigate, but he found all the roads into the area barricaded. Eaton had been on the Vallow-Daybell story since the beginning, even following Chad and Lori to Hawaii. Now, anxious to discover what was happening, he monitored police radio channels while securing a charter helicopter's services and got airborne. He streamed chilling live video of the Daybell residence as teams swarmed across the yard, marking out search grids, erecting blue-tarped shelters, and working cadaver dogs across the four-acre property.

Chad's phone rang as he sat in his car, and a recorded voice said: *"This is a call from and paid for by 'Lori,' an inmate at Madison County Jail. This call is subject to recording and monitoring. If you don't wish to talk, hang up now. Thank you for using Telemate."*

His wife was calling from jail in her breathy, Barbie-doll voice:

Lori: Hi, babe.

Chad: Hello.

Lori: Are you OK?

Chad: Well, they're searching the property.

Lori: The house right now?

Chad: Yeah, yeah (unintelligible). So, Mark Means will be talking to you.

Lori: OK, what, are they in the house?

Chad: No, they're out on the property.

Lori: Are they seizing stuff . . . Again?

Chad: They're searching.

Lori: Mmm.

Chad: There's a search warrant and so (unintelligible) to take evidence with the kids.

Lori: OK, mmm.

Chad: Yeah, I saw you tried to set up a call; I'm glad you called.

Lori: Yeah.

Chad: So, we'll see what transpires.

Lori: Kay.

Chad: Yeah, I don't really . . .

Lori: What do you want me to do . . . ?

Chad: What?

Lori: . . . pray?

Lori: What do you want me . . . ?

Chad: Yeah, pray and . . . yeah.

Lori: OK, what can I do for you?

Chad: I'm feeling pretty calm; I would call Mark, though, maybe. Just talk with him.

Lori: Have you talked to him already?

Chad: I did call him, yes.

Lori: So he knows what they're doing?

Chad: Yes. Looks like I got a call from somebody else that I need to talk to, but I love you so much.

Lori: OK, I love you. Should I try to call you later?

Chad: Um, I don't know, I . . . I don't know. You can try, yeah. I'll answer if I can.

Lori: OK.

Chad: I love you, and we'll talk soon.

Lori: OK, baby. Love you.

Chad: Love you, bye.

Every jail call begins with the warning that the calls are recorded. Chad and Lori knew their calls were monitored, so they tried to speak without giving too much away. Nonetheless, it's evident that Lori is trying to find out how bad it was when she asked, "Are they seizing . . . stuff . . . again?" Her real question was, Have they found them yet? When Lori asks if she should call Chad later, he telegraphs that the situation is bad: "Um, I don't know, I . . . I don't know. You can try, yeah. I'll answer if I can." The next time they would speak on the phone would be two years later when their attorneys arranged for a single unmonitored phone call to allow the codefendants to talk to each other about a possible plea.

Det. Hermosillo stamped his feet on the cold ground and slid his hands in his pockets. He had been a member of the Rexburg, Idaho, police department for nearly twenty years on the morning he served the search warrant on Chad. During those years, his city had more than doubled to 39,000 residents. Rexburg is a Mormon community founded in 1883 by The Church of Jesus Christ of Latter-day Saints (LDS). Today, about 95 percent of Rexburg residents are members of the church. The imposing, eternally illuminated Rexburg LDS temple, with its sharp, prow-shaped entrance and soaring spire, is perched on the hillside above Rexburg, where it can be seen from almost anywhere in town. On overcast days, it glowers out of the gray sky, looking down on the campus of Brigham Young University that sprawls across the hillside below it. Rexburg is in an area of the United States called the Great Basin. At more than 4,800 feet above sea level, daytime temperatures rarely rise above freezing between late November and February, and the ground often remains frozen deep into spring. Madison County and neighboring Fremont County are rural; the residents are primarily farmers and ranchers who hunt, fish, and ride snow machines in winter. The city of Rexburg is in Madison County, but many outlying farms, including the Daybell property, extend into neighboring Fremont County.

Det. Hermosillo worked on the ground while newsman Nate Eaton's chartered helicopter wop-wopped overhead. Hermosillo's first assignment was in the cinder block fire ring behind the Daybell home. He and other officers sifted through the ash. They recovered bits of cloth, what looked like bone shards, teeth, and a silver necklace and charm. The necklace was from the Pura Vida brand, a company that originated in Costa Rica.

The brand sells jewelry featuring tropical themes like waves, palm trees, and mountains and is popular with teenagers. Tylee Ryan had been photographed wearing that necklace. Nearby, FBI Evidence Recovery Team (ERT) technicians moved a small black statue of a dog out of the way and began to excavate what the family called their pet cemetery. Hermosillo recalled Chad's text message to Tammy at 11:53 A.M. on September 9, 2019:

> Well, I've had an interesting morning! I felt I should burn all of the limb debris in the fire pit before it got too soaked by the coming storms. While I did so, I spotted a big raccoon walking along the fence. I hurried and got my gun, and he was still walking along. I got close enough that one shot did the trick. He is now in our pet cemetery. Fun Times." A few minutes later, Chad texted, "Gonna shower now and then go write for a while at BYU. Love you!

Nearly three hours later, Tammy replied, "Good for you!" Investigators turned up the remains of a dog and cat but no raccoon. The last proof that Tylee Ryan was alive was a picture taken at Yellowstone the day before that text. His reference to burning limb debris would prove chillingly Freudian. Technicians began to excavate the pet cemetery using a small backhoe to scrape layers of soil away, but when they discovered a bone fragment and began to smell the odor of decomposition, they switched to hand tools. The team dug slowly and delicately, using small trowels and paintbrushes. It was painstaking work, and the officers were forced to trade off working in the pit every two or three minutes because of the overwhelming stench of burnt and decomposing flesh. As they carefully scraped away the soil, the scene became confusing. It took the investigators some time to realize that what they were looking at was charred flesh clinging to bone. They uncovered more masses of charred flesh and long bones that a forensic anthropologist on the scene confirmed were human arms and legs. A large, melted, and deformed green bucket emerged from the moist soil, full of more charred bones, flesh, and what appeared to be internal organs. When the officers tried to lift the bucket and its delicate contents out of the hole, the mass fell apart, forcing them to pick up the scattered body pieces with their gloved hands. Under the green bucket, they found a jawbone and part of a human skull.

Hermosillo took a break from digging and straightened to look across the surrounding pastures. Irrigation canals bordered the Daybell property on three sides, with the road on the fourth. Tammy Daybell loved raising ducks, and a line of fuzzy ducklings could often be found paddling in the canals behind their mother. Most of the trees on the Daybell property were clustered near the house and barn, but at the back of the property, a single bushy outlier tree stood next to a dry irrigation retention pond. The investigators would all come to think of it as JJ's tree. As the long day continued, clouds moved in, the overcast only adding to the already chilled, somber atmosphere. From under JJ's tree, an FBI officer beckoned Hermosillo to join him, pointing out an area of interest.

When Hermosillo approached the tree, he saw an oblong spot where the grass was shorter than the surrounding natural growth. An FBI special agent said he ran his hands over the area and felt a seam where the sod had been cut and replaced. Det. Hermosillo watched as other officers carefully began removing layers from that spot. They removed the top inch of sod and soil to reveal three flat, white paving stones. It was then that Hermosillo said he could smell a decomposing human body.

The objective precision which police officers strive for sometimes makes them masters of understatement; during Lori Vallow Daybell's trial, when Hermosillo testified that he "could smell the odor of a decomposing body," his matter-of-fact delivery belied the depth of that statement. Still, you could hear the emotion in his voice. Like most law enforcement officers, Hermosillo was familiar with the signature odor of decomposing human flesh. It's a smell like no other. Some people describe it as the sweet-bitter smell of rotting pork, overlain with an oily, old fish odor and often accompanied by the outhouse stink of a body's final release of urine and feces. Ray Hermosillo had been working the case of Lori Vallow Daybell's missing children since he first heard Lori's name in November 2019. By the time he testified at Lori's 2023 trial, he had seen hundreds of photographs, reviewed hours of video, studied thousands of text messages and GPS plots, and Tylee and JJ had been his constant companions for 1,257 days.

As the officers excavated in the shadow of JJ's tree, they found a sheet of thin wood paneling under the paving stones. When they removed the paneling, there was a round object wrapped in black plastic protruding from the soil. One of the officers cut the thick black plastic, only to find another thinner layer of white waffle-textured kitchen garbage bag. When they sliced into the white plastic, the officers saw brown hair beneath and knew they had uncovered a human head. The bundle they revealed when the dirt was shoveled from around it was a child-sized body wrapped tightly in a black plastic tarp, secured with yards of duct tape. Hermosillo stepped into the hole to help lift the small body out of its grave. There was no need for the gurney from the coroner's van; they simply carried JJ Vallow's small body to the waiting vehicle. There would be no need for the gurney for JJ's sister, Tylee, either. What they were able to recover of her charred and dismembered body was carefully placed in body bags and carried to the waiting van. The next day, Det. Hermosillo accompanied the children's remains on a 275-mile drive to the Boise, Idaho, office of the Ada County Coroner. Later that evening, Fremont County Sheriff Len Humphries stood before the news cameras and confirmed that the bodies found buried in Chad Daybell's backyard were those of JJ Vallow and Tylee Ryan. The public was shocked to learn Tylee's body had been cut into pieces and burned.

For months, as his wife spent her days in the Madison County jail, Chad Daybell had stood at his kitchen window and looked out over Tylee's and JJ's graves. That morning, Chad had watched, first from the vantage in his car and later from the front window of Emma's home across the street. Within moments of law enforcement announcing on their radio network that they had found human remains, Chad pulled out of Emma's driveway and sped away. Patrol officer Eric Wheeler was in his marked vehicle and followed Chad, pulling him over still in sight of the operation in Chad's backyard. Passersby snapped blurry pictures of him, head down, hands cuffed behind, being loaded into a police car. Chad's daughter, Emma rushed to the scene. Police allowed her to talk to her father as he sat in the back of the patrol car. A camera focused on the back seat of the car captured their conversation. Chad gave Emma his wallet and explained how to take care of his financial matters. He told her he would not be coming home.

A few days earlier, authorities in Idaho alerted Kay and Larry Woodcock that a possible recovery operation would be happening. Kay and Larry immediately flew to Idaho to be on hand. When Brandon Boudreaux, the ex-husband of Lori's niece, Melani Pawlowski, heard that Tylee and JJ's bodies had been found in Chad's backyard, he drove straight through the 922 miles to Rexburg from Gilbert, Arizona. The fourteen-hour drive left him exhausted; still, the first thing he did was check in on Kay and Larry. When he reached their hotel room, he found Larry in bed, laid low by a vicious bout of vertigo. To make matters worse, authorities had just called and asked Kay and Larry to come down and identify JJ's body. Rest would have to wait. Brandon took one look at Larry and knew he was in no condition to leave the hotel room, let alone take care of the terrible job. Brandon, who had known JJ all his life, insisted on going in Larry's place. Brandon said it was a horrible task, but he was glad to spare Larry that last sad goodbye.

As the setting sun silhouetted JJ's tree, police began to secure the site, and an impromptu memorial sprung up on the fence, running the length of the Daybell property. Blue and purple, the children's favorite colors, had come to symbolize the search for them. Well-wishers festooned the fence with pictures, colorful ribbons, balloons, signs, cards, flowers, candles, stuffed animals, and at least one rosary. When Chad's children tore down the monument, the neighbors across the street offered to host the memorial on their fence so community members had a place to pay their respects. It would remain in place for nearly three years while Lori and Chad's legal process dragged on. Local Rexburg resident Janine Hansen and her family made a special project of tending the fence display until Lori's trial. One of the many small, positive developments from the tragedy was the close friendship that grew between Janine, her husband, Clint, and Kay and Larry Woodcock.

With Chad and Lori safely in jail and the FBI involved, police continued to piece together cases in Idaho and Arizona. Like a million-piece jigsaw puzzle, they sifted through data measured in terabytes—bank and credit card records, GPS locations, tens of thousands of text messages, phone calls, photos and emails, videos, social media, forensic test data, and reports from medical examiners. With each discovery, the picture grew: Lori Vallow, Chad Daybell, and Alex Cox were murderers who thought they were above the law because God had chosen them to be leaders and saviors in the coming end of days. When the children's bodies were found, the prosecutor charged Lori Vallow Daybell with two counts of conspiracy to commit the destruction, alteration, or concealment of evidence, one for each child. Chad Daybell was also charged with two counts of conspiracy to commit the destruction, alteration, or concealment of evidence, one for each child, as well as two counts of the actual crime of destruction, alteration, or concealment of evidence. Each of them had bail set at $1 million.

Before his arrest and Lori's new charges, Chad had pleaded with friends and family for help with Lori's bail. Chad needed to put up 10 percent of her million-dollar bail to get Lori out, amounting to $100,000 in cash; he would also have had to pledge to the court at least one million dollars in assets to secure the remainder. Between them, Lori and Chad's assets were nowhere near that. Lori's luxury homes in Hawaii and Arizona had all been rentals, and she had received none of Charles's million-dollar life insurance settlement. At best, Chad's home had about $80,000 in equity, and when he returned from Hawaii, he had just $130,000 left of the $430,000 he'd received from Tammy's life insurance. Before he was arrested, Chad begged Lori's family for help and even asked his neighbors, Alice and Tim Gilbert, who had been Tammy's close friends, to pledge their farm as security for Lori's bail. Lori had Chad call her cousin, Braxton Southwick, looking for financial help to bail her out. Braxton and the Gilberts all declined to pledge their homes to secure Lori's attendance in court.

The unexpected happened as law enforcement continued to methodically collect and analyze evidence. The world was suddenly thrown into the COVID-19 pandemic. In April 2020, the Idaho court system sharply curtailed in-person court appearances, and by the time police found the children's bodies and arrested Chad in June 2020, the county had suspended grand juries and ordered all court proceedings be conducted by video conference. Shutdowns and backlogs at the state and FBI forensic labs also delayed the investigation. As the months dragged on, the public expressed outrage that neither Chad nor Lori had been charged with murder.

The US Constitution requires a preliminary finding that there is probable cause to charge a defendant with a felony and bind them over for trial. That probable cause finding can be determined either at a preliminary hearing or by a grand jury. Some states favor grand juries, while others prefer preliminary hearings. In Idaho, prosecutors usually use preliminary hearings, and grand juries are rare. On August 3, 2020, the public finally got their first look at the evidence against the couple when the Fremont County Court held a preliminary hearing for Chad Daybell on the charges of destroying, altering, or concealing evidence. The hearing was livestreamed to the public. The impact of COVID-19 could be seen in the courtroom: in-person attendance was limited, a plexiglass enclosure surrounded the judge and the witness stand, the clerk disinfected the entire witness stand after every witness, and most of the people in the courtroom wore N-95 masks.

When Det. Ray Hermosillo took the stand for the first time, the chilling testimony he gave about how and where the children's bodies were found was sufficient to bind Chad over for trial. After seeing the evidence against Chad, Lori waived her right to a similar hearing and stipulated that there was probable cause for her indictment. With the awful evidence out in the open, the public waited for the state to stop pussyfooting around and charge them both with murder. The wait was agonizing. Then, nearly a year later, in May 2021, Court TV released leaked information that Fremont County had issued grand jury subpoenas. They reported that Fremont County would convene a grand jury to review the deaths of Tylee Ryan, JJ Vallow, and Tammy Daybell. Grand jury proceedings are secret. The only participants are the panel members, the prosecutor, a court reporter, and witnesses called to testify. Judges do not oversee the process. Instead, a presiding grand jury foreman leads the proceedings. What happens in the grand jury is never revealed. While the proceedings are recorded, only the prosecutor, the accused, and their attorney receive a copy of the recording or written transcripts. If the grand jury finds enough evidence to charge the accused, they issue an indictment.

Thousands of people took to social media to celebrate, breathing a collective sigh of relief, when prosecutors Lindsey Blake and Rob Wood called a press conference on May 25, 2021, to announce that Lori Vallow and Chad Daybell had finally been indicted for the murders of Tylee, JJ, and Tammy. The process was far from over; no one could have foreseen that it would be two more years before the first trial. With indictments pending for both defendants, Judge Stephen Boyce set arraignment dates. Chad was arraigned on June 9, 2021, and pled not guilty; on August 6, 2021, the prosecutor filed a Notice of Intent to Seek the Death Penalty against Chad, and he waived his right to a speedy trial. In Arizona, the investigations into Charles Vallow's murder and the attempt on Brandon Boudreaux continued.

Before Lori could be arraigned on the murder charges, her attorney, Mark Means, filed a motion with the court, asking for Lori's mental competence to be examined. Means was concerned about Lori's mental state, believing she could not aid and assist in her defense. The judge ordered a psychological examination by a state-certified expert, who confirmed Means's suspicions: Lori was mentally incompetent. Judge Boyce entered an order committing Lori to the state mental hospital where she would receive treatment to restore her competence. When Lori refused medication, Boyce ordered treating doctors to medicate her forcibly if necessary. Her case was stayed for ten months while she received treatment in the state hospital.

It would take nearly four years for Lori Vallow Daybell to stand trial for the murders of her children and Tammy. In the meantime, officials in Arizona announced they had charged Lori with conspiracy to murder both her fourth husband, Charles Vallow, and her niece's ex-husband, Brandon Boudreaux. Kay and Larry Woodcock, whose call for a welfare check had set the entire case in motion, let themselves hope they would finally see justice for Tylee, JJ, Tammy, and Charles.

8

SOMETIMES SOCIAL MEDIA ISN'T THAT SOCIAL

Social media has been involved in the Vallow and Daybell case since the public was made aware that Tylee and JJ were missing. With the rise of the internet and the availability of cheap, fast bandwidth, the face of journalism has changed; suddenly, anyone can be a reporter, and everyone has an opinion. You could say it all started with Twitter, Facebook, and Jodi Arias. While it was big news when Jodi Arias murdered Travis Alexander in his Mesa, Arizona, home in 2008, it was her bizarre antics during her police investigation that first sparked the public's interest. In the police interview room, she stared directly at the camera while combing her fingers through her hair and then performed a headstand against the wall. She laughed, talked to herself, sang, and pawed through the trash.

Like the 1994 trial of football legend O. J. Simpson for the murder of his wife, Nicole Simpson, and her friend Ron Goldman, Jodi Arias's trial was televised. The difference between Arias and O. J. was the number of people watching and the immediacy of a live broadcast where viewers could watch and post their impressions in real time. People who couldn't watch every minute of the Arias trial didn't have to wait until the evening news for a summary of the day's events the way they had during the O. J. trial. A steady stream of tweets on Twitter and posts to Facebook interest groups kept people up-to-the-minute, fanning interest in the case. The Arias case was filled with salacious moments; from the testimony that Jodi was a spurned lover who slashed Travis's tires and crawled into his house through the doggy door to the playing of their phone sex tape in court, the public was consumed.

Highly publicized trials are hard on judges, court staff, and attorneys. Judge Lance Ito's career was never the same after the O. J. Simpson trial, nor was prosecutor Marcia Clark's. By the time the Arias trial was over, both the prosecutor, Juan Martinez, and the defense attorney, Kirk Nurmi, were accused of misconduct that would get them disbarred. Martinez's habit of sexually harassing women in his office and allegations that during the Arias trial he leaked information to a blogger with whom he was having an affair led him to consent to disbarment. Arias's defense attorney, Kirk Nurmi, was also disbarred later, accused of revealing client confidences in his book about the case. Similarly, in 2023, the public was privy to the livestreamed murder trial of prominent South Carolina attorney Alex Murdaugh and the subsequent controversy when the clerk of the court, Becky Hill, was accused of jury tampering and plagiarism after she wrote a book about the trial.

Questions arose about cameras in the Idaho courtroom almost immediately after charges were filed against Lori Vallow. The desire for televised coverage of the case was further fueled by the lack of access to the court because of its remote location and the COVID-19 restrictions. In the early days of the case, the court in Hawaii and Magistrate Farin Eddins, the Madison County, Idaho, magistrate, allowed cameras to broadcast the proceedings. Any hearings held by video conference were streamed on the court's YouTube channel. When Magistrate Eddins conducted Chad Daybell's preliminary hearing in August 2020, pool cameras captured the hearing and streamed it on many media platforms. All of the early motion and status hearings in the murder cases were streamed from Fremont County District Judge Stephen Boyce's court YouTube channel or by

Court TV's pool coverage. Then, in August 2022, Lori Vallow's attorneys filed a motion asking the court to ban cameras in the courtroom because of something that happened during an earlier hearing. As in past hearings, Court TV provided pool coverage. However, the defense complained there were microphones on the defense counsel table that could pick up their private conversations, and the camera focused too long on Vallow's face as she listened to arguments and conversed with her attorneys. The prosecution agreed, and their agreement proved persuasive to Judge Stephen Boyce. While he confirmed that the media had not violated the court's earlier order regarding the use of cameras, he ordered both still and video cameras out of the courtroom during pretrial proceedings. He refused to permit the audio from the hearings to be transmitted live, so the media was reduced to obtaining and releasing the court's audio recordings after the hearings. The judge continued the same prohibitions during Lori Vallow's trial in April 2023, citing concern that televising Lori's trial could jeopardize Chad's ability to get a fair trial later. The court continued to release recordings of each day's proceedings at the close of court.

The issue of cameras in the courtroom and the conduct of the media, in general, has become an issue in every high-profile case since the O. J. Simpson trial, with judges in each jurisdiction handling it differently. Cameras are never permitted in federal courts. In the Wagner family murder case in Pike County, Ohio, where Billy Wagner, Angela Wagner, and their two sons, George and Jake, were prosecuted for the murders of eight victims, including Hanna May Rhoden, the mother of Jake's daughter, over a child custody dispute, the judge permitted witnesses to opt out of having their testimony streamed. In the Colorado trial of Letecia Stauch for the murder of her eleven-year-old stepson, Gannon Stauch, a fixed camera covered the entire courtroom, and another showed the witness stand. Those cameras were not permitted to zoom in for closeups.

The question of cameras in the courtroom puts two fundamental constitutional rights, the right to a fair trial and freedom of speech, in conflict, creating tension no matter what a judge decides. The Sixth Amendment of the US Constitution assures, "In all criminal prosecutions, the accused shall enjoy the right to a speedy and public trial, by an impartial jury of the State and district wherein the crime shall have been committed, which district shall have been previously ascertained by law, and to be informed of the nature and cause of the accusation; to be confronted with the witnesses against him; to have compulsory process for obtaining witnesses in his favor, and to have the Assistance of Counsel for his defence." The Fifth Amendment says, "No person shall be held to answer for a capital or otherwise infamous crime, unless on a presentment or indictment of a Grand Jury, except in cases arising in the land or naval forces, or in the Militia, when in actual service in time of War or public danger; nor shall any person be subject for the same offence to be twice put in jeopardy of life or limb; nor shall be compelled in any criminal case to be a witness against himself, nor be deprived of life, liberty, or property, without due process of law; nor shall private property be taken for public use, without just compensation." The First Amendment provides, "Congress shall make no law respecting an establishment of religion, or prohibiting the free exercise thereof; or abridging the freedom of speech, or of the press; or the right of the people peaceably to assemble, and to petition the Government for a redress of grievances." The United States Supreme Court is responsible for interpreting the Constitution and determining whether laws or other government rulings, such as court decisions, violate its terms. One of the most significant of the many questions they must answer is, what is to be done when provisions of the Constitution conflict? How do we decide which takes precedence?

There was an important reason the Founding Fathers built protection for free speech and a free press into the foundation of our democracy—they believed that the free exchange of ideas, even wrong or distasteful ideas, was crucial to preserving democracy. They also thought the government should operate in the open to avoid corruption and abuse of power. Thus, the Constitution is filled with checks and balances. We often hear how the three branches of government, legislative, judicial, and executive, act to balance and check one another. Another of those checks and balances relies heavily on the right of free speech and a free press. When free media access the government and its functions, the government is likelier to stay in its lane, do the people's work, and not abuse its power. The right to a public trial is for the benefit of both the people and the defendant. The public has the right to be sure their elected officials do their jobs honestly and fairly as they conduct the people's business. The accused also has a right to a public trial to assure fairness. As Supreme Court Justice Louis Brandeis said more than a hundred years ago, "Publicity is justly commended as a remedy for social and industrial diseases. Sunlight is said to be the best of disinfectants; electric light the most efficient policeman."[1]

But what happens when the right of a free press runs up against an individual's right to a fair trial and due process of law? It's an often-asked question in the current media climate, where anyone with a YouTube channel or a blog can claim to be a journalist. The days when courts could rely on well-known commercial news organizations with officially issued press credentials that employed journalists who subscribed to a canon of journalistic ethics are gone. It was just these questions that permeated the Lori Vallow trial. The trial was moved from rural Fremont County, in the eastern part of Idaho, to Ada County, the largest population center in the state, to access a deeper and more diverse jury pool. Likewise, the judge reasoned that prohibiting livestream video of pretrial hearings would preserve the pool of likely jurors. In the Vallow case, the judge justified continuing the prohibition after Lori Vallow's trial, because Chad Daybell was still awaiting trial.

Before Lori's trial, journalists began asking how the court planned to ensure free press access to the trial when video coverage was unavailable, but the definition of journalist had blurred. Indeed, a reporter for an organization like East Idaho News, a purely digital news organization, is a journalist, but what about the YouTube show creator with one hundred thousand subscribers? What about the blogger with a few hundred followers? Which story creators get priority? Judge Stephen Boyce's answer: no one. He ordered that the seats in the courtroom be allotted by daily lottery. Mainstream media had to compete with bloggers, YouTube creators, and interested citizens for the limited courtroom seats. Those who could not get a seat in the courtroom for Lori's trial watched from a remote location in the courthouse where the video was transmitted by closed circuit. The closed-circuit video was not recorded or stored, and those attending were strictly forbidden to record the proceedings or take photographs. One news organization went so far as to hire a courtroom sketch artist to record the courtroom. The Ada County Courthouse made extensive and careful plans for the Vallow trial and managed the logistics of getting hundreds of people through court security and into the viewing areas. Deputies wrangled spectators in the courtroom and patrolled the overflow room, assuring people were not surreptitiously filming or photographing the video stream or anyone in the courtroom. Judge Stephen Boyce permitted creators with laptops or phones to use the internet during the trial, and a steady stream of tweets, Instagram posts, and Facebook updates narrated the trial in an unbroken stream of consciousness. No filming was allowed inside the courthouse, so the front steps were populated with local and national camera crews, and content creators stood in corners, talking into the cameras on their phones.

The question also became what impact the entertainment industry would have on the outcome of Lori Vallow's trial as authors, streaming services, and networks scrambled to get books and documentaries out while interest in a particular case was high. The Netflix documentary series *Sins of Our Mother* premiered in September 2022, six months before the Vallow trial began. The series told the story from the perspective of Lori's son, Colby Ryan. The judge and attorneys asked potential jurors whether they had seen the series. News shows such as *Dateline* and *20/20* covered the story extensively in the run-up to the trial; a Lifetime movie and several books were released long before Lori's trial began. But it wasn't just commercial media that contributed to the buzz about the case. Followers flooded Facebook interest groups, Twitter, and Reddit. Several of the Facebook interest groups had more than twenty thousand followers during the height of the case's popularity. Established YouTube true-crime channels covered the case extensively, and new channels popped up to focus on the case. Some of those channels grew from hundreds of followers to hundreds of thousands.

Ann Bremner is the attorney who represented Amanda Knox. You may recall that Knox, an American college student on a semester abroad in Italy, was accused of murdering her roommate, Meredith Kercher. Bremner's book, *Justice in the Age of Judgment*, discusses media coverage and social media's effect on many famous cases, including Knox's. As she points out, widespread publicity can be both a blessing and a curse. When Knox was detained and on trial in Italy, Americans interested in the case dissected the evidence, pointing out the deficiencies in the Italian investigation. American supporters pressured both the American and Italian governments to intervene. Knox was convicted in three separate Italian trials but ultimately exonerated on appeal to the Italian Supreme Court.

As Bremner notes,

> We all have fears that we've carried along from childhood . . .
> It's easy to put the source of our fears on someone else—the
> movie we watched too close to bedtime, the storybook read to
> us in primary school . . . That same inclination—to pass blame,
> to find an outlet for discomfort or uncertainty, is why people
> pass judgment in the court of public opinion. That's why they
> flock to Twitter, blogs, and Facebook groups about the terrifying
> cases outlined in this book. When we find an online community
> that shares our biases and prejudices, it brings a sense of relief.
> Suddenly judgments about horrible crimes, our political beliefs,
> or fears are legitimized . . . But that's not how this country is
> supposed to work. It's not how our courts are supposed to work.
> Yet, the court of public opinion continues to encroach on the
> American justice system. [2]

The diffuse government power that balances the American system of democracy also creates confusion. Each state is responsible for its own criminal justice system as long as it fits within the framework of the United States Constitution. Within each state, individual judges, most of whom are elected by the citizens, decide how cases will be tried in their courtrooms.

It's no wonder Americans and people who follow American cases from abroad find the outcomes bewildering. One judge may ban cameras, another may allow them, and a third may permit witnesses to opt out of being livestreamed because, ultimately, each judge must balance the rights of the First, Fifth, and Sixth Amendments of the US Constitution as they apply to their courtroom and their particular case.

Public opinion about the worldwide obsession with true crime is mixed. Some feel that interest in the tragedy of others diminishes the suffering of the victims and sensationalizes or even popularizes the perpetrators. Others believe that the publicity surrounding notorious cases brings a deeper understanding of the criminal justice system and casts sunlight on a process that desperately needs it. While some complain that news organizations and online creators are simply profiting off of the misery of others, many believe the public interest in crime stories still serves the purpose the Constitution intended: to ensure the power of the government is limited by insisting that it operate under the watchful eye of the public. For many, true crime also serves as a cautionary tale to help us avoid the same pitfalls or recognize the red flags in our lives before something terrible happens.

9

HE CAN PIERCE THE VEIL

As the months went on with Chad in jail, Lori receiving psychiatric treatment at the state hospital, and COVID-19 slowing everything down, people interested in the case began to ask, Who are these people, really?

Chad Daybell, like most members of the mainstream Church of Jesus Christ of Latter-day Saints, believed that the Biblical end times were imminent. Although the Bible cautions, "No one knows when that day or hour will come, even the angels in heaven and the Son don't know, only the Father knows."[1] Chad and Lori believed they knew. They believed June 21, 2020, was the day. They believed it so fervently that they staked everything on it. They believed it so completely they killed their family members for it.

Chad didn't grow up believing he was a prophet, but from an early age, he looked for ways to stand out and feel special. He was raised in Utah as the oldest son of devout LDS members Jack and Sheila Daybell. He was born on August 11, 1968, and grew up in Provo, Utah, where his father worked at Geneva Steel. After high school, Chad attended Brigham Young University for a year before taking a break from college to serve his two-year church mission. Sometimes, Chad felt lost at the huge university during his first year. He wrote, "I vividly remember walking slowly across the BYU campus during a January snowstorm and thinking, 'There isn't a soul on earth who cares what I'm doing right now.' I knew that statement wasn't completely true, but at home, it seemed life revolved around my other siblings' activities, and at BYU, I had taken general education classes, meaning I was seated with hundreds of students in large auditoriums where I rarely sat by the same person twice."[2] Chad felt neglected by his parents; as the oldest of five children, there were always younger siblings that needed more parental attention. His high school years reflected a continued pattern of trying to attract attention and feel important. He was involved in the student council and liked the attention he got from performing in student assemblies. Chad returned to BYU after serving two years as a missionary in New Jersey and graduated with a bachelor's degree in journalism.

Chad said he remembered seeing Tammy Douglas around high school, although she was two grades behind him. Within weeks of returning from his mission, he renewed his acquaintance with her in a young singles group. In those days, Tammy worked as the secretary for the municipal department that oversaw the local cemetery and suggested Chad apply for a job working in the cemetery. Chad got the job and worked there for the remainder of his student days at BYU. Later, he would fall back on the work experience during his life. During their courtship, Tammy saw Chad when she delivered paperwork to the cemetery; they even took their engagement photographs in the graveyard, Chad hiding from Tammy on the opposite side of a headstone. In those giddy, early days, Tammy could not have imagined that thirty years later, she would be murdered by that same man and buried in that same cemetery.

Chad and Tammy had a typically brief Mormon courtship and marriage. They were married on March 9, 1990, when Tammy was nineteen and Chad was twenty-two. In their wedding pictures, Tammy wore a modest wedding gown with a high neckline and long sleeves. Chad was dressed in an all-white tuxedo. The rest of the men wore black tuxedos, and the women in the wedding party wore prairie-style dresses with wide lace collars. Chad continued classes at BYU while working a few hours weekly at the cemetery. Tammy was promoted to full-time employment in Springville's city office, where she created a computer index and database out of the cemetery's handwritten ledgers.

Thus began the trend in the Daybell family of Tammy working while Chad chased his dreams and visions. Chad worked as an intern at the *Springville Herald* and then, in his final year of college, began working as assistant city editor for the *Daily Universe* newspaper. During his last year at BYU, Tammy decided it was time for them to start a family. Their son, Garth, was born just a month after Chad graduated from BYU. Chad was hired as a copy editor by the *Ogden Standard-Examiner*, and the couple moved to Ogden, Utah. After three years in Ogden, they decided to return to Springville to be closer to their families. Chad's brother told him the sexton at the Springville cemetery was retiring, and Chad was hired as his replacement. Chad said gravedigging paid better than newspaper work. He liked the regular hours and the fresh air and reported several encounters with the spirits of the dead in his autobiographies, *Living on the Edge of Heaven* and *One Foot in the Grave*.

The couple had four children when Chad said he heard a voice tell him it was time to start writing books. His first book was published in 1999 by Cedar Fort Publishing and became a regional bestseller. Although sold as fiction, Chad later claimed his books were based on his visions of the future. The first book in what became a trilogy, *An Errand for Emma*, told the story of a character based on his eldest daughter, who travels back in time and meets Brigham Young. The second, *A Dilemma for Doug*, had Emma's brother traveling back to World War II. But it wasn't until the third book, *Escape to Zion*, where Emma went into the future and found herself amid the tribulation that preceded the second coming of Jesus Christ, that Chad began writing about the expected end times. About the tribulation, Chad said, "I don't know when an earthquake will come, but I have seen in vision the damage it will cause. I hope we still have a few years before it strikes, but it would be best to be prepared if it comes sooner. One certainty is that the Lord Jesus Christ is in charge. His prophet and apostles will guide the Saints and lead the righteous to safety at the proper time."[3]

Chad quit the cemetery and began working as the Utah area manager for Access Computers. But then, the owner of his publisher, Cedar Fort Publishing, offered him a job as their managing editor. The job provided lower pay, but Chad believed the Holy Spirit was guiding him into the choice. After three years, Chad had learned the business and left to start his own publishing company, Spring Creek Book Company. LDS books were becoming more popular, and by 2004, with Tammy working behind the scenes and Tammy's mother, Phyllis, handling sales, they had published twenty-four books and secured a position as the Small Wholesaler of the Year. The success would not last, however. When the 2008 recession began, Tammy was forced to work part-time in the computer lab at the local elementary school while Chad returned to gravedigging as the cemetery sexton in Spanish Fork City.

According to his autobiography, Chad had always felt his faith deeply. He said during the training for his church mission, "I was on a spiritual high in the MTC (Missionary Training Center), similar to when the energy particles had bombarded me during my near-death experience. Spiritual light was continually being poured through my torn veil. MTC President George Durrant's powerful talks always filled me with great enthusiasm, and I felt closer to the Savior there than ever before. One time during our classroom study, our teacher shared with us a poem about the Savior leaving his heavenly home to suffer the indignities of earth life to die for us. As the teacher read it, I could visualize the scenes of what was happening in the poem, and I started sobbing in gratitude. I couldn't stop."[4]

Chad claimed he'd had visions during his mission. He said, "My companion was talking with the other family members, so I told Rafael, 'I have visions, too, but I don't dare tell anyone. Back in Utah they'd think I'm crazy. My bishop probably would have called you into his office to chastise you after your testimony today.'

"Rafael looked at me in shock. 'The Mormons in Utah don't talk about these things?'

"I shook my head, and Rafael responded, 'That's a key reason I knew the church is true. The First Vision, the angel Moroni, John the Baptist appearing, Peter, James, and John giving the priesthood, and angels at the Kirtland temple. It's the whole foundation of the church!'

"'Oh, they'll mention those visions as historical events during Sunday School, but it's as if the members in Utah don't believe visions can still happen now.'"[5]

Mormons believe in preexistence—that before they were born, their souls existed in heaven, with lives and missions and relationships—but when they are born, God places a veil over their knowledge of that time before. Chad claimed he had two near-death experiences that caused this veil first to thin and later to be torn open completely. "My novels are filled with many trials and triumphs that will occur among the Saints in the coming years. The most common question I receive is, 'What parts of your books are based on what you've seen in vision, and what parts did you make up?' The short answer is that I don't fictionalize any of the events portrayed. I'm really not that creative. Let me describe how my writing process occurs. My torn veil allows information to be downloaded into my brain from the other side. The scenes I am shown are real events that will happen, but it is my job to fit them into the lives of the fictional families in my novels."[6]

Near-death experiences (NDEs) and their accompanying visions are a popular subject among LDS members, and many who report NDEs say they experience visions of what will happen in the end times. Chad took particular interest in authors who claimed to have near-death experiences, including Suzanne Freeman, whose three books Chad published. The first of Freeman's books, *Led by the Hand of Christ*, was published by Chad in 2004.

Members of the mainstream LDS Church are encouraged to be prepared for the time of tribulation or any other disaster. They are told of the importance of having a year's worth of food storage and a year's worth of income saved in case of emergency. While the church says the practice is purely common sense, intended to guard against any natural or man-made misfortune, their implicit intent is to prepare the faithful for the end times. It's in the very name of the church: *Latter-day* Saints, and in their mission statement. Joseph Smith Jr. believed the true church had been led astray or subverted over the years and that God had called his only true believers to restore the one true church because Jesus can't return until the true church is restored. Even though the Christian Bible says no one knows when Jesus will return, throughout Christian history, prophets have claimed to see the date and time of Christ's return, and there are always those who interpret current events as signs that the end of days has come. Some LDS faithful take preparing to the extreme, cashing out retirement funds to buy tents and camping equipment. These so-called preppers gather at conventions and conferences to share ideas and belong to social media platforms for people with similar interests. It was on just such a platform that Chad Daybell first discovered Julie Rowe.

Chad Daybell was on a chat platform called Another Voice of Warning (AVOW), a subscription-based site where like-minded Latter-day Saints exchanged ideas about the second coming of Jesus Christ. Chad was intrigued when he discovered posts on the site from a woman who claimed to have prophetic visions about the world's impending end. Julie Rowe claimed to have had near-death experiences. Chad Daybell approached Julie, telling her he wanted her to write a book he would publish; the result was Rowe's book, *A Greater Tomorrow: My Journey Beyond the Veil*. Like many other near-death experiences (NDEs), Julie believes that while she was ill, her spirit left her body, and she visited heaven, where she received prophecies about the coming end of days. When the book was released, many LDS members took her warnings seriously and began stockpiling survival supplies. Both Chad and Julie Rowe were surprised by the book's popularity. Rowe, who claimed to be a clairvoyant and an energy healer who could speak with angels, began giving seminars. Chad's publication of the book in 2014 brought Spring Creek Book Company its most significant success, and it was only after that success that, in 2017, Daybell published his autobiography, which tells the story of his own NDEs. Notably, there is no record of Chad telling anyone about his near-death experiences, including his close family, before the publication of Julie Rowe's book.

The popularity of Rowe's book can, in some part, be credited to the conflation of her story with apocalyptic predictions made around the same time by Christian pastors John Hagee and Mark Biltz about the 2015 Blood Moon. The church even found the need to issue a statement about the occurrence.

> A rare confluence of a lunar eclipse and a supermoon set to happen this weekend has prompted such widespread fear of an impending apocalypse that the Mormon Church was compelled to issue a statement cautioning the faithful not to get caught up in speculation about a major calamity.
>
> Sunday night's 'blood moon' and recent natural disasters and political unrest around the world have led to a rise in sales at emergency-preparedness retailers. Apocalyptic statements by a Mormon author have only heightened fears among a small number of Mormon followers about the looming end of time. The eclipse will give the moon a red tint and make it look larger than usual. It won't happen again for 18 years. [7]

Julie Rowe posted on AVOW that she knew the end times were coming, and she knew they would be terrifying because she had seen it in visions. Chad's interest in the end times and his claims of near-death experiences would put him on a collision course with Lori Vallow. Like so many others, Chad predicted that the end of days was already upon them. The Seventh Seal had been broken, and the half hour of silence in heaven was nearly over, and a terror was coming that would eclipse all past wars and disasters, leaving only a handful of God's chosen to rebuild.

In January 2019, just a few weeks after they met, Chad sent Lori an email listing "Seven missions to accomplish together." The seven things listed are:

1. "Translate ancient records." This appears to be a reference to Joseph Smith Jr. translating ancient scripture. It suggests that Chad believed God would similarly endow him to translate newly discovered scripture, perhaps the sealed portion of the Book of

Mormon that God is said to have withheld from Joseph Smith Jr.
to be revealed in the last days.

2. "Write a book about the translation process." Once the ancient
   documents were translated, it would be essential to describe the
   translation process to give the documents credibility.

3. "Identify locations in northeast Arizona for white camps."
   Northeastern Arizona is sparsely populated. Both Spencer, in
   Visions of Glory, and Julie Rowe, in *A Greater Tomorrow*, predict
   that those Saints who have prepared will gather in tent cities in
   the early days of the tribulation. Some visionaries reported seeing
   row upon row of white tents.

4. "Presidency of the Church of the Firstborn." Mormon history is
   full of references to the Church of the Firstborn. Most refer to this
   passage in the Bible's Book of Hebrews: "And as members of the
   church of the firstborn all our names have been legally registered
   as citizens of heaven! And we have come before God who judges
   all, and who lives among the spirits of the righteous who have
   been made perfect in his eyes!"[8] While most Biblical scholars
   believe this is a reference to the difference between the Old
   Testament covenants with God and the more accessible
   New Testament covenants, Mormons interpret the Church of
   the Firstborn as the highest level of heaven, welcoming only an
   elect few who have proven their worthiness. Bruce R. McConkie,
   LDS author and member of the Quorum of the Twelve
   Apostles, wrote, "As the Church of Jesus Christ is God's earthly
   church, so the Church of the Firstborn is God's heavenly church,
   albeit its members are limited to exalted beings for who the family
   unit continues and who gain an inheritance in the highest heaven
   of the celestial world."[9] McConkie further describes the Church of
   the Firstborn. "The purpose of the church on earth is to prepare us
   for an inheritance in the church in heaven."[10] It is unclear whether
   Chad believed a Church of the Firstborn would be established on
   earth or if he was referring to the church as it is said to exist in

heaven. It's also unclear if he believed he would someday be the president of either or simply believed it was in his power to appoint the president of this elite body. Many believe that when the City of Zion is built, the Church of the Firstborn will succeed The Church of Jesus Christ of Latter-day Saints.

5. "Help establish the food distribution as the tribulations start and delegate." It appears Chad believed that his authority in the chosen 144,000 would require that he and Lori organize the process of distributing the food stores among those in the white camps and then move on to other, more critical jobs.

6. "Ordain individuals to translation as the camps begin." The word *translation* as used here may have more than one meaning. As we saw above, Chad believed he and Lori would be given the power to translate ancient documents, as Joseph Smith Jr. was given. There is also the concept in LDS theology of "translated beings," meaning they have already become immortal but remain on the earth rather than in heaven. This item could be interpreted either as Lori and Chad having the authority to empower others to translate ancient documents, or it could be construed that they have the authority to translate or exalt other beings, thereby making them immortal.

7. "Provide supplies to righteous members of families." This refers back to item number five, clarifying that Chad and Lori believed they had the authority to make life-and-death decisions for people.

Chad also believed that his near-death experiences had thinned his veil so that he could determine whether people were light or possessed by demons and therefore dark. On October 30, 2018, just days after they met, he emailed Lori about his light and dark rating scale.

Family History Information
Current numbers on Earth at this time of each estate level.

These totals represent the "light" spirits. The "dark" has equal numbers.

Estate	Males	Females
6	5	2
5.3	0	0
5.2	71	0
5.1	133	4
4.3	700	1,300
4.2	7,000	13,000
4.1	70,000	130,000
3	700,000	2.3 million
2	Billions	Billions

Most LDS members are level 2.

Most bishops and ward leaders are level 3.

Most stake presidents and general authorities are level 4.

Most apostles are level 5. A few are level 6.

The dark side can only match the light number, not exceed them. That is why there are a few 5s on earth right now. It limits the dark's power.

2s and 3s are fluid and can change sides during earthly life.

4.1 and above have made covenants to their side. They rarely switch sides.

Chad also gave Lori a list of her family members and his assessment of whether they were light or dark. The parenthetical references are Chad's and appear to reflect the period of their previous lives. The author added the italicized notations of each entry's relationship to Lori. Chad's assessments of her family changed over time, as one by one, they went dark.

Barry Cox—3L (1500s France) *Lori's father*

Janice Cox—3L (1600s England) *Lori's mother*

Stacey—Was 3L on earth, has graduated to 4.1L *Lori's deceased sister*

Alex Cox—2L *Lori's brother*

Adam Cox—3L *Lori's brother*

Laura—Was 3L on earth, has graduated to 4.1L *Lori's sister who died in infancy*

Lori—4.3L

Summer Cox Shiflet—3L *Lori's sister*

Husband is 2L, but borderline 2D

First husband—2L *Nelson Yanes*

Second husband: William Lagioia—2D

Son: Colby Ryan—3L Kelsee Ryan—3D *Colby Ryan's wife*

Third husband: Joseph Ryan—4.3D Is now sealed away *Died April 2018*

Daughter: Tylee Ryan—4.1D *Only her father, Joseph Ryan, rated darker*

Fourth husband: Charles Vallow—3L (1700s London)

First wife: 2D *Charles's first wife, Cheryl Wheeler*

Cole Vallow—3D *Charles's son with Cheryl Wheeler*

Zach Vallow—3L *Charles's son with Cheryl Wheeler*

Joshua Vallow—4.2L *Lori and Charles's adopted son. Son of Charles's nephew, Todd Trahan, and his partner, Mandy Leger*

Niece: Melani Boudreaux—3L *Melani is the daughter of Lori's deceased sister, Stacey, and her former husband, Steve Cope.*

Husband: Brandon—3D

4 kids—Both boys are 3L, Older girl—3L, Younger girl—4.1L

Later, Chad would identify two of these children as dark.

In early January 2019, Lori invited Zulema Pastenes out for lunch. When Lori arrived, Melanie Gibb was with her, and they told Zulema the news about Charles Vallow being possessed by a demon. Lori said, "I've been told" that Charles has become a zombie. As Lori explained it, Charles's body had been taken over by a succession of evil spirits. No sooner did they drive one out than a new and stronger one moved in. First, it had been someone named Garrett, then Ned Schneider, and finally, a powerful and multiple-demon entity called Hiplos. Lori even admitted she had sex twice with Charles after his body was taken over. It was clear Lori was receiving this information from Chad.

The idea that dark spirits are all around and that they can inhabit people is not new, nor is it antithetical to mainstream LDS doctrine. President Wilford Woodruff said, "We are surrounded by those evil spirits that are at war against God and against everything looking to the building up of the Kingdom of God, and we need this Holy Spirit to enable us to overcome these influences."[11] Brigham Young taught that every person who strives to be a Saint is closely watched by fallen spirits, continually prompting them to do wrong.[12] According to the church, Satan and his evil spirits are essential to God's plan of salvation because, without them, Saints could not prove their worthiness. Authors and podcasters Scott and Kylie Gillespie give a detailed and carefully annotated review of Mormon belief on this subject in their paper, *Possession by Devils and Unclean Spirits* (2017).[13] The document is widely available online and would have been accessible to Chad and Lori. The essay points out that "if you are steeped in the wisdom of the world, the statement 'possession by evil spirits is the single most common affliction of mankind' will seem dissonant to your carnal (secular) mind. It's only by superior spiritual wisdom that you can see the truth that people are possessed of demons, and others have the power to cast them out." Certainly, Chad and Lori believed this was true. They also believed it was their calling to cast the demons out. It is a seductive argument. Any resistance is blamed on the secular mind, and the doubter is told that their faith is not strong enough to believe. Joseph Smith Jr. taught, and the modern church still believes, that Lucifer was punished by being banished from heaven without a body. He travels the earth looking for people to destroy and takes possession of the body of anyone who yields to him. Interestingly, the essay also explains that we can understand how evil spirits possess someone by reading accounts of near-death experiences, including that of Dr. George Ritchie and "Spencer" from John Pontius's book, *Visions of Glory*. The pervasive influence of *Visions of Glory* will be explored further in later chapters.

The need to clear the earth of evil spirits was urgent because Lori believed that the tribulation would begin on July 21, 2020, but evil spirits could delay Jesus's return if they were not dealt with first. There is an explanation for why Lori chose that date, but the answer requires some assumptions. First, one must assume that God applies the traditional way of marking earthly years and that the time since the fall of Adam has been calculated without error. The Book of Revelation has Christ opening a book sealed with seven seals. He opens one every thousand years. Presuming the dates are correct and allowing that in the "Lord's time," a day in heaven is a thousand years on earth, Christ would have opened the Seventh Seal in 2000. The Book of Revelation announces that when the Seventh Seal is broken, there will be silence in heaven for the space of about half an hour. In the Lord's time, half an hour would be 20.8 years. That places the beginning of the time of tribulation somewhere in mid-2020. [14] The calculation requires many assumptions and overlooks the Bible's admonition that no one will know the day or hour Jesus will return. Still, it appears Lori was convinced that, like the apostle Paul, an earthquake in July 2020 would cause the prison doors to fly open, and she would be free to complete her mission of gathering the 144,000. The Bible says: "About midnight, Paul and Silas were praying and singing hymns to God, and the other prisoners were listening to them. Suddenly there was such a violent earthquake that the foundations of the prison were shaken. At once, all the prison doors flew open, and everyone's chains came loose." [15] Lori and Chad were also convinced that once the tribulation began, no one would pay a bit of attention to their affair, two missing children, or the mysterious death of Lori's husband and Chad's wife.

Lori deferred to Chad in all visionary things; he was, after all, her prophet and priesthood holder. Lori told friends that while she occasionally was visited by angels or had dreams that seemed visionary, she relied on Chad to communicate with the spirit world and relay God's direction. On July 21, 2020, the world did not end. A mighty earthquake did not rattle the Wasatch Front, and Lori and Chad's prison doors and chains stayed stubbornly locked. There was nothing to distract law enforcement from the investigation into Chad and Lori's crimes. One might wonder if Lori began to have doubts.

10

YOUR YOUNG MEN
WILL SEE VISIONS

"Those who can make you believe absurdities can make you commit atrocities."

—Voltaire

Lori Vallow had been on a spiritual quest long before she met Chad Daybell. Likewise, before he met Lori, Chad was also seeking a deeper understanding of Mormon doctrine. Chad's novels already focused on the end of days, and he was an active contributor to the doomsday site Another Voice of Warning (AVOW). Since Lori first received a copy of *Visions of Glory* from her cousin, Braxton, she had been aligned with the neo-fundamental wing of the church.

Author Eric J. Smith was a contemporary of Chad's. The two men met through their shared association with author Julie Rowe. Eric Smith heard Julie speak for the first time in his hometown of Rexburg, Idaho, at an event to publicize her first book. Julie's editor and publisher, Chad Daybell, was also there. Rowe's story so moved Eric that he asked if there was a way he could assist in her movement. Julie had recently begun a fundraising program to establish what she called "safe houses" for the Saints who she was sure would be on the roads, displaced by the callout, natural disasters, and wars as they traveled to safe mountain camps or to gather in Missouri. Eric Smith was a lifelong LDS member seeking deeper meaning when he began researching outside of church-endorsed sources. Smith said,

Sometime in June or July of 2017, I stumbled across a belief system that sounded like reincarnation. I don't remember where it came from, but I think it was mentioned in several different podcasts and websites I had visited. My curiosity grew, and I began looking in the scriptures to verify the possibilities of this as a lost doctrine. I found before long that it was actually scriptural, but had likely been scrubbed out by Emperor Constantine in the events surrounding that infamous council of Nicaea. I performed a lot of research and asked the Lord questions along the way and found out for myself that it is indeed a true doctrine. Before long I was sharing this belief system I had come to know as "Multiple Probations" with a couple close friends. One of which was Julie Rowe, and another was (Redacted). Julie felt as I did, but (Redacted) resisted it for a couple months. I have a lengthy journal entry from September 12 of 2017 that captured several insights and (Redacted's) new enthusiasm for this doctrine. He became even more studious in this doctrine than me and I rode his coattails for a while as he learned new things, much of which did not resonate with me as true. He told me he pitched the concepts to Chad Daybell, who at first resisted it, and after another conversation or two, he took it really well. I listened to Chad and (Redacted's) ideas, believing some and discarding others, meanwhile I had my own journey of beliefs which were more grounded in the scriptures and what I considered at that time to be authoritative sources. My thoughts were compiled with a friend named Greg Christensen, who I wrote a book with entitled *Multiple Probations—a Lost Doctrine Remembered.*[1] I felt the scriptural nature of our arguments put me on solid ground. Meanwhile Chad had found a necklace at church one day and began using it to help him in his work of classifying people and doing "family history," which was a code name for basically prying into people's personal lives and determining who they had been, and whether they were light or dark individuals or not. I went along with some of what he was doing, but never felt good about the light and dark classification system.

Eric Smith believed that Chad Daybell had genuine spiritual gifts. "Anybody who says otherwise are probably not being truthful with themselves." Smith believed Chad's thin veil made it possible for him to "see and discern things on the other side of the veil."[2] But Smith said when people are that open, they can also be open to dark forces. Eric Smith said he sensed a change in Chad about a year before the story broke that Lori Vallow's children were missing, which would have been about the time Chad met Lori. Eric Smith defended the ideas he discussed with Chad Daybell and Julie Rowe. In their book, *The Church of the Firstborn*, Eric Smith and Gregory Christiansen said, "The teachings of Jesus of Nazareth might have been best categorized as fringe doctrines to the orthodox Jews of the day. This teaching could be supported in scriptures, but they required one to have a deeper understanding . . . Ultimately those fringe doctrines led to his own persecution and that of his followers; it led to their excommunications and executions in some cases."[3] Smith and Christiansen used this to justify their fringe teachings, insisting the teachings of Jesus require a deeper understanding of scripture, including the underlying symbolism. They took great care to begin the book by adopting well-accepted mainstream LDS doctrine before radically departing from it. They discussed these ideas with like-minded people, including Chad Daybell and Julie Rowe. These are ideas that Chad would later expand upon to share with Lori Vallow and her friends. Smith and Christiansen's ideas relied heavily on the Mormon canon. They used the King James version of the Bible as revised by Joseph Smith, the Book of Mormon, Doctrine and Covenants, and the Pearl of Great Price. Using these sources, they came to some unconventional conclusions.

They began by introducing the Church of the Firstborn. It's a common Mormon belief that there will be a time of trial and tribulation before Christ returns and that during that time, the Saints will build the City of Zion (also called the New Jerusalem) in Missouri. Eric Smith believed the City of Zion would become home to all observant believers. From that group, those who have been exalted for their devotion will form the Church of the Firstborn. These people will lead the City of Zion and live in the presence of Jesus when he returns to reign. As Smith and Christiansen said,

> In other words, the establishment of the Church of the Firstborn upon the Earth is all about the coming together of heaven and Earth. It is about the fulfillment of the covenant which Enoch secured from the Lord that he and his people would have an inheritance upon the earth in a day when its inhabitants were prepared for terrestrial glory . . . It is plain in scripture that the Church of the Firstborn is the Millennial church, and its missionaries are a group referred to as the 144,000 . . . They are ordained by angels . . . Their authority will not come from The Church of Jesus Christ of Latter-day Saints.[4]

It's here that Smith and Christiansen made a controversial shift. They believed that not all members of the LDS Church would be part of the elect that would make up the Church of the Firstborn. They claimed that because the mainstream church has diverged from the original teachings of Joseph Smith Jr., they considered most members of the mainstream church Gentiles, who would not be elevated to the Church of the Firstborn. In effect, the Church of the Firstborn would reform God's reformed church (The Church of Jesus Christ of Latter-day Saints) and bring it back to its original roots. Their next contention is that women and men would play equal roles in the Church of the Firstborn. This was a drastic departure from the patriarchal system of most Mormon organizations, where women do not hold priesthood power and may not serve in leadership positions over men. The current Church of Jesus Christ of Latter-day Saints is led exclusively by elderly white men.

In her book, *The September Six and the Struggle for the Soul of Mormonism*, Sara M. Patterson records the excommunication of six LDS intellectuals in September 1993. It was a period when church leadership attempted to standardize and contain the church's message. In an Orwellian move reminiscent of 1984, the church leadership had recently established the Strengthening Church Members Committee (SCMC) to ensure doctrinal purity by searching church members' speeches and publications for any instances that "did not correlate with doctrine."[5] One can only imagine what that job might entail now, in the age of instant news and the internet.

Biblical studies scholar David Wright experienced a faith crisis of his own as he studied the excommunication of the Six:

> The struggles between the institutional church and the September Six had at their foundation different understandings of what it meant to be a restoration church. When Joseph Smith Jr. first founded the church in 1830, he asserted that it was the restoration of the 'true church,' one that had been absent from the earth since the time of Jesus and his disciples. While Smith declared that his was the true church, what the restoration looked like was not a one-and-done deal. Restoration was a process, and not everyone agreed on its end goal. This was true during Smith's lifetime, and it continues to be true in the various branches of the Mormon tradition that sprang from his movement. What Wright and his contemporaries in the LDS Church struggled over were different visions of the restoration, struggles that shaped their view of the church's past, present, and future.[6]

The Six were intellectuals who asked questions about church history, the revision of doctrine, and the roles of women and members of the

LGBTQ community in the church. Like the Six, Wright was confronted by his bishop about an article he had written. The article discussed ways to view historical texts. Ironically, Wright's article was an attempt to convince the faithful that Joseph Smith Jr.'s prophecies could still be true even if they found the history contained in the Book of Mormon suspect. Despite Wright's decidedly apologetic view, the church could not suffer any suggestion that the history of the church was not true. When Wright suggested the bishop was looking for a reason to excommunicate him, the bishop agreed. He was not trying to hide it. He said that their goal was to get Wright "to be orthodox" or "[they would] hold a disciplinary council."[7] Wright was excommunicated in 1994.

The inquiry into what constitutes LDS orthodoxy is an open question today because LDS orthodoxy changes so frequently. At the time the Six were excommunicated in 1993, any discussion of women holding priesthood power and any study of the deity the church calls "Heavenly Mother" was forbidden. Although there was ample evidence that the women of Joseph Smith Jr.'s time performed healings and other priesthood rituals, any suggestion that Joseph Smith Jr. endowed women with any form of priesthood power was quickly suppressed by the modern church. In 1993, the post-Brigham era view of women as powerless helpmates was the only view the church would entertain. By 2019, the church's position was more nuanced. "Often, we women don't realize that the power through which we accomplish 'much good' in our callings and in our homes is an expression of priesthood power. As a matter of fact, all the good that is done in the world is done through God's power . . . Knowing that women have access to that priesthood power strengthens us to be able to do what is asked in whatever responsibilities or assignments are ours."[8] In other words, women may "access" or "express" God's power, but that expression does not translate into any influence over policy or decisions. Dr. Sara Patterson makes clear in *The September Six* that the church is in a very real and ongoing struggle for its soul in an environment where women, people of color, and members of the LGBTQ community no longer feel constrained by church leadership to conform to the accepted teachings. This was evident in the beliefs of Chad and Lori.

The danger in this push-pull dynamic occurs in every sector of American society and politics. As some church members advocate for a more progressive approach to the LDS faith, those who are grounded in traditional LDS doctrine push back by moving further to the conservative side, giving rise to the prepper movement and social media platforms like AVOW. Mainstream church leadership walks a tightrope. On one side is the dissipation of the church as its more progressive members leave the faith. On the other hand, its more conservative members desire to return to the social mores of the past century. Dr. Ryan Cragun, a scholar studying sociology and religion at the University of Tampa, studies the secularization of America. His work notes that most churches, regardless of denomination, are seeing declines in membership. He observes that for the first time since its settlement in 1847, Mormons are no longer the majority in the state of Utah. [9]

For those excommunicated from the church, the decision may come with a sense of profound grief. While the church no longer calls the action "excommunication" or even "disfellowship," preferring to say instead, in yet another act of Orwellian doublespeak, that members are given "formal membership restrictions," the result is the same. People who have lived their entire lives within the embrace of the church are suddenly strangers in a strange land, cut off from the one thing that gives them a sense of identity and community. Because the culture of Mormonism encourages members to insulate themselves from the Gentile world, those who are excommunicated suddenly find themselves cut off from the people, rituals, and institutions that gave meaning to their lives. While the church says it does not actively promote shunning excommunicated members as some faiths do, friends and family who are still active members are discouraged from having contact with those who are no longer in the fold and encouraged to avoid anyone having a faith crisis. Despite his excommunication, scholar David Wright remained a believer. He wrote in his journal, "I am inescapably a Mormon. I am not on the outside looking in. I just have another way of being inside." [10]

In their book, *The Church of the Firstborn*, Eric Smith and Gregory Christiansen attempt to reconcile some of the conflict. Like Denver Snuffer, they encourage an expanded role for women while still calling for the church to return to some of the doctrines the modern church has deprecated. In their chapter titled "Gender and the Last Day," Smith and Christiansen make a most astonishing claim. While their claim may be shocking to mainstream members, it isn't without support in intellectual circles of the church. We've discussed Joseph Smith Jr.'s prophecy of the One Mighty and Strong and the church's history of men who claim they are the One. Many have asked if Chad Daybell considered himself the One, but Eric's conversations with Chad suggest a radically different idea. No person can rise to the celestial kingdom in the Mormon faith unless they are baptized and married. Taking that reasoning to the next level, the church also teaches that Jesus Christ must have been married. As mentioned previously, the idea that Jesus may have been married is not exclusive to Smith and Christiansen. Many scholars and religious leaders in various faith traditions argue that Jesus must have had a wife. Smith and Christiansen remind readers that since the Mormon pantheon includes God's wife, Heavenly Mother, Christ must also have such a partner. "Should we be surprised at the idea that Christ has an equal partner to His work, who has Her own Mission to accomplish. No. To the contrary, we should see that there is no other way. If there is a male deity, there must also be a female deity." [11]

Smith and Christiansen then make the thunderous leap to posit that the One Mighty and Strong that Joseph Smith Jr. prophesied is a woman. They believe she is the wife of Jesus Christ and has her own mission and group of helpers to assist her in fulfilling her mission.

> Yet what could be a more fitting duty for the equal partner of Christ? Surely, she must have a mission to fulfill upon the Earth, which is unique to Her, and yet which is equally important to the ministry of the Savior in the meridian of time and His many labors to exalt the Earth and its inhabitants. Surely also She does not come alone, just as Christ had his John the Baptist to herald him, and his Peter, James, and John to work beside Him, it only stands to reason that the bride will have her retinue as well. [12]

It's a small leap to the belief for Chad, that his goddess, Lori Vallow Daybell, is a handmaid of the One.

Reincarnation or "multiple mortal probations," plays a pivotal role in the beliefs shared by Eric Smith and Chad Daybell. Dr. Robert Beckstead, an excommunicated member of the LDS Church, Utah emergency room doctor, and author, claims the concept of reincarnation is "eloquently embedded" in the writings of prophet Joseph Smith Jr.[13] Beckstead believes that Smith began to talk about multiple probations after meeting Alexander Neibaur. Neibaur was a Jewish convert to the church and a student of the Kabbalah, a doctrine that teaches reincarnation. The ancient beliefs of the Jews were of interest to Joseph Smith Jr., who taught that members of The Church of Jesus Christ of Latter-day Saints were members of lost Jewish tribes. After Smith met with Neibaur, Beckstead claims Smith began teaching about what he called "plural probations." Most references to Smith's teachings around plural probations are anecdotal, and few published writings confirm it. According to Beckstead, in April 1843, Smith taught that "the purpose of successive probations or 'worlds' was to permit the gradual accumulation of intelligence." Beckstead also reports, "Around this time, Joseph Lee Robinson, another Smith confidant, reported that Smith 'discussed the idea that we have passed through probations prior to this and surmised that we must have been married and been given in marriage in those probations."[14] Some argue that the idea was introduced to Joseph Smith Jr. late in his life and that he did not have time before his death to fully flesh out and confirm the idea with God before he was murdered. Heber C. Kimball, one of Joseph Smith Jr.'s apostles, taught that if your spirit is not brought into subjugation in this probation, it could have another chance. Kimball said "Joseph always told us that we would have to pass by the sentinels that are placed between us and our Father and God. Then, of course, we are conducted along from this probation to other probations, or from this dispensation to another, by those who conducted those dispensations."[15] Kimble said, "What I do not today when the sun goes down, I lay down to sleep, which is typical of death; and in the morning, I rise and commence my work where I left it yesterday. That course is typical of the probations we take."[16]

If the goal of every Saint is to achieve exaltation to the celestial kingdom, and the only way to accomplish that is through good works and faithfulness during life in a body, then perhaps Beckstead is right. LDS prophet Lorenzo Snow is quoted as saying, "That sacrifice of the divine Being was effectual to destroy the powers of Satan. I believe that every man and woman who comes into this life and passes through it, that life will be a success in the end. It may not be in this life."[17] The mainstream church vehemently denies that Joseph Smith Jr. ever taught reincarnation. The church points to the Book of Mormon and the words of Nephi and Jesus that we cannot repent after death as proof of that. Proponents say this is precisely why souls must be reborn for another chance at repentance. Like many other faiths, the doctrine of The Church of Jesus Christ of Latter-day Saints is full of contradictions. For instance, if there can be no repentance after death, why would the LDS Church baptize and marry the dead? It's no surprise that curious but faithful Mormons like Chad Daybell and Lori Vallow might explore these questions.

Exalted couples remain together for "time and eternity" in the celestial kingdom. Before a man can become exalted, he must be sealed to a wife. For a woman to be exalted, her husband must call her through the veil by her secret name. But what happens in families like Tammy Daybell's when a wife dies and a husband remarries? While it presents little concern to the church, it causes endless consternation to members because the church still believes in polygamy in the celestial kingdom. The church has only recently begun openly discussing Heavenly Mother because, in doing so, it admits that there are countless Heavenly Mothers. You see, exalted men practice eternal polygamy, taking many wives in the celestial kingdom, with whom they produce spirit babies. In her book *The Ghost of Eternal Polygamy*, Carol Lynne Pearson points to the belief as the source of tremendous anxiety among the faithful.[18] A young widow, who was sealed to her now-deceased husband, would be of little interest to any other young man because she can't be sealed to him for time and eternity. Likewise, if someone like Chad Daybell remarries after the death of his wife, the church teaches that the man will be married to both women in the celestial kingdom. In the allocution Lori Vallow gave at her sentencing, she called

her victim, Tammy Daybell, her "eternal friend," but she may as well have
called Tammy her sister wife.

As the Daybell case illustrates, there is a strange tension in the church.
On the one hand, some believe Joseph Smith Jr.'s creation of the new church
was a democratization of religion, making "new experiences and spiritual
authority open to everyone . . . They wanted to unearth a history that they
thought was rich with equality, the Spirit, and emphasis on being driven by
personal conscience and personal revelation."[19] Still, the church hierarchy
stressed a pure, centralized, consistent message that began by acknowledging
the absolute authority of church leadership. It's no coincidence that this
development in the church in the 1990s coincided with its alignment with
the religious right and the Evangelical Christian movements that were also
burgeoning at the time. The church worked hard to align itself politically
with conservatives on the religious right on social issues like homosexuality
and the roles of women.

It is into this stew of change that Chad Daybell was born. By 2015,
Chad discussed his ideas with his small group of like-minded people.
Daybell was active on the AVOW website. Chad and Christopher Parrett,
who owns the site whose tagline is "Prepping like there is NO tomorrow,"
were acquainted. There was frequent talk on the site about the "callout."
A term that refers to a time when the mainstream church leaders will call
all members to bring their food storage and supplies to their ward, where
they will be loaded on trucks and taken to "white camps." Their supplies
will be distributed to the masses in an echo of Joseph Smith Jr.'s com-
munist Law of Consecration. The tent camps will be established to house
the faithful during the tribulation that precedes the return of Jesus Christ.
Parrett originally predicted that the callout would occur between 2010
and 2012. Chad also had definite beliefs about the end of the world and
unclean spirits possessing bodies. On October 1, 2019, less than a month
after Tylee and JJ were last seen and a few days before Tammy Daybell was
murdered, Chad posted a comment to one of Parrett's articles. "Excellent
article Chris. So are you considering moving farther away from the far-
left liberal city of Idaho Falls? Or do we just shoot the zombies as they

approach the UCON overpass on Highway 20?" As his books illustrate, Chad didn't see a problem with stealing ideas or conflating fact and fiction, and the zombies of *The Walking Dead* became Chad's bodies possessed by evil spirits of LDS doctrine.

Christopher Parrett published several books, and Chad Daybell sometimes collaborated with Parrett. Three of Parrett's books were simply collections of followers' posts on the AVOW website that Parrett calls *Dreams, Visions and Testimonies of the Last Days*. In the books, members recounted their prophetic visions and dreams of the coming tribulation. The dreams are always of tent cities, war, famine, floods, and earthquakes. Again and again, the contributors report dreams in which only the LDS faithful are spared.

There can be no question that by the summer of 2019, Chad was convinced he could see the storm clouds of the apocalypse gathering. He predicted its arrival in July 2020. It was imperative that he and Lori gather, consolidate, and plan. It was more than simply amassing food supplies and tents. For Chad, it was also about attracting followers and consolidating and condensing power. He sent Lori a message cautioning her about who among their circle could be trusted; he gave her the level of trustworthiness of each person as a percentage:

Mel G 97
Mel B 85
Zulema 96
Sarena 18
Christina 8
Nicole 86
April 7
Thor 94
Jason 31
Al 94
Summer 40
Janie [*sic*] 15

Barry 8
Adam 0
Stacie [*sic*], Talia, Audrey, Raphael 100

According to Chad, Melanie Gibb, Melani Boudreaux, Zulema Pastenes, Nicole Earle, Thor Furuseth, and Alex were trustworthy; Lori's other friends, April Raymond, Serena, and Christina, not so much. At the same time, Stacie [*sic*] (Lori's deceased sister), Audrey Barattiero, and Raphael were rated as 100 percent trustworthy. Raphael was one of the names Chad used to refer to himself. This was sent to Lori during the period when Chad was encouraging Audrey Barattiero to befriend Lori and keep her happy while Chad tried to figure out how to extricate himself from his marriage to Tammy. Of course, Lori's parents, Barry and Janis, her sister Summer, and her brother Adam, all people who had expressed concern about Lori's delusions, were rated as untrustworthy. Notably, none of Chad's family members are on the list. It's unclear why there is never any mention of Chad's five adult children, his siblings, or his parents, and nothing was said about Chad's nieces and nephews going dark, as we saw with Melani Boudreaux Pawlowski's children. At Chad's trial, Zulema revealed a document Lori had given her that contained dark and light scales. On it, Lori had written in Chad's children, all of whom were light. The difference makes many wonder if Chad truly believed what he was teaching. People close to him said Chad sometimes said he was a prophet, but there were also times he believed he was or had been a deity in an earlier life. Julie Rowe's prediction that Chad would be the Davidic Servant in the new Jerusalem bolstered his belief. In Mormonism, the Davidic Servant and the One Mighty and Strong are often used interchangeably. Chad told people he had been reincarnated as the Holy Ghost three times.

Within the growing neo-fundamentalist movement, many saw Chad as just another wannabe. However, Chad saw himself as the savior of the church; he was the Davidic servant, the reincarnation of Methuselah, The One, the Holy Ghost incarnate with a direct line through the veil to God himself.

11

YOU WILL BE ACCOUNTABLE FOR YOUR KNOWLEDGE

The Saints of The Church of Jesus Christ of Latter-Day Saints are cautioned, "A man is saved no faster than he gets knowledge, for if he does not get knowledge, he will be brought into captivity by some evil power in the other world . . ."[1] This is what Lori Vallow meant when she told Melanie Gibb during their taped phone call that Gibb would be accountable for her knowledge. As God's appointed representative, it was Lori's responsibility to keep her followers in line. She did so with a combination of charm and threats.

Lori's charm and enthusiasm were irresistible, and each woman in her orbit was delighted when Lori beamed her undivided attention on them. Trips to the temple with Lori were profoundly spiritual and magical. On one occasion, Lori and Melanie Gibb were in the temple when Melanie said she felt heat on her head, and Lori said, "It's happening." Lori told Gibb that God had given Lori the power to ordain Gibb to be part of the 144,000 because the angel Moroni had personally given Lori the priesthood key to ordain people. A woman with priesthood keys is impossible in the mainstream LDS Church, but Gibb believed Lori; after all, they were in the Temple when Lori said it, and surely Lori couldn't lie there.

Even before Lori met Chad Daybell, Jason Mow told Lori and Melanie he recognized them as "gatherers," ordained by God to gather the 144,000 in preparation for the end of days. Mow's statement affirmed to Lori and Melanie their significance in the blossoming Mormon neo-fundamentalism movement. Likewise, everything Lori heard in podcasts and read in books confirmed her suspicions that there were mysteries in her church that she still didn't know. Jason Mow was a former police officer, podcaster, and author who wrote a fictional book series called The War Chapters. He lived in the same area and attended the same Temple as Lori and Melanie Gibb. Mow's novels focused on larger-than-life heroes in epic historical battles from the Book of Mormon. He was a podcaster who also spoke at prepper events. He, too, believed that the second coming of Christ was imminent and that God was beginning to gather the 144,000 who would survive the tribulation preceding Christ's return. He invited Lori and Melanie to his *Time to Warrior Up* podcast. Lori's association with Mow started when Lori contacted him by email, told him she had read two of his books, and asked him if he would be interested in speaking to the youth at her church. She also requested Mow "put her in touch with like-minded people." He suggested she get in touch with Melanie Gibb.

Later, Lori and Melanie started their podcast and had Mow, Chad Daybell, and David Warwick on as guests. They also called their podcast *Time to Warrior Up*. During one recorded session, Lori explained her past life experiences and her role in the coming battle. Jason Mow and another sympathizer, Thor Furuseth, can be heard in the background as Lori claimed to be a "personal witness of the resurrected Jesus Christ." For Lori, this meant she had seen the Second Comforter, Jesus Christ, in person. Lori explained that she "sat down with him" in the premortal life. For most LDS members, this premortal life is unremembered because God places that "veil" between heaven and Earthly existence. However, Lori claimed that she saw beyond the veil into the memories of her premortal life. She also claimed to have been ministered to by the angel Moroni, an important figure in LDS teachings.

Lori says she was frequently awakened at night by angels. In the beginning, she had many questions. She asked,

> Why? . . . You made me this super-sweet person. I'm so sensitive—my whole life, everything hurt my feelings; I was totally sweet and innocent, and I was like, why would you ask me to fight this life and be this warrior? Why did you send me here? You know my personality; you know I hate to fight. I will avoid a fight at all costs. And he gave me a premortal memory . . . of me. And I got to see myself as a warrior, fighting for the Savior, in the premortal world, and I went to other worlds, and I fought, and I was one of His strongest warriors, and I saw it. And he showed me so that I could never deny it again. I was not sweet, and I was not innocent. I am old; I have fought. I have fought in this war for millennia. And that's who I am.

As Lori Vallow searched for something deeper, she became more and more confident that the truth lay in the doctrines the mainstream church discouraged or hid. Lori treated *Visions of Glory* and *The Second Comforter* as scripture. She shared Snuffer's belief that the mainstream church had become too "rabbinical," in other words, too academic. Lori embraced Snuffer's condemnation of the mainstream church's teaching that the Saints should "leave the mysteries alone." Instead, Snuffer suggests that the church should return to its roots in the mysteries of spiritual folk magic and divination. Lori also believed that God had endowed some chosen few with the ability to prophesy and envision the future.

According to Snuffer, the second comforter is a personal experience of Jesus Christ. Joseph Smith claimed to have been visited by the "personage of Jesus Christ." "Therefore," says Snuffer, "he had a personal knowledge about the Second Comforter. Joseph wanted the Saints to understand that his visitations from Christ were actual, literal, and physical. Similarly . . .

Christ will be comforting you by coming to visit with you."[2] Snuffer says, "The reason Christ calls Himself the 'Comforter' is because when He comes, you will need comfort. You will pass through distresses, sorrows, and difficulties first, and then he will provide comfort."[3] Lori Vallow was no stranger to distress and sorrow. She had experienced the disintegration of four marriages and been involved in an endless bitter custody dispute with her third husband, Joseph Ryan. She had a teenage daughter testing her autonomy and an adopted autistic son who required near-constant attention. The idea that the actual physical presence of Jesus Christ could visit her to comfort her must have charmed her. While Snuffer's message was enthusiastically received by many of the LDS faithful who became part of his "Remnant" movement, his book was not well received by the mainstream Church of Jesus Christ of Latter-day Saints, and he was excommunicated in 2013. *The Second Comforter* may have been the first time in Lori's life that she had ever received the message that it was acceptable to question the church.

The Second Comforter was only the beginning, though, because Lori would soon discover even more radical ideas in *Visions of Glory*, a strange book made up entirely of retelling the near-death visions and dreams of a man the author calls "Spencer." Spencer claimed that during several near-death experiences, he received prophetic dreams that foretold the second coming of Jesus Christ and the tribulations that would precede it and usher in a golden age of peace. Spencer's dreams cast a new perspective on LDS doctrine and introduced new concepts that many found seductive. After the book was published, Thom Harrison, who is a well-known LDS mental health professional, admitted that he was Spencer and the visions were his. The book only seemed to validate many of the things Chad Daybell wrote about in his novels. On the afternoon that a bikini-clad Lori was filmed being served at the swimming pool in Hawaii with documents demanding she produce her children to prove they were safe, an open copy of *Visions of Glory* can be seen next to her on her lounge. In text messages, Lori often referred to Chad as "Spencer," acknowledging his role as a visionary.

The modern church has a history of groups splitting off because they seek something deeper or a return to what they see as the pure doctrines taught by Joseph Smith Jr. The common themes of those doctrines are plural marriage, the law of consecration, in which the Saints promise to dedicate their lives and material goods to the church, the idea that Saints may live multiple mortal probations, and the gathering—the idea that the elect of Israel should gather together in one place. These were teachings Chad and Lori "received" and passed on to their followers. Truthfully, Chad and Lori were only a tiny part of a much larger movement in Mormon circles. The difference between them and others, such as independent fundamentalists Ogden Kraut or James Harmston, who claimed to be the reincarnation of Joseph Smith Jr., or even Denver Snuffer, was Lori and Chad's willingness to murder for their beliefs.

In November 2018, Chad sat on the coffee table while Lori, Serena, and Melanie Gibb sat facing him on the couch. They had all stayed at Lori's house during that Mesa, Arizona, PAP conference. This was Lori and Chad's second time together, and she was utterly infatuated with Chad and his beliefs. He told the women he had information about translation. Lori, like an attentive acolyte, begged him to teach them. Chad described the three steps to translation: physical, emotional, and spiritual. He told them he could tell how people were progressing and explained his scoring system. Chad's attachment of numbers and percentages to his ideas made them feel more concrete. He explained that when a demon possessed a person, their spirit was locked in a kind of spirit prison while their body was still alive. The original spirit can't be released from prison until the body dies. He told the women he had an information portal in his home where he went to work with spiritual beings who were beyond the veil to usher in the Second Coming of Jesus Christ.

The women coalescing around Lori included Zulema Pastenes, Melanie Gibb, Melani Boudreaux, Serena Sharp, Christina Atwood, and Nicole Earle. Zulema said they believed everything Chad told them because of the way he presented the information. Melanie Gibb met Zulema when she became Zulema's visiting teacher and introduced her to Lori. The women all became closer on the long drive to St. George, Utah, for the October 2018 Preparing a People conference. Shortly after that conference, Zulema told Lori that God told her she was to protect Lori. Lori was their goddess, and Chad was Lori's prophet. Lori was the conduit through which the faithful received Chad's visions and dreams.

In early 2019, Zulema reported she'd had a vision that she could "create storms and fire and will have the eye of the Lord." Lori elicited help from the women to "work on" Charles. In March 2019, Lori asked the women to gather in a secluded, safe area. These unedited text messages between Lori and Zulema describe the plan:

> Zulema: We can always meet at my house too . . . I have great shields up and no one will bother us here.

> Lori: Awesome! I never even thought of that so let's keep it in mind. We will see if the others are on board.

> Zulema: Lori, I have a strong feeling that the meeting needs to happen, no matter what. I think we should move forward no matter what. The Lord will have there who is supposed to be there.

> Lori: Hi beautiful. Is it still ok if we try to have the retreat at your house? It's only sarena and I, maybe Mel who will stay overnight.

> Zulema: Of course it's ok!

> Lori: You are awesome! I'm happy to get us a hotel but we might be more protected at your house.

> Lori: Mel (Gibb) is going to need to say she is going out of town. It's imperative that Brendon (Gibb—Melanie's husband at the time) not know where we are. He could cause some trouble. Other than that I see shields protecting us.

They met at Zulema's house. There, Lori, Serena, Melanie Gibb, Christina, and Nicole did what would become known as a casting. This was during the fifty-eight days Lori was missing from her family. Lori had been staying in Hawaii but had come to Arizona for the casting. She told them that because she was a translated being with such high vibration, she didn't come from Hawaii to Arizona by airplane; instead, she had come through a portal. Zulema found this suspicious because she had seen Lori's airline ticket. Still, she wanted to believe. At that gathering, Lori told the group she had perfected how to cast the demon out of Charles Vallow through group prayer. They each called down the spiritual weapons they believed they controlled and disconnected the energy cords between Satan and Charles. The group prayed intensely about Charles, and when Lori called Chad, he confirmed it had worked. However, a couple of days later, Chad told Lori that another demon had entered Charles, this one more powerful than the last. Following this visit, Lori went to Texas with Charles. Zulema asked Lori why she would return to a zombie, and Lori told her she needed to "get his finances in order."

During the spring of 2019, Lori and Zulema exchanged text messages about how their exaltation affected them physically. Lori was convinced they were getting younger by four days for every day they lived. She and Zulema agreed that their menopause symptoms had vanished and that they were both experiencing menstrual periods like much younger women. They compared notes and discovered they both had started their periods the same day after they visited the LDS temple together. The texts continue:

Zulema: No! You are so. Powerful. A powerful goddess that can do this and so much more. I felt the power from your hand! It pulsated energy into mine!

Lori: We are becoming one! We have important things to do and the time is now to get started! We Will succeed! You are amazing!

Zulema: Namaste. The goddess in me recognizes the goddess in you. I love you so much and I am grateful that heavenly father brought us together.

Lori: Me Too!! You are such a powerful goddess and you lift me!! We have worked together for eons and I'm so grateful for you!!

Lori: How can I calm the wind??

Zulema: Put your arms out, connect to Mother Earth, lift your arms with a breath, then bring your arms together on the front of your chest, then place your palms facing out and push the wind out, like parting it out.

Lori: Thank you! I'm working on it.

Zulema: I had a super weird and dark dream last night. I was laying down like on a beach with my body barely under the water. I had tentacles going all over the my back. I could see the tentacles they were black. Then it appeared that the tentacles had passed except for some that were left on my thighs. I keep feeling them so much that it woke me up. I woke up casting out. I'm not sure what that was but it was definitely dark! What do you think?

Lori: Sounds dark like they are trying to attach darkness to you. But you are too powerful! U will be triumphant!!! I know it! Be strong my sister.

Zulema: they had put some dark creatures that were still attached to your aura. They were like leeches trying to suck out my light energy. Chad had to remove them from me! I could feel them yesterday. My energy was low, I had body pains and I felt a disconnect.

Zulema: Did you come to me in my dreams last night? Were you and Chad working on something? I could see you and hear you. It was so real!

Lori: We were!

Lori: What did we say?

Zulema: Chad had been given the gift of healing. Then you two were working on something but I could only hear your voices. I couldn't decipher what you were saying.

Lori: We were healing and blessing and protecting you so that you can complete your mission. The dark side has had council meetings on how to stop you . . . so we listened in so that we could combat anything and everything they try! You have been given powers protections and priesthoods.

Zulema: I felt it. I heard Chad say he had been given healing power and he was going to heal me. I was there!

Lori and Zulema fed off one another. At first, Lori had no idea what she'd said in Zulema's dream, but by the end of the text thread, Lori was telling Zulema, and Zulema was confirming everything Lori said. It's a case of confirmation bias, where neither wanted to admit they didn't know what the other was talking about.

With Melanie Gibb, the exchanges were more philosophical.

Melanie: D&C 88_32 And they who remain shall also be quickened; nevertheless, they shall return again to their own place, to enjoy that which they are willing to receive, because they were not willing to enjoy that which they might have received. The remnant return to their own place? Where is that at? Back to the spirit world? To await another probation? Another creation?

Lori: My understanding is that according to our own mission. Different people will do different things. Some will stay and help. Some will go to the next round. Some will come back during the millennium.

Melanie: That makes sense, the remnant will go to the next round.

Lori: Yep!! That's so cool right cause basically the multiple creations are done when the Savior comes again. Yay! Then you will go off with your eternal companion (David) and create your own world. Then we will all come back to help fight at the end of the millennium.

Melanie: Very cool! I've been studying and getting more knowledge about the priesthood we have. Adamic or familial priesthood. We have it together with our husband. Can we use it individually and without our husbands physically here? The reason I ask is that we're in the middle of warfare. I have been casting out and I know I get rid of some but not others (higher level darks and demons) but Chad can. Because he uses the priesthood. Can we use our priesthood to cast out and destroy weapons? Chad found swords and helmets on Sarena and I today that were causing us headaches and muffled communication with the Lord.

Lori: Yes, you and I can use the priesthood. We have it.

Lori told Zulema she'd had a dream that Charles would die in a car crash. She was convinced it would happen and said it was part of the plan for her and Chad to be together. In late May 2019, Charles was in Texas with JJ. Zulema and Lori decided to use their power to cause Charles to have a fatal car crash. They seemed unconcerned that JJ might also be injured or killed. Zulema texted Lori, "I will go in spirit when the bomb goes off, and I'll be there to see JJ's spirit to go to the presence of the Lord. Then I and the angels will protect the bodies and not allow them to be possessed by evil."

A flurry of text messages on June 2, 2019, between the two women at around noon revealed what they intended:

Zulema: I'm ready!

Lori: Let's go now.

Zulema: That's powerful! I'm still sending fire.

Lori: Yes it is. I'm blinding him with light

Zulema: Ooh that's awesome

Lori: I'm feeling it big time Raphael is with us (Raphael is one of the names Lori used for Chad)

Zulema: I feel him

Lori: Did he leave?

Zulema: I can't see him. I felt like I was chasing him because I saw me running after someone.

Lori: Get him

Zulema: Oh I'm chasing!

Lori: You r amazing lady!!! I love you????

Zulema: I'm tired now . . . lol

Lori: Me too. I'll keep the light abs fire gong until he's gone.

Zulema: Me too! I'm still sending it

On June 3, 2019, Lori: OK I listened last night. Prayed over it and surrendered. Flying home today to gave the literal demon. He is still fine as of this morning. I love you for being so diligent and wise.

Zulema: How are you? I've been thinking about you all day

Lori: Just got home and got jj to sleep. Let's go spiritually tonight and work on him. We give the timing to the Lord but we don't want to relent. This is war.

Charles didn't die in a car accident that day, and Lori claimed it was because Satan interfered with their plan and saved Charles.

Lori moved back to Arizona from Texas three weeks before Charles was murdered. It was then that she told Zulema Alex's status had changed. He was, in fact, a multiple creation who was already exalted. Lori produced a map and claimed she had been given a new calling to eradicate all dark, earthbound spirits who had not passed over. She showed Zulema the areas on the map she had already cleared. She claimed to be clearing millions of dark spirits each day.

Over and over, Lori said that because she was already exalted, man's rules did not apply to her. She did not have to eat, sleep, or use the bathroom. She didn't have to follow the prohibitions of the church or wear her temple garments, which were for lesser mortals. She would wave her hand or slap the table and say, "Doesn't count for me!"

On July 8, 2019, just three days before Charles was murdered, Lori wrote to Zulema:

> Ask if we can call up a California earthquake tomorrow. Hiplos (their name for the demon inhabiting Charles) will be heading there tomorrow. In Valencia. Sadly He is still ok. But we r going to continue to work on him. The Elements will obey eventually.

On July 11, 2019, at almost midnight, Zulema wrote:

> As I was working on Hiplos today in the temple I was told "he will be taken as he is," idk what that means. Then I was shown to only put light, the brightest light, from the top and the bottom at the same time. Meeting in the middle. So I've been doing that all day. I hope this is a good day for all this to end. (Zulema didn't know Charles had died that morning.)

On July 12, 2019, Zulema sent a text message to Julie Clement:

> Hiplos is gone It was a Nephi and Laban ending. I will tell you more when I see you or when you see Lori in person.

The Book of Mormon references Nephi and Laban. Nephi was a prophet who was commanded by his father, Lehi, to return to Jerusalem to obtain brass plates containing genealogy records held by Laban. After several attempts to get Laban's plates, Nephi finds Laban drunk at home. God tells Nephi that Laban has been delivered into his hands and commands Nephi to slay him. Nephi pulls Laban's own sword and kills him.

Lori never liked it when her followers contacted Chad directly. She preferred to take their questions to Chad and return with his answers.

Still, Zulema frequently texted Chad directly with questions and requests for blessings.

On July 13, 2019, Chad responded to a text from Zulema:

> Hi Zulema, I would be happy to give you a blessing! Possibly this evening or tomorrow. It is crazy about Charles, but such a relief.

Zulema answers:

> Thank you Chad! I'm working until 8 P.M. but let me know when you're ready and I'll take break at that time . . . Yes the Charles thing feels surreal but still progressing that. Big Relief that he's gone!

Before Lori moved to Rexburg, she told Zulema that Tylee had been taken over by an evil spirit named Hillary. On August 31, 2019, Lori and Alex left for Rexburg, or, as Lori refers to it, "Zion." Two days later, on September 2, 2019, Zulema texted Alex, "How was the trip?"

> Alex: Pretty good considering the dark portal we brought with us.

> Zulema: ?

> Alex: Tylee. Can you call a tornado for a single person?

> Zulema: I think you will be led to deal with the dark one when its time

A few days later, Melanie talked to Lori as she unpacked in Rexburg. During the call, Lori told Melanie that Tylee was a dark spirit, and Tylee was heard in the background saying, "Not me, Mom!" Within days first Tylee, then JJ disappeared.

By December 8, 2019, the heat was on. It had been twelve days since Kay Woodcock asked the police for a welfare check and Lori and Chad had fled Idaho for sunny Hawaii, ghosting most of their followers. By then, law enforcement had been in touch with Melanie Gibb several times, and she, like Alex before her, was beginning to wonder if she might somehow be Lori and Chad's fall guy. She called Lori and Chad and recorded the conversation.

Chad: Hello, sweet Melanie . . .

Melanie: I was wondering where are you guys? Are you in Idaho?

Chad: We're nowhere near Idaho . . .

Melanie: I just wanted to ask you a question, if you don't mind, Lori . . . remember when we talked about JJ going to Kay's house, and you told me they went there, and now he's not there? I was wondering what happened.

Lori: (long pause) Well, I had to move him somewhere else because of her actions, so . . .

Melanie was surprised that JJ wasn't with Kay Woodcock. When Melanie saw Lori in Rexburg, Lori had a plan: she was going to lie and tell Kay that she had breast cancer and needed Kay to take JJ for a while so she could focus on her treatment. Earlier, Lori told Melanie that she took JJ to the airport, where she gave him to Kay, who had taken him back to Louisiana.

Melanie then asked Lori why Chad had told her they didn't want Melanie to know where JJ was for her security. She asked if there was a reason she should be concerned. Lori assured Melanie it wasn't her security that was at issue but JJ's. Lori corrected Chad when he said, "We were afraid if you knew it would put you in danger," saying they didn't want to put Melanie in a bad position. She then confronted Lori about why she told the police JJ was with Melanie when he was not. Lori said she needed to say something without telling anyone where JJ was. When Melanie asked, "Is JJ safe?" Lori responded, "He is safe . . .

and happy." Lori's answers were facile and breezy. "I know exactly where he is; he's perfectly fine and safe." In fact, JJ had been buried in Chad's backyard for the past seventy-seven days.

Melanie then asked if she could share a scripture, and Lori agreed but asked Melanie a question first.

> Lori: Did Alma turn himself into King Noah? What was he required to do?

> Melanie: Well, King Noah was incredibly wicked, and so he fled his evil ways, which was adultery, and living riotously, and breaking all the commandments.

> Lori: Right, so what was he required to do, Alma?

> Melanie: He had to go and flee so that he would be safe and then help other people realize how jacked up the system and the government was.

> Lori: What about Moroni? What was he required to do at the end?

> Melanie: To carry on those plates and bury them.

> Lori: What did he have to do to do that? Did he hide in the rocks?

> Melanie: He had to hide because they were so um . . . everybody was killing everybody in that society, everybody was dying.

> Lori: Who else had to hide in the cavity of a rock by day and go out by night?

> Melanie: The prophets did.

> Lori: They did.

Melanie: Well, this scripture may be thoughtful for you. This is Doctrine and Covenants section three, verses seven and eight, "For behold, you should not have feared man more than God. Although men set at naught the counsels of God and despise his words—yet you should have been faithful, and he would have extended his arm and supported you against all the fiery darts of the adversary, and he would have been with you in every time and trouble." So when we work with the Lord and are obedient, he's going to protect us from adversarial darts and all kinds of negativity, but when we open the door to Satan, he comes in, and he attacks, and then he takes away to make it look like somebody else took it away. That's not how God works; he doesn't work in darkness.

Lori: I agree with you a hundred percent, and that's what the Lord is doing for me. That's exactly what he's doing for me.

Melanie: Uh, it just sounds weird.

Lori: We have not opened the door to darkness, Mel, darkness is knocking on the door all the time because that's the way dark works with the light, and I promise you that I have done nothing wrong in this case, but sometimes you have to hide in the cavity of a rock for your own life's safety, and that's what the Lord requires of you, sometimes that's how it is because there's a lot of darkness on the Earth. It's been after me for zero reasons, except for the darkness of Kay, which you already know she's dark.

Melanie: I haven't met her enough to know if she is dark or not. I've just met her slightly; I haven't engaged with her that much, so I don't know that personally . . .

Lori then went on to complain about Kay receiving Charles's life insurance, and Melanie denied having seen the documents that Lori claims prove Kay stole the money. Lori then asked Melanie if she was recording the conversation for the police, and Melanie quickly changed the subject and said, "If you really loved me, you wouldn't have told the police that I had JJ."

> Melanie: I believe that you have been very deceived by Satan. I believe that he has tricked you. I just don't believe what you are doing is correct, I mean, Tammy dies, and then your husband died, and then he's missing; it just doesn't sound like God's plan to me . . . in my gut, it feels weird, it doesn't feel right, I don't have peace about it . . .

> Lori: You know me, Mel, you know me. This does not sound like you; this sounds like you've been influenced by somebody dark who wants you to believe dark things and have fear of the celestial world . . .

Lori cautioned Melanie that the Lord was coming soon, and when they stood before the Lord, Melanie would see that Lori was right. Chad then chimed in and told Melanie that it was his sister-in-law's fault that there were conspiracy theories about Tammy's death. He repeated that Tammy had been getting weaker and sicker for some time, and she "just passed away . . . I've been told for years that Tammy would pass away at a young age, and I had no idea that Lori would be a part of my life." Lori and Chad expressed concern that Melanie's boyfriend, David Warwick, was putting doubts in Melanie's head. Melanie, again, told them she was relying on her gut feelings.

> Lori: Well, I'm sorry I included you in those teachings, then, for your own safety. I wish that you didn't have as much knowledge as have because you will be accountable for the knowledge you do have, Mel.

Melanie then told Lori and Chad she was reading about Korihor, a figure in the Book of Mormon who was the anti-Christ and preached that what the prophets had said about Jesus being the savior was not true.

Melanie said, "He thought at the very end, because of his carnal and natural desires . . ."

Lori cut Melanie off, and you could hear the outrage in Lori's voice as she asked, "That's me? Carnal and natural desires?"

Melanie answered flippantly, "Well, honey, you got a lot of natural desires; we all know that."

"That's what you think is me, Korihor? Are you kidding me right now?"

Melanie then said she thought Lori was similar to Korihor. When Lori pointed out that she lived by the scriptures, Melanie reminded her that "we can wrest the scriptures for our own vainglory." When Lori protested, Melanie told her she believed Lori was using the scriptures to support an evil belief system. Melanie claimed Lori had been opening dark portals instead of obeying God. The call ended with Lori accusing Melanie of not wanting Lori to protect her children and with Lori saying she was sorry Melanie had turned against her as Joseph Smith's friends turned against him.

Another telephone recording, made about a month after Melanie's recorded conversation with Lori and Chad, surfaced in 2021. It added insight into Melanie Gibb and her relationship with Lori. In January 2020, a woman who had read Melanie Gibb's book reached out to her on Facebook. The woman's name was Sharie Dowdle. She discovered Gibb after listening to podcasts by Mike Stroud. Stroud is another in the pantheon of leaders espousing a Chad Daybell neo-fundamentalist brand of Mormonism. Stroud, who was a seminary teacher for twenty-seven years and who taught Jason Mow, was excommunicated from the mainstream LDS Church for his beliefs. After several conversations on Facebook Messenger, Melanie Gibb and Sharie Dowdle had a telephone call.

Sharie became uncomfortable when the conversation turned to Lori Vallow and her children and began recording the call. During the call, Melanie told her about when she asked Alex if she really wanted to know what happened to Lori's children, and Alex answered, "You don't want to know." Melanie went on, "You know Alex, bless his heart, who passed away, he just thought he was doing a favor to his sister; he didn't really care so much about Charles or this or that, but he just thought he was helping her."

You could hear the alarm in Dowdle's voice as she asked, "Did she ask him to kill him?"

"Well, to self-defense, yes, because they planned it," was Gibb's laconic answer. Gibb continued talking about Charles and the days surrounding his attempt to have Lori picked up on a mental health hold. She told Sharie that Charles had Lori's cell phone and posed as her to get Melanie to come to the Vallow house. "I get there, and it's him, and I'm like, oh my gosh . . . so I talk to him, and he says, 'You know, Melanie, Lori's crazy, like she thinks I'm this guy named Ned and that she's trying to destroy my life,' and I'm like uhhhhh."

Melanie told Sharie that Lori was stupid for telling Charles what she planned to do. "I just stood there, and he hugged me, and he was crying." Charles told Melanie that he thought Lori was going to kill him. Melanie told Dowdle that she knew the children were with Lori when she moved to Rexburg because she talked to Lori on the phone and heard the children in the background. Then Melanie told Dowdle about her visit with Lori in late September 2019. Authorities would later identify it as the weekend JJ was last seen. Melanie described when she asked Lori about Tylee. "I'm like, Tylee went to BYU? And she goes, yeah, but she gave me this really creepy look. Yeah, it was creepy. It was like yes, she's dead really. You know, that kind of look." Melanie said, "JJ's there, and she tells me he's a zombie now, and so was Tylee . . . Yeah, so people that are zombies don't end up staying alive, as you can probably see the pattern here." Melanie also talked about Tammy Daybell. Lori told Melanie that Tammy became a zombie after she began questioning whether Chad was having an affair. This call occurred before the children were located, and Dowdle was deeply concerned that the missing children were dead. She sent the recording to the authorities, but Dowdle lives in a state where it is not legal to record someone if they don't know they are being recorded, which is likely why the recording was not introduced at trial. Later, when Dowdle saw Melanie's May 31, 2020, interview with Nate Eaton of East Idaho News, she was shocked at how different Melanie's story was from what she had said in her phone call with Dowdle.[4]

Melanie also explained zombies to the police. The interviewing officer testified, "I asked Melanie if these people were living beings. She then provided an example using the police station. They would first check to see how many zombies there were. They would then say their prayer, and Chad would check his pendulum. Chad would then come back with the number of how many had died. I asked Melanie if these people would experience a physical death, and she stated that they would. Again, using the example of the police station, she indicated that their prayer would have physically killed the people at the station. Melanie indicated that there would be no evidence that their prayers had caused the deaths because people die every day."

Dowdle's recorded call was leaked publicly on social media, which created a new wrinkle. Lori's attorney, Mark Means, was in contact with a YouTube true-crime creator who went by the alias Awen Rees. She offered to help Means organize the volumes of discovery as an unpaid volunteer. It's unclear what the agreement was between Means and the YouTuber, but Rees began dropping hints on her channel that she had access to information no one else had, including sealed court documents. The Dowdle recording was provided to Means in discovery and made its way to a Facebook group about the case that Rees was active in. A woman who collaborated with Rees later confirmed Rees had been the source of the leak. The Facebook group released the recording to their members. Rees's supporters, who were vocal in their calls for justice for Tylee and JJ, were outraged when they learned she was assisting the defense. The leak was reported to law enforcement, and Rees disappeared from YouTube.

Over time, Zulema Pastenes drew closer to both Lori and Chad. She frequently texted Chad, asking for his advice and soliciting blessings to help with physical ailments. It was evident she saw him as her spiritual leader. Chad and Lori believed, as all Mormons do, that one can only enter the celestial kingdom if they are married. They encouraged Zulema to marry Lori's brother, Alex, to secure their places in heaven. Likewise, they were thrilled when Lori's niece, Melani Boudreaux, married Ian Pawlowski after only knowing him for ten days. Both marriages secured the women's places in the afterlife. Surely, Lori must have been concerned when Melanie Gibb filed for divorce from her husband, Brendon Gibb, worried that Melanie's place in heaven could be at risk, but Lori didn't like Melanie's boyfriend, David Warwick, and didn't encourage them to marry. Warwick shared some of their beliefs about the imminence of the coming tribulation, but he believed guidance should come from the leadership of the church and thought Chad's light/dark scale and their talk of prior probations were silly, and he told them so.

12

THE PET CEMETERY

While Lori and Chad basked in the Hawaiian sunshine, law enforcement began assembling the pieces of a complex puzzle spanning three states, two years, and thousands of miles. The police in Gilbert and Chandler, Arizona, and Rexburg, Idaho, the sheriffs and prosecutors in Fremont and Madison counties, and the FBI worked together to amass and analyze information. The picture that emerged was chilling as they wrote warrants and obtained thousands of text messages, emails, photographs, and GPS location coordinates.

When Lori discovered she was not entitled to Charles Vallow's life insurance, she investigated how much money she would receive from Social Security. She received benefits for Tylee because her father, Joseph Ryan, Lori's third husband, was deceased. Shortly after Charles Vallow died, Lori applied for the same benefits for JJ. A review of Social Security records revealed Lori Vallow continued to collect the Social Security benefits for several months after the children were dead and that she did not notify the Social Security Administration as required by law. The financial documents reflect that Tylee had a bank account she used frequently, but after moving to Rexburg, Lori closed Tylee's account and transferred all Tylee's money into her own account. The prosecutors believed the financial crimes contributed to the motive for the murders.

A picture of Lori's true attitude toward her children also emerged, and the picture wasn't flattering. Lori was finished with motherhood. Perhaps it was easier to admit her true feelings once she convinced herself they were zombies. When Alex set up the internet router in her apartment in Rexburg, he named the network "anti-Laban," referencing the Book of Mormon story where Nephi kills Laban. The password he chose for the new system was "toomanykids." When he texted the information to Lori, her response was, "funny." Alex had texted Zulema that he felt they'd brought the evil with them from Arizona in the form of sixteen-year-old Tylee. In reality, Tylee was simply a headstrong young woman with opinions of her own. Her lifelong upbringing in the LDS Church made her deeply suspicious of her mother's new prophet and his ideas.

After Lori moved to Rexburg, Chad Daybell struggled to keep Lori interested and committed while he figured out what to do about Tammy. Like Joseph Smith Jr. trying to marry Fanny Alger while still married to Emma, Chad needed to find a solution that allowed him to have both. His new church would frown on someone so influential divorcing, but the death of the first spouse would ensure he could have them both in the celestial kingdom. On October 4, he texted Lori, "Thank you for sending me that paragraph, beautiful Lili. I'm eager to see you soon. Trying to hasten her departure. I love you endlessly." The following day, he sent this message, "The short version is that she has been switched. Tammy is in Limbo, and a level 3 demonic entity named Viola is in her body. It happened at about 10 pm and was done by Tammy's sister, Sam, who I always knew was a 3D, but it turns out she is multiple creation."

When detectives searched Lori's Rexburg townhouse in November 2019, there was virtually no sign that JJ or Tylee had ever lived there. One of the only things they found was an outdated prescription for JJ's medication. Police did find other, more troubling items. They found JJ's empty Star Wars suitcase and three or four seventy-two-hour preparedness kits in the crawl space under the stairs. The go-bags contained water, flares, and military

Meals Ready to Eat (MREs). Although Alex Cox had his own apartment in the complex, it was empty, and it appeared to law enforcement that he'd been living with Lori. They found a plastic tub containing his mail and belongings in a bedroom closet. In that same bedroom, they discovered two Tyvek suits, like the ones painters wear to protect their clothing. In Lori's garage, they found guns and more guns, including a handgun and a Grendel AR-style rifle with the barrel threaded to receive a suppressor. They found a lot of ammunition of different calibers, silencers, and military-style knives, including a machete. They also recovered a camouflage ghillie suit that hunters and snipers wear to blend in with foliage, duct tape, tarps, gloves, and a scary rubber Halloween mask. They found pages of documents authored by Chad Daybell outlining his beliefs, his trust scales, and the light and dark rubrics.

Law enforcement found a rental agreement from a local self-storage unit on the printer in Lori's apartment. They used the document to apply for a search warrant for the storage unit, and when they opened it, they found the children's missing personal property. The unit contained clothing, personalized blankets made with their pictures, old schoolwork, JJ's backpack, and their bicycles.

Digital devices are the most critical component of any inquiry in a twenty-first-century criminal investigation. Law enforcement wrote search warrants and began collecting data from cloud-based storage systems. As arrests were made and devices were seized, they also ran extraction software designed to download information from the individual devices. Synthesizing that data into usable and understandable formats is tedious work. The GPS location data collected from Chad's, Lori's, and Alex's phones gave law enforcement probable cause to search Chad's backyard. Once Tylee's and JJ's bodies were discovered, the deeper meaning of some of the data emerged.

FBI agent Rick Wright said he was confident Tylee returned with the family from their visit to Yellowstone on September 8, 2019. The family returned from Yellowstone at 8:37 P.M. At 9:35 P.M., Alex left Lori's apartment and went to the Maverick gas and convenience store on Main Street. He returned to Lori's apartment and stayed there until 11:44 P.M., when he returned to his apartment. Law enforcement found it odd that Alex

Cox's phone showed up back at Lori's in the middle of that night because it wasn't Alex's habit to be at Lori's late at night. But that night, he went to Lori's at midnight, returned to his apartment at 12:44 A.M., and then was at Lori's again from 2:42 A.M. until 3:37 A.M. Law enforcement then placed him on Chad's property from 9:21 A.M., which would have been shortly after Tammy Daybell left for work, until 11:39 A.M. When Alex Cox left the Daybell property, probably after helping Chad Daybell dismember and burn Tylee's body, he stopped by a local Mexican fast-food restaurant for lunch. Tylee's DNA was found on tools in Chad's shed, confirming most of the damage to her body probably occurred there.

Alex Cox's phone was also in Chad's backyard on September 23, 2019, the morning after Alex was seen carrying JJ into Lori's apartment asleep. Alex was on Chad's property near the pond from 9:55 A.M. to 10:12 A.M. He spent less time at the property that morning, leading to the conclusion that Chad, the former cemetery sexton, was probably the person who did most of the work to prepare JJ's shallow grave and bury him under the tree near the retention pond. On both of those days, texts and voice calls flew furiously back and forth with Lori while Alex and Chad worked in Chad's backyard.

The weekend JJ disappeared, Melanie Gibb and her boyfriend, David Warwick, were at Lori's apartment for a visit. On the morning after JJ was last seen, as David Warwick and Melanie Gibb prepared to leave, David asked to say goodbye to JJ. Lori said he wasn't there. She told David JJ was acting like a zombie, climbing up to crawl along the space between the upper cabinets and the ceiling. Lori complained that JJ had knocked her picture of Jesus Christ on the floor and that Alex had taken him to give her a break. The following day, September 24, 2019, Lori called JJ's school and told them JJ had gone to Louisiana with his grandparents for several weeks. That was also when Lori told her new babysitter she wouldn't need her for a while because JJ was in Louisiana.

Rexburg Police Det. Chuck Kunsaitis noticed a news story from Utah about satellite imagery of Chad Daybell's property on the days after the children went missing. He followed up and received the images from Apollo Mapping. One of the images Kunsaitis obtained was taken September 9, 2019, the day after Tylee is thought to have been murdered and less than an hour after Alex Cox is believed to have left the property. Kunsaitis noticed a discolored circular area in the pet cemetery, where the soil had recently been disturbed. Law enforcement used the satellite images to support their application for a warrant for the Daybell property. When the Evidence Recovery Team began excavating the adjacent pet cemetery, they focused on the areas in the photos where the soil had appeared moist and disturbed. During Lori's trial, Kunsaitis choked up as he testified that the area of discoloration was the exact spot where Tylee's remains were found, stuffed in a melted green bucket.

Special Agent Steve Daniels was the FBI agent leading the Evidence Recovery Team (ERT) on the morning the bodies were located. The first area the team focused on was the backyard firepit. Stacked cinder blocks bordered the fire ring. Agents could see ash outside the fire pit and expanded the grid search to include the circular pit's surrounding area. As they began by carefully removing layer after layer of dirt and ash and sifting it through a fine mesh, they could smell a strong odor of what seemed to be an accelerant. David Sincerbeaux of the Idaho State Police lab analyzed the fire pit debris for the presence of accelerants and confirmed gasoline had been poured on Tylee's remains.

Tylee's and JJ's bodies were transported to Ada County for autopsy. Tylee's remains were then sent to the FBI forensic lab in Quantico, Virginia, for further analysis. A forensic anthropologist and an expert on tool marks analyzed her bones. The FBI tool mark expert, Douglas Halepska, looked at areas of the bones for damage that would indicate some sort of force was used on them. He then looked at the tools sent to the lab from Chad's shed. The tools had Tylee's DNA on them. Halepska said there was a serrated blade and a pickax used on Tylee, and the damage indicates that the tools were used in a chopping motion. The FBI forensic anthropologist, Dr. Angi Christensen, who analyzed Tylee's bones, said the marks made by the tools were not in locations that are typical in dismemberments, leading to the conclusion that the tools may have been used to kill Tylee before her body was cut up.

DNA analysis also played a part in the case. The science surrounding DNA analysis is rapidly developing. Until recently, the analysis of human hair was limited to hair with a root attached, and hair analysis actually involved analyzing the tissue attached to the hair. Bode Technology has developed a proprietary technology that generates a DNA profile from a rootless hair. It was this technology that was applied in the Vallow case. In November 2022, just weeks before Lori Vallow's January 2023 trial was scheduled to begin, the prosecution notified the defense that the crime lab had discovered an additional human hair in the duct tape used to wrap JJ Vallow. The Idaho crime lab could not test the rootless hair, so it was sent to Bode Technology for analysis. The hair was identified as belonging to Lori Vallow.

Human hair at a crime scene is some of the least persuasive evidence. This is because humans are constantly shedding hair. When human hair is found at a crime scene, it's impossible to tell when it might have been shed. Since hair is easily transferred, it's also impossible to determine how it arrived at the crime scene. It could have come directly from the owner or been carried in on someone else's clothing. In the Vallow case, it was well known that JJ often slept in Lori's room and sometimes in her bed. The presence of Lori's hair in the duct tape binding him did not mean she was present when JJ was bound. The hair could just as easily have come from JJ's pajamas or Alex Cox's or Chad Daybell's clothing. While the public was convinced the information was bad for Lori, neither side took great notice of the results during the trial. The prosecution presented it and left it there. Surprisingly, the defense didn't do more to argue that the hair could have come from anywhere and been deposited at any time. Those sorts of decisions are tactical, and some attorneys choose to treat a bad fact as if it isn't important so they don't draw additional attention to it.

The businesslike police reports and calm trial testimony cannot begin to describe the impact of what those associated with the case experienced.

The teams tasked with collecting evidence and recovering Tylee's and JJ's remains are professionals, but they are also human. They are people who choose careers that put them in contact daily with the terrible reality of what humans do to one another. The signature smell of death is their constant companion. The job is even harder when the victims are children. The terrible circumstances surrounding the Vallow case were not a common experience for small-town law enforcement, who were more accustomed to barking dog complaints and the occasional stolen bicycle. During the trial, the public heard again and again the sensory reality of the job. Officers reported what the ground felt like around JJ's burial site, their frustration as the mass of Tylee's remains fell apart in their hands, and the way the searchers forced themselves to overcome their bodies' own natural aversion to death and decay to care for the victims. Both prosecutors and defense attorneys spent months poring over grisly crime scene photographs, searching for clues and explanations. "Even though Tylee and JJ didn't live in our community for very long, they were still our children," Prosecutor Rob Wood said.

Still, no one in Rexburg could have prepared for the media firestorm that descended on their small rural community. Even as the weeks turned to months, while Lori received mental health treatment, public interest remained high through the long run-up to the trial.

13

THE LONG RUN-UP

By the time Lori Vallow and Chad Daybell were charged with murdering Tylee Ryan, JJ Vallow, and Tammy Daybell on May 24, 2021, the prosecution and defense teams had already been dueling with motions instead of swords for nearly two years. If an indictment is the fencing equivalent of the state claiming "en garde!" the motions are "fleche" (an explosive running attack) followed by "parry and riposte" (defensive block followed by a responding offensive action). The cases began in Madison County, where the City of Rexburg was located, but spilled over into neighboring Fremont County, where the children's bodies were found. Fremont County prosecutor Lindsey Blake took the lead in the case, with Madison County prosecutor Rob Wood appointed as special prosecutor. By the time the murder charges were filed, Wood and Blake had already been in the choreographed dance of motion and answer for the better part of two years. It would be nearly another two before the first jury would finally hear evidence.

One of the early issues prosecutors raised was their concern that Lori's attorney, Mark Means, had an ethical conflict of interest. Means became something of a lightning rod in the case. It was evident from the beginning that Means had little or no criminal law experience. Before the children's bodies were found and charges were brought against Chad, Means advised both Lori and Chad. On the morning of the search, it was Means that Chad called to talk about what to do about the search warrant, and it was Means whom Chad told Lori to call. When Lori appeared on her early charges, Means appeared for Lori but told the judge he represented both her and Chad. Then, after Chad's arrest, John Prior appeared with him for his first appearance on the destruction of evidence charges. Prior's office was in the same building as Mark Means. Unlike Means, Prior was an experienced criminal attorney. With Prior on Chad's case, Mark Means continued to represent Lori. Representing codefendants in a criminal case is usually an obvious conflict of interest because the lawyer will likely have to blame one to save the other. It is also a conflict for an attorney to represent someone if they have previously represented a codefendant. This is because the attorney could be privy to confidential information from each codefendant. The prosecution raised the issue that Means might have a conflict, and the judge reviewed the issue in chambers; for the time being, Means remained on the case. It isn't unusual for a conflict question to be discussed privately to ensure attorney-client confidences are not disclosed.

Means was an interesting character. When the court ordered anyone appearing in person to wear a mask because of COVID-19, Means stood at the counsel table wearing a camouflage bandanna over the lower part of his face, looking more like a bank robber than a defense attorney. Means's website advertised his expertise in divorce and personal injury law, and prosecutors expressed concern that he had never tried a felony case before. For the moment, at least, he was Lori Vallow's chosen, privately retained counsel. Means was outspoken, rough around the edges, and unfamiliar with the rules of criminal procedure and usual practices in criminal court. Despite his inexperience, he tried his best to look out for Lori. Shortly after the murder indictment was filed, he informed the court that he did not believe Lori was competent to stand trial.

Competency is a complex issue. It is different from a claim of insanity. An insanity claim is usually made as a defense to a crime, alleging that at the time of the crime, the defendant did not have the mental capacity to understand what they were doing or that it was wrong. Idaho is one of four states in America that does not permit the use of an insanity defense. A defense of insanity differs from a claim that the defendant presently cannot understand the charges or participate in their defense. The judge ordered an independent psychological examination by a court-certified psychologist. The expert concurred with Means; Lori was not competent for trial. The judge committed Lori to the state mental health system, and she was placed in the state hospital. There, she received services aimed at helping her return to competency. Minimum competency is not a high standard. The defendant must be oriented to time and place, understand the charges against her, and the roles of all the people in a criminal trial. Lori was under the supervision of the state hospital for ten months before her treatment providers notified the court that she had been restored to competence. Lori's speedy trial deadline was tolled while she was in treatment.

During those months, while Lori's speedy trial time was suspended, the clock continued to tick for Chad. The law in Idaho requires that a criminal defendant be tried within six months of the date of their arraignment unless they waive that right or the time is otherwise tolled. Civil commitment is one of the situations that trigger a tolling of the speedy trial statute. In the meantime, that meant that Chad Daybell was in limbo. The legal water would have been muddier, except that Chad had already waived his right to a speedy trial, unlike Lori, who consistently insisted on her speedy trial rights. The advantage for Chad and his attorney was that they now had extra time to prepare his case. The downside was that Chad remained in jail, unable to post the one-million-dollar bail.

While Lori was still receiving treatment, Mark Means filed a notice informing the court that Lori Vallow was indigent. The court appointed Jim Archibald, an experienced, death penalty certified public defender, as Lori's co-counsel but ordered Means to remain lead counsel. Means continued to file odd motions that illustrated his lack of experience in criminal matters. While Lori was being treated at the state hospital, Means filed motions regarding an incident he claimed happened there. The facts may never be known, but Means claimed that Lori and one of her treatment providers listened in on Chad's change of venue motion. What transpired next is disputed. According to Lori, the provider recommended Lori contact The Church of Jesus Christ of Latter-day Saints to discuss her case and ask for help getting different legal counsel. The clinician told Lori it was treatment "homework." When Lori called the law firm that regularly represents the church, according to her, the lawyer who took her call said he had more than thirty years of experience in criminal litigation and that he knew every detail of her case. Means claims that this caused Lori to make disclosures that she would not have otherwise made and that should have been protected by attorney-client privilege. The law firm denies all of it. They claim that when Lori called, they informed her that because she was currently represented by counsel, they could not speak to her. It ended up being much ado about nothing and made Means appear foolish.

Likewise, he attempted to subpoena Melanie Gibb's telephone records following her testimony before the grand jury. When Melanie ignored the subpoena, Means tried to hold her in contempt for not complying. Through it all, Lori insisted she wanted Means to continue as her counsel. More than one person close to the case suggested that Means believed at least some of the same things Lori and Chad did about the coming end times. News shows like *Dateline* and *20/20* had already run segments about Lori and Chad since the children were first reported missing. Then, in 2021, the Lifetime Network released a scripted movie about the case titled *Doomsday Mom*. In the film, Lori tells a cellmate that in another life, Mark Means was her blue-eyed son, conceived from her marriage to an archangel. It is unclear where the script writer obtained that information or whether a cellmate said anything of the sort, but the movie illustrates the lengths to which the media went to cover the story.

Mark Means's motion to hold Melanie Gibb in contempt was dropped when, in December 2021, the court revisited the conflict issue and disqualified Means. He may have also run afoul of the Idaho State Bar, which regulates lawyer performance. Each state bar treats attorney discipline a bit differently. In many states, attorney disciplinary records are public, but in Idaho, the records only become public if a final decision is made on a disciplinary complaint. Shortly after Means was dismissed from Lori Vallow's case, he closed his Idaho office. The Idaho State Bar records reflect his resignation from the Idaho Bar Association. His LinkedIn page lists himself as "Attorney/Professor at Means Law Office, PLLC" in Troy, Missouri, but he is not listed on the Missouri State Bar membership roster. Missouri is said to be where the City of Zion will be built when Jesus Christ returns.

With Means's removal, Jim Archibald became Lori's lead counsel and asked the court to appoint John Thomas as cocounsel. It is typical for at least two attorneys to be appointed in death penalty cases. In Idaho, defendants may choose any attorney if the lawyer is privately retained. It is up to the defendant to make sure their retained counsel is qualified to represent them. If, on the other hand, the state is paying for appointed counsel, the state requires that counsel meet minimum qualification standards. Means did not meet the minimum requirements for death penalty certification. Chad's attorney, John Prior, was also not death penalty qualified under the state standards. However, since Prior was retained and not court-appointed, he did not need to be. He was, however, an experienced criminal attorney and likely could have been state-certified. Chad Daybell was not indigent, and his attorney continued on his case, although the specifics of his fee agreement with Daybell were unclear. When Chad returned from Hawaii, he had about $130,000 in his bank account, presumably what remained of Tammy's $430,000 life insurance proceeds. He also became their home's sole owner, with about $80,000 in equity. When Lori initially appeared in court in March 2020, she was represented by Boise, Idaho, attorneys Edwina Elcox and Brian Webb. They argued the bail issue and withdrew after the first appearance. Mark Means also appeared for Lori at that bail hearing. It was unclear if Elcox and Webb's representation was intended to be limited to the bail hearing or if they decided after the hearing that they didn't want to be involved in the case further.

Lawyer fee agreements are private contracts that are not generally disclosed, so the public does not know if any of Chad's $130,000 went to pay Lori's attorneys and how much was paid to John Prior as a retainer. As the case dragged on, Chad Daybell deeded his interest in his home to John Prior in lieu of further attorney fees. This arrangement is not unusual in cases where clients do not have cash to continue paying their attorneys. In January 2023, in a closed and sealed proceeding, John Prior asked the court to declare Chad Daybell indigent. While John Prior asked to remain Chad's attorney of record, Judge Boyce approved Prior's request for state funds to hire a death penalty qualified public defender to assist him.

Before Mark Means's disqualification, he and John Prior each filed motions to change the trial's location. The prosecution opposed moving the trial. In a community that is lightly populated and predominantly LDS, nearly everyone knew Chad Daybell or someone who knew him. The Vallow/Daybell case was the main topic of conversation in town for not just weeks but months. Over the prosecution's objection, Judge Boyce ordered the trial moved from tiny St. Anthony, Idaho, to Boise in hopes of finding a more diverse jury pool with less contamination from the relentless media. For the two years before the trial began, Lori and Chad's cases had been joined for trial. Chad's attorney filed multiple motions asking that the cases be severed and the defendants tried separately. Judge Stephen Boyce repeatedly denied those motions until shortly before the trial commenced.

Criminal cases have different legal requirements than civil cases. In criminal cases, the prosecution represents the state, and they have the power and resources of the government behind them. One of the checks on that power requires that the prosecution turn over all investigative materials to the defense. The process is called "discovery." The prosecution must reveal all its cards, especially information that could help acquit the defendant, known as exculpatory information. The prosecution must also give the defense any information that could lead them to exculpatory information. That's a wide net.

Throughout the run-up to the trial, the defense teams sparred with the prosecution over discovery. Both defense teams repeatedly complained that the prosecution had not complied with the discovery rules and turned over all their investigative materials; numerous motions were filed to compel the prosecution to provide more discovery. Prosecutors insisted they had given the defense everything. Each time the judge heard their complaints, he questioned the prosecution and received assurances that all the information had been supplied. Every prosecutor's office has a system for indexing discovery materials and accounting for when and how each piece is given to the defense. Each time the prosecution assured the judge that the defense had received all the discovery, they also complained about how "voluminous" the amount of discovery they were responsible to index and turn over was. Still, the defense attorneys for both Lori and Chad continued to say that not all materials had been provided, and as it happened, they were right. In every case, the judge sets deadlines for filing motions and turning over discovery before trial. In the Vallow case, the prosecution violated the deadline for discovery, admitting just days before the trial that some materials had still not been turned over. Some of the information involved the recently discovered hair DNA, but there were also hundreds of hours of jail calls and recorded FBI interviews that the defense had never been given.

Now, Judge Boyce had a tough decision—how to make the upcoming trial fair in light of the missing information. The prosecution said they thought the proper remedy was simply for the court to rule they couldn't use any of the information. But, as the defense attorneys rightly pointed out, that defeats the purpose of the discovery rules. The prosecution does not get to decide whether the information is relevant to the case or how it might be used at trial before they turn it over. The defense has a right to see and investigate everything, whether the prosecution thinks it's relevant or not. Chad Daybell's lawyer asked for more time to investigate the information and perhaps have the new DNA independently tested. While that solution made sense for Chad, it couldn't work for Lori because although Chad had waived his right to a speedy trial early in the case, Lori had not. Moreover, Lori had repeatedly confirmed she wanted her trial set within the speedy trial limits.

After Lori was ruled competent in April 2022, her trial was set for January 2023, barely within the speedy trial window. Then, in late October 2022, Lori's attorneys again filed motions with the court, questioning Lori's competence to stand trial. The judge decided to stay the proceedings while Lori was reevaluated, and he took the January 2023 trial off the Ada County Court's docket. The evaluation was accomplished quickly, and the results were presented to the court on November 9, 2022. The judge found Lori competent to continue. In hindsight, the parties likely could have been ready for trial in January, but Judge Boyce, recognizing the lengths the court in Boise had gone to in preparation, opted to postpone. The next available window for a lengthy trial was in April 2023. The new trial date on April 3, 2023, was forty-one days outside her six-month speedy trial window. With Chad asking for extra time, the judge had no choice but to sever the trials. Giving Chad extra time would compensate him for the discovery delay, but that was not an alternative for Lori.

Lori's attorneys suggested instead that the judge dismiss the death penalty to compensate for the prosecution's lack of attention to their discovery obligations. After reviewing the Idaho law, Judge Boyce believed he had the authority to dismiss the death penalty, but there was no precedent in Idaho case law. He drew from precedent in other states as well as federal cases and ordered the death penalty dismissed as it applied to Lori. Lori's case went forward as scheduled, with life in prison without the possibility of parole as the maximum possible sentence. Chad Daybell's trial was set a year into the future, in April 2024, and death remained the maximum sentence for him.

Once Jim Archibald and John Thomas took over Lori's case, they filed many more of the typical death penalty motions. Before the judge threw out the death penalty, they filed motions asking the judge to declare it unconstitutional. Throughout America, attorneys who do death penalty work routinely file these sorts of motions, not because they expect the trial judge to grant them but because they want to preserve the arguments for the appellate courts. New law in death penalty cases is made by lawyers filing motions and appealing decisions. Sometimes, the cumulative effect of all those motions in many cases begins to move the needle on a particular issue. In preparation for the death penalty, the defense also began a mitigation investigation.

The death penalty in America has a checkered past. In June 1972, the US Supreme Court ruled that the death penalty, as it applied to three cases it reviewed, was unconstitutional. The court said capital punishment was legal in America, but only under certain circumstances. The states then rewrote their statutes to conform to the Supreme Court ruling. In doing so, they created a bifurcated system where death penalty cases occur in two phases. In the first phase, a jury determines whether the charged person is guilty or innocent. Then, if the prosecution has asked for the death penalty and the defendant is found guilty, the same jury hears the sentencing portion of the trial. During the sentencing portion, the jury is presented with information that could convince them to recommend a sentence of life in prison without parole instead of death. The penalty phase requires at least as much preparation, if not more. Defense teams usually hire a mitigation specialist who investigates the defendant and their background. The American Bar Association recommends going back three generations into the defendant's history, examining medical, work, education, mental health, and military records. They investigate the defendant's criminal background, delving into the facts surrounding any past convictions and much more. They interview witnesses and pore over documents. The goal is to find information that could either explain or excuse the defendant's behavior in hopes the jury will be convinced to spare their client's life.

There are standard ways to approach every criminal case. One of the first avenues of defense is to attack the underlying procedural process that initiates the case. That means scrutinizing the grand jury or preliminary hearing process and examining the charging document for defects. Most states' criminal rules of procedure require that if that defense is going to challenge those processes, it must be done before trial. While grand juries are conducted in secret, they are recorded, and transcripts are made available to the defense. The defense scrutinizes the makeup of the grand jury and reviews whether the process is fair and impartial. They also examine the indictment to ensure the written charges match the grand jury's findings and the alleged crimes match the statutes listed in the indictment. Motions for discovery, motions to suppress evidence, sever charges or defendants, and motions to dismiss for double jeopardy must also be filed pretrial.[1] Chad Daybell's attorney, John Prior, requested the grand jury transcripts and filed motions to dismiss the indictment. The court records of those documents were sealed because they involved the secret grand jury process. The judge denied Prior's motions.

The grand jury motions were not the only documents the judge sealed. Judge Stephen Boyce began sealing court documents and holding closed hearings in the case almost immediately. The practice continued throughout the trial, limiting information available to the public. Some information contained in court records should be sealed. The Idaho rules require that pleadings, motions, affidavits, responses, memoranda, briefs, and other documents, along with minutes, orders, opinions, findings of fact, conclusions of law, judgments, and notices, be available to the public with some exceptions. Those exceptions are for personal data, such as birthdates, social security numbers, and addresses, and medical and mental health records, including evaluations.[2]

The hearings that had to do with whether Lori Vallow was competent and the reports and evaluations on her mental health were properly sealed, as were the hearings and pleadings that had to do with the grand jury. Other sealing of documents and hearings were more suspect. Facebook interest groups about the case formed early, and some eagle-eyed amateur sleuths discovered a few troubling posts. Folks in Rexburg were active on Facebook, some in interest groups for city and county employees. In one of those groups comprised of people involved in the court system, including law enforcement officers, prosecutors, and judges, members posted photographs and opinions about the case. At least one person found the posts concerning and sent screenshots to defense lawyers and prosecutors. What followed was a storm of motions seeking to disqualify the prosecutors. At least, that's what can be surmised from the limited information available in the index to the court's records. More isn't known because all of the motions and the hearings about the motions were sealed by the judge. If the documents were sealed to protect the reputations of the attorneys and judge, it would be an inappropriate use of the court's power. The controversy set off a feud between this author and Judge Boyce, culminating with the judge publicly ejecting the author from the courtroom in retaliation during Lori Vallow's trial. The author was permitted to view the trial from the overflow remote viewing area and was permitted back in the courtroom for Chad's trial. In a questionable ruling at the conclusion of Chad's trial, the judge ordered all of the previously sealed documents sealed indefinitely leaving the public to question exactly what the court is hiding.

14

ALL RISE—
LORI VALLOW'S TRIAL

For twenty-seven days in 2023, the case of the State of Idaho vs. Lori Norene Vallow took center stage, captivating American audiences and drawing attention worldwide. The internet buzzed with information and speculation about the cases for nearly four years before the first Vallow-Daybell cases finally came to trial. Thousands had joined Facebook groups and hung on the words of true crime podcasters and YouTube creators. People traveled from as far away as Australia and England to attend the trial, and it took nearly a week and hundreds of interviews to select a jury of people who had not formed an opinion about Lori's guilt or innocence.

The Ada County Courthouse is a large, modern brick edifice in downtown Boise, Idaho. It's a far cry from the small rural courthouse in Fremont County. Built in 1909, the Fremont County courthouse is located in St. Anthony, Idaho, the seat of Fremont County, population 13,592. The reason for moving the trial 319 miles to the west was straightforward. The task of seating an impartial jury from a tiny community made up almost entirely of members of The Church of Jesus Christ of Latter-day Saints would be daunting in a case with such heavy religious overtones.

However, the logistics of moving the trial were anything but straightfor-ward, and prosecutors fought to keep the trial in Fremont County because of the staggering cost. Lodging and transportation had to be found and paid for, for the judge and his staff, the five lawyers of the prosecution team and their staff, and the two defense attorneys and their staff. The courthouse in Boise would have to rearrange its dockets and security protocols to free up the largest courtroom to accommodate the size of the crowds seeking to view the trial. Limiting public access to the trial by closing it to cameras put further pressure on the courthouse. The county commissioner's meeting space was used as an overflow viewing area. Trial Court Administrator Sandra Barrios and her masterful staff worked for months to ensure the trial ran smoothly. Fremont County had to provide security personnel and pay for Lori Vallow's space in the Ada County jail. By the time Lori's trial began, taxpayers of tiny Fremont County had already spent more than $3 million, or $273 per county resident, on the case. The last-minute decision to sever the cases meant doing it all again for Chad's trial. Lindsey Blake and Rob Wood, the elected prosecuting attorneys, were caught between two competing interests: on the one hand, they were expected to pursue justice for Tylee, JJ, and Tammy, while on the other, to be good stewards of their constituents' hard-earned tax dol-lars. There were times you could see them visibly cringe as the expenses mounted.

Many trial watchers skipped jury selection, which was done primarily in private interviews. On the first day of testimony, spectators made their way through metal detectors and checked in with court staff. They were checked off a reservation list and handed a colored paper ticket like the ones you get in a school raffle. Each day, the color of the ticket changed. There was a certain amount of jockeying and vying for seats with good views of the jury or the defendant. The first rows in the center were reserved for law enforcement and the families of the victims. The defense staff and their investigator sat closest to the defense table in the first row. The prosecution's victims' advocate sat with the family, holding hands, handing out tissues, and assisting with their movement through the courthouse.

The clerk gaveled court into session, Judge Boyce took the bench, and the jury was brought in. Those in the gallery waited for Lori to be ushered into the courtroom. When defendants are in custody and attend their trial, they wear street clothes. This is so the jury won't be prejudiced by seeing them in jail garb and assume they are guilty. Their families can provide the clothing, but more often, it's the responsibility of the defense team to ensure their client has proper court attire. Some public defenders maintain a clothing closet for clients. Others may use a small state stipend to shop for clothing at thrift stores or Walmart. The clothing must be modest and accommodate the restraints sometimes used when prisoners appear in court. The restraints should not be visible to the jury, so they are often covered by clothing. Some devices fit on the prisoner's leg to prevent them from running and are worn under slacks or a skirt. The jail staff generally decides what sort of device will be used.

On the first day, Lori was ushered into the courtroom wearing black slacks, a white shirt, and a black cardigan sweater. She was in ankle shackles. She entered the courtroom and was seated behind her counsel table before the jury came in so they did not see her shamble into court in chains. Her ankle shackles were locked to a ring in the floor. As the trial went on, it appeared the level of shackling was relaxed, and she wasn't locked to the floor. Those close to the defense table could hear the chains at Lori's feet rattle when she moved. The courtroom was arranged with the defense table across the courtroom facing the jury, which put the defense table at a ninety-degree angle from the prosecutor and the judge.

As the trial continued, Lori appeared in white leggings with black zebra stripes and green-and-brown camouflage leggings. The unfashionable choices appeared to have been culled from a discount bin. She was permitted some basic makeup and grooming items. She wore her long, wavy hair down during most of the trial and, at times, used it to shield her face. Without access to hair color, her hair had darkened to an ash blond.

Lori Vallow Daybell sat motionless as Fremont County Prosecutor Lindsey Blake stepped to the podium to give the opening statement. Insiders reported that while Lori was at the defense table, she rated everyone in the courtroom as either dark or light. Lindsey Blake, undoubtedly dark on Lori's scale, wore a checked blazer over a navy dress and knee-high brown boots. Lori's motionlessness looked a lot like her stillness in the Chandler Police Department interview room on the morning of Charles Vallow's murder. Her composure and her seeming lack of concern would not last, however. Prosecutor Blake told the jury the case was about money, power, and sex. She said Lori Vallow Daybell "used money, power, and sex, or the promise of those things, to get what she wanted. What she wanted was money, power, and sex." The case was not easy; there had been no eyewitnesses, and no one, except the defendants, knew for sure where the murders had occurred or whose hands had killed Tylee Ryan, JJ Vallow, and Tammy Daybell.

The jury was educated about circumstantial evidence. They were told circumstantial evidence is as good as direct evidence. While true, a circumstantial case requires more work for both the lawyers and the jurors. A circumstantial case is like a chain, where each piece of evidence is a link. To convict, the jury must be able to connect those links to form a logical path from the crime to the perpetrator. During her opening statement, Blake illustrated her remarks with several photographs, including images of JJ Vallow's body still wrapped in black plastic and duct tape, Tylee Ryan's lower jaw, and Tammy Daybell's exhumed body, dressed in her LDS temple clothing. It was only a preview of the disturbing images the jury would see. Kay and Larry Woodcock sat, heads touching, quietly crying. For them, it was the start of a long, painful month. As Prosecutor Blake began talking about Lori's belief that she was a translated being, Lori began to rock from side to side.

Before the trial even started, there had been controversy. There was disagreement over who was considered family to the victims. Most states have adopted some form of a victim's bill of rights. Many have incorporated the rights into their state constitutions. Idaho's definition of who is a victim is restrictive and somewhat vague. The law has not kept up in an era where the social definition of family constantly changes. Following his adoption, Kay Woodcock became JJ's legal aunt. Biologically, she remained his paternal grandmother. Kay's husband, Larry, JJ's step-grandfather, legally became his step-uncle after the adoption. The law in Idaho extends "victim" status only to the "immediate families" of homicide victims and defines immediate family as "parent, mother-in-law, father-in-law, husband, wife, sister, brother, brother-in-law, sister-in-law, son-in-law, daughter-in-law or son or daughter."[1] Aunts, uncles, and grandparents don't make the cut. The designation, or lack of it, impacted many family members. As in all criminal trials, witnesses were excluded from the courtroom until after they testified. Victims were exempt from that exclusion, meaning they could remain in the courtroom and hear the other witnesses' testimony. The judge found that although Kay Woodcock did not qualify as an immediate family member, another section of the statute allowed him to appoint a representative to exercise the rights of a deceased family member. The judge appointed Kay as the representative in place of JJ's father and her deceased brother, Charles Vallow. That meant Kay could remain in the courtroom during the testimony, but her husband, Larry Woodcock, could not. The prosecution decided not to call Larry Woodcock as a witness so that he could remain in the courtroom with his wife. The issue would become significant once again at Lori's sentencing.

Lori's attorney Jim Archibald gave the opening statement on her behalf. Archibald was a tall, broad-shouldered man. His hair was shot with gray with a sweep of white at each temple. His complexion was ruddy, his eyes heavy-lidded, and he wore a short goatee. Archibald had been an attorney for more than thirty years. He was a public defender, qualified to represent people in death penalty cases, and had represented defendants accused of murder twenty-seven times. In January 2003, Archibald had been appointed to the bench as a magistrate. He served for nearly eighteen months but resigned just two weeks before the end of his probationary period after allegations surfaced that he had been drunk in public and groped two women at a juvenile drug court conference in Florida. It was a shocking accusation for an active member of the LDS Church. One of the women, an Idaho attorney, complained to the Idaho Judicial Council, but Archibald resigned his position before the council could take any action.

He acknowledged the allegations in a letter to the editor, published in the Idaho Falls *Post Register*, but claimed his resignation was because of depression and the pressures of the bench.

Unlike Prosecutor Blake's opening, which had been organized and pointed, Archibald's opening statement was unfocused and rambling. He explained that his services for Lori were paid for by taxpayers and thanked the jury for paying their taxes. He explained that his job was to protect a defendant's rights and ensure the prosecution did its job properly. He told the jury that being a defense attorney wasn't always a popular job and invited them to be respectful of him as he would be of them. In an odd admission, he then told them that eight years before, his law office had been bombed. Archibald explained that Lori believed in life after death and believed she would see her loved ones, including her deceased children, again. He went into the juror's responsibilities and the need to find her not guilty if there was reasonable doubt. His opening statement ended with a whimper rather than a bang.

Kay Vallow Woodcock was the prosecution's first witness. She explained her relationship to Charles and discussed their decision to allow Lori and Charles to adopt their grandson, JJ. She said she and her husband, Larry, frequently visited Lori and Charles in Arizona and maintained a close relationship with JJ. She said that Lori initially was a great mother to JJ, and she and Larry enjoyed visiting with Lori and Charles. She told the jury that in early 2019, Lori and Charles separated, and no one knew where Lori was for nearly two months before she unexpectedly showed up in Houston and moved back in with Charles. During Lori's absence, Kay went to Houston frequently to care for JJ while Charles traveled for work. She had also helped Charles with some administrative work for his business. Kay saw JJ in person for the last time on May 17, 2019, when he and Charles visited her home in Lake Charles, Louisiana. She remembered vividly because they had an early birthday party for JJ at a local pizza parlor while he was there. She testified that her last conversation with JJ was a thirty-five-second FaceTime call on August 10, 2019. Kay attempted to arrange for JJ to visit and attend his father's memorial service in Louisiana, but Lori refused to let him go. Shortly after that, Lori moved to Rexburg. JJ would be seen for the last time forty-three days later, wearing his red pajamas in Lori Vallow's Rexburg apartment.

While Kay was helping Charles with his business, he gave her access to his online accounts. On November 4, 2019, she found a delivery notice from Amazon in Charles's email. When Kay looked through Charles's Amazon browsing history, she discovered plenty of account activity after Charles's death. As early as August 2019, Lori searched for malachite wedding bands, beach wedding dresses, and men's white linen pants and shirts. Lori ordered things using Charles's Amazon account, and the deliveries were made to a townhouse in Rexburg, Idaho. The timing was suspect; Kay learned that Tammy Daybell had died on October 19, 2023. A day after Kay found the Amazon email, Lori married Chad on the beach in Hawaii.

The prosecution called Brandon Boudreaux as the next witness. He testified about his close relationship with the family, Lori's changing beliefs, and how, on the day the children's bodies were found, he drove from his home in Arizona to Rexburg, where he identified JJ's body by viewing images at the coroner's office.

During the first week of the trial, lead prosecutor Lindsey Blake's father, Jim Blake, died. Although Blake's father had had dementia, his death was unexpected. Born and raised in Fremont County, Blake was elected in 2020 after the Vallow and Daybell cases were already underway. The judge ordered Lori's trial recessed early on Friday, and no court was held on Monday to permit those who wished, to attend services for Jim Blake. Lindsey Blake courageously returned to court on Tuesday to resume the direction of Lori Vallow's trial.

As he had been at Chad's preliminary hearing two years before, Rexburg Police Det. Ray Hermosillo was an essential witness for the prosecution at Lori's trial. As the lead detective, he gave the jury an overview of the case. Although Hermosillo was professional and understated, the jury could hear the emotion in his voice as he described his experience. There was no doubt that the murders of Tammy, Tylee, and JJ had left a permanent scar on the officer. Hermosillo was on the stand for the better part of two days as the prosecution methodically introduced exhibit after exhibit. He described the room-by-room photographs of Lori's apartment, including the room where Alex Cox had been staying. Police found mail addressed to Alex in the room along with two Tyvek protective suits like the ones that painters wear. In the garage, they found ammunition of several calibers, a camouflage ghillie suit, several rifles, a pistol, silencers, military-style knives, documents, printed emails from Chad Daybell, a Walmart bag full of rope and duct tape, and an eerie rubber Halloween mask. The pace and emotional pitch of the first morning was relentless, and the judge called a well-earned early lunch.

When the court reconvened, the prosecution asked Det. Hermosillo to turn his attention to the day the children were found. Lori appeared agitated, and her attorneys immediately asked for a sidebar. Lori's counsel knew both disturbing information and graphic photographs were coming. After a short conversation with all the attorneys beside the bench, the sound of which was masked by a white noise machine, the judge called for a meeting of the attorneys in his chambers. Twenty minutes later, when the court reconvened, the defense made a motion. Jim Archibald asked the judge to excuse Lori Vallow from the courtroom. He said Lori didn't want to be exposed to the graphic testimony and photographs that would be presented in that portion of the trial. Archibald reminded the court of Lori's mental illness and her fragile emotional state. The judge denied the request. If the jury had to view the photographs and hear the gruesome testimony, so should Lori. The judge ordered that none of the pictures be shown splashed across the courtroom's large viewing screen. Instead, the most graphic images would only be projected on computer screens for the jury and counsel and not depicted for the public. Lori sat back, arms crossed, wearing an angry expression, as she slumped between her lawyers, letting her hair fall in her face to hide from scrutiny. She stared into space, avoiding the monitor on the table in front of her. Lori was on a cocktail of psychotropic drugs to help with her mental state, and later in the afternoon, she appeared to nod off. Since this was the only time it happened during the trial, it led to speculation that she had been given something to help calm her earlier agitation.

The jury watched Lori intently as the graphic photographs scrolled across the monitors in front of them. Some jurors wiped away tears, others scowled. Spectators in the gallery began intently watching juror number eight, Saul Hernandez. His seat was in the front row of the jury box, closest to the gallery, and his expressions said a great deal about what the jury was feeling: shock as they heard about the death of Charles Vallow, disgust when they heard about the way the children's bodies were found. He often leaned forward, listening intently as experts presented the DNA and GPS data. Jurors may speak to the media after the trial, but do not have to. Juror number eight would break his silence after the trial and discuss his impressions and his experience in media interviews. Much of what he said confirmed the observations of the jury watchers.

The rules of evidence dictate what information the jury hears. The judge decides how those rules should be applied, using the statutes and the case law to interpret them. In Lori's case, evidence rule 404 was often at issue. The rule states, "Evidence of a crime, wrong, or other act is not admissible to prove a person's character in order to show that on a particular occasion the person acted in accordance with their character."[2] The rule goes on to say that "This evidence may be admissible for another purpose, such as proving motive, opportunity, intent, preparation, plan, knowledge, identity, absence of mistake, or lack of accident."[3] In Lori's case, the prosecution wanted the jury to hear how Charles Vallow had died and how Brandon Boudreaux's death had been attempted. The judge ruled that the jury could hear the information because it was used to show motive, preparation, and course of conduct. The prosecution argued that the conspiracy to commit the murders of Tammy, Tylee, and JJ was simply a continuation of the plan that began in Arizona with the murder of Charles Vallow. The judge issued a limiting instruction that outlined the parameters of what could be presented to the jury. This issue would later become one of the central complaints in Lori's appeal when the defense claimed the prosecution exceeded the judge's order. There is another legal concept that applies to character evidence. If one side "opens the door" on a particular subject, the other can walk through it. For example, if the defense offers a witness who claims the defendant is not a violent person, the prosecution can then bring in a witness to testify about an incident where the defendant violently attacked a domestic partner, even though the prior incident is unrelated to the crimes being tried and would otherwise be excluded by rule 404. While both sides were cautious in their questioning, there were a few instances where one side opened the door.

The faces of the jury reflected dismay as they heard the details of Charles's murder. The jury was not told that Lori had already been charged with conspiracy to commit murder in Charles's death because of Idaho Rule of Evidence 403: "The court may exclude relevant evidence if its probative value is substantially outweighed by a danger of one or more of the following: unfair prejudice, confusing the issues, misleading the jury, undue delay, wasting time, or needlessly presenting cumulative evidence." The rule permits a judge to keep out relevant evidence if the prejudice outweighs the probative value. In this case, the judge ruled that the jury could be unfairly prejudiced if they knew the state of Arizona thought Lori was responsible for planning Charles's death.

Each piece of evidence that is introduced must be accompanied by a foundation for its reliability. That foundation consists of the who, what, where, when, and how of the evidence. What the evidence is, who collected it, where they got it, how it was collected, who had it in their possession, how it was analyzed, and how the chain of custody was preserved to guard against tampering. The prosecution spent painstaking time laying the foundation for each bit of evidence. The officer who was in charge of preserving jail calls testified about how calls are intercepted, recorded, and stored before the prosecution introduced the call between Lori and Chad that occurred on the morning Tylee's and JJ's bodies were found. Then the state played the recorded call. They similarly laid the foundation for hundreds of pieces of information, including cell phone extractions, GPS data, satellite photos, DNA testing, and more. This is an often technical process that requires a mind-numbing level of detail. Despite this, the jury took notes and appeared engaged and attentive.

One of the most anticipated witnesses was Lori's close friend Melanie Gibb. She testified about how Lori met Chad at the Preparing a People conference on October 26, 2018. This was the jury's introduction to multiple mortal probations and Chad's belief that he and Lori had been married in other lives. The prosecution used Melanie Gibb to introduce the jury to Chad and Lori's belief system. The state had to approach the information methodically, building one idea on another until the jury formed a complete picture. Surprisingly, neither side offered much beyond cursory foundational information about the underlying beliefs of The Church of Jesus Christ of Latter-day Saints or how those beliefs may have led to Chad and Lori's disappearance down the historical rabbit hole of "restoring" the church. A deep dive into LDS theology would likely have drawn an objection on relevance grounds. Still, some discussion of Lori's and Chad's upbringing in the church might have helped the jury better understand how Chad and Lori arrived at their aberrant beliefs. As mentioned, both Fremont and Madison counties are populated almost exclusively by church members. Thus, most of the participants in the trial were church members. Prosecutor Rob Wood was the bishop of his ward when the case began. Prosecutor Lindsey Blake, Judge Stephen Boyce, and defense attorneys John Thomas and Jim Archibald were also church members. Special Prosecutor Rachel Smith apologized during Lori's trial for not being as conversant in LDS doctrine because she was the only person on the team who was not a member of the LDS Church. Religion was considered during jury selection; each juror was questioned privately about their religious beliefs and attitude toward The Church of Jesus Christ of Latter-day Saints. The public was not privy to those discussions, so it is unclear how many, if any, of the sitting jurors were members of the LDS Church. The prosecution and defense were both concerned with whether a juror's church membership might cause them to be biased about the case.

Melanie Gibb testified that Lori told her about Chad's light and dark rubric and how people signed light contracts with Jesus or dark contracts with Satan while they were in heaven in premortality. Lori taught Melanie and several other friends that dark spirits could possess bodies. That teaching began after Chad told Lori that a dark spirit had possessed the body of her husband, Charles. Lori told Melanie that she had a dream that Charles died in an auto accident and believed it would occur. When the accident didn't happen, Lori said it was because Satan interfered. Melanie understood that because Charles was dark, he would have to die. She explained that Lori believed the prayer circle they called a casting could force a dark spirit from a body. During those castings, they used words like "cutting spiritual cords" and other terms that Gibb said "sounded like energy work." After each session, Lori would call Chad and ask him if their spiritual work had been effective. When Charles remained alive, Chad told them their casting had worked, but another spirit had moved into Charles's body; Ned Schneider became Garrett, who then became an entity made up of many dark spirits called Hiplos. Lori and Zulema spent hours in the LDS temple attempting to cast out Hiplos.

Melanie now realized that when she introduced Lori to Chad, it sparked a firestorm. Like when a massive wildfire begins making its own weather, the consequences of Lori and Chad's meeting were far-reaching and fatal. The stakes could not have been higher as Lori and Chad began meddling in everything, dictating divorces, marriages, and relocations, and soon, deciding life and death. They told their new followers that nothing was more important than their mission. They would allow no one to stand in their way and would align the world and their followers as they saw fit. Lori told Melanie that Chad had foreseen that Tammy would die soon. When Melanie asked Lori why she and Chad didn't get divorced from their spouses so they could be together, Lori told her Chad would lose his place with the lord and his exaltation. Both their spouses must die to preserve their standing as leaders of the 144,000. The day Chad called Melanie to tell her the police would be calling her and not to answer, Melanie wasn't surprised. She and her boyfriend, David Warwick, were the last people outside Lori's family to see JJ Vallow alive.

Melanie testified Lori had only been living in Rexburg for a few weeks when Melanie and David visited from Arizona. Late summer is when Idaho is at its best. The sky was impossibly blue, the lush green fields were ready for harvest, and cattle and sheep fattened by summer's bounty browsed in the pastures. The couple stayed with Lori in her townhouse. They saw JJ but not Tylee. David Warwick testified that he saw JJ playing in Lori's apartment on September 21, 2019, cutting windows and doors out of a large cardboard box. JJ, like many autistic people, found interactions with strangers difficult or confusing, and he resisted any attempt by David to talk to him about what he was doing. Melanie and Lori wanted to record an episode of their podcast with David while they were all together. Later that evening, as they set up to record in Lori's kitchen, Lori told them her brother, Alex Cox, had taken JJ to his apartment so they would not be disturbed. Warwick said Alex brought JJ back at about 10:30 P.M. He remembered it vividly because JJ appeared to be sweetly sleeping on Alex's shoulder. Alex took JJ upstairs to Lori's room and left shortly after. Melanie said she didn't think JJ liked Chad. While they were there, there had been an incident where JJ was acting up, and Chad tried to take him upstairs. A few minutes later, Chad came downstairs, rubbing a spot on his neck where he said JJ had scratched him.

Chad took David to see some property in Rexburg the next day. First, he took them to a vacant lot beside an LDS church. Reminiscent of the story where Joseph Smith Jr. claimed to see a church on vacant land, saying, "I see it, and it will be so," [4] Chad claimed he and Lori could see a glorious temple that was there "in spirit." David said he couldn't see anything, but Lori and Chad insisted the temple was there. Chad also took David to look at eighty acres for sale near Chad's house. David was a general contractor and said he might know an investor interested in building in Rexburg, but Chad had a different use in mind. He envisioned a white camp, a gathering place there for the faithful during the coming tribulation. Lori and Chad were intent on consolidating their followers in one place and wanted David and Melanie Gibb to move to Rexburg. Despite David telling Chad repeatedly that he didn't work on Sundays, Chad met David at the site with a realtor in tow. David said he would think about it and perhaps call the realtor during the business week, but nothing more came of it.

Chad thought he had found an ally in David. After all, Warwick had never been shy about sharing his visions and dreams of the end times. He admitted he had spoken on podcasts about his belief that there are "secret combinations" taking place in Washington, DC, England, and Saudi Arabia and that he has seen visions of China and Russia attacking the US military and defeating them in three days as the United States is "sacrificed for a one-world government." Warwick testified that the night he stayed at Lori Vallow's apartment, he had a terrible nightmare. Melanie Gibb, who was in the room with him, woke him up. She testified that David was shaking and upset. They believed the terrible and graphic nightmare was sent from Satan or one of his angels, and Melanie wanted Lori to call Chad to give David a blessing. She went to Lori's room and knocked on the door, but no one answered. When she tried the doorknob, the door was locked. This was the same night JJ Vallow was seen for the last time in his red pajamas, asleep on Alex Cox's shoulder. The next morning, Alex Cox and Chad Daybell buried JJ in Chad's backyard.

David Warwick clarified that while Melanie Gibb believed Lori and Chad's teachings, he did not, despite sharing a more general belief in prepping and government conspiracies. Melanie claimed to the police later that she was never entirely sure about Lori and Chad's teachings but went along with them; the evidence says otherwise. Melanie was one of Lori's biggest supporters. She often served as Lori's Greek chorus, offering background and vouching to others for Lori's claims. Warwick was skeptical that Chad Daybell had been given some sort of superior keys to the priesthood. As a faithful LDS member, he believed only the president, seer, and revelator of the church had the authority to direct the church, particularly in matters concerning the end times and the callout. While Warwick shared Chad's belief the end times were imminent, he believed God had created the hierarchy of their church to lead the faithful through the tribulation, and he couldn't see why God would depart from that plan to single out Chad Daybell as a leader. Echoing Denver Snuffer in *The Second Comforter*, Chad claimed the mainstream church itself was

in apostasy and that it was time for a second LDS restoration with the
formation of the Church of the Firstborn. Chad was nowhere near the first
to make this claim. Nearly every splinter group, from the FLDS to
the Lafferty and LeBaron brothers, have claimed they were restoring the
mainstream church from apostasy.

Zulema Pastenes was the next witness the prosecution called to flesh
out how Lori and Chad's beliefs had led to murder. She approached the
witness stand, wearing a modest gray skirt and jacket. She was accompanied by her lawyer, Garrett Smith, who sat in the gallery. This is the same
attorney whom Brandon Boudreaux sued for defamation. Smith and his
law partner represented several of Lori and Chad's family and followers,
including Zulema; Lori's sister, Summer Shiflet; and Lori's niece, Melani
Pawlowski. Zulema had been with Lori, Melanie Gibb, and two other
women when they drove to St. George, Utah, for the Preparing a People
conference, where Lori met Chad. Zulema quickly became part of Lori
and Chad's inner circle.

The prosecution had Zulema explain Chad's light and dark scales to
the jury, and she told them about Lori's and Chad's beliefs in past lives.
According to Chad, both Zulema and Melanie Gibb were Lori's daughters in their former lives. Chad told Zulema that during the time of the
Book of Mormon, she had been Lori's daughter and had been raped,
murdered, and dismembered by the Lamanites. The story echoed eerily
when the jury later heard from the medical examiner about the condition
of Tylee's body.

Zulema described a meeting with Lori, Nicole, Serena, Christina, and
Melanie Gibb at Zulema's home. Lori brought out a whiteboard and drew
a diagram to explain multiple probations and the worlds a person could be
born on. She presented each woman with a sticky note with their past lives
written on it and told them she needed their help to perform a casting to
rid Charles Vallow of his evil spirit. Over the months, there were many of
these casting meetings. Before each, Lori reinforced that each woman was
powerful and gifted by God. Each was assigned a different spiritual power
to call down against the demon. Zulema's was fire. After each had called

down their spiritual element, Lori finished by sealing the casting. Zulema said she believed Lori when she said she had special knowledge and power. Lori claimed to have been visited by Jesus and angels, and Zulema did not think someone who had been in the presence of Jesus would lie.

Zulema said Lori's brother Alex believed Lori and Chad wholeheartedly. When she asked him how he felt about shooting Charles, he shrugged, saying, "Zulema, he was a zombie." In light of all the later developments, Zulema sometimes wondered if Alex was responsible for his own death. On November 24, 2019, two weeks before Alex's death, Chad gave Alex a patriarchal blessing. Two days later, police would knock on Lori's door to do a welfare check on JJ. When they searched Alex's Ford F-150 pickup, police found a printed copy of the blessing in the glove box. Typically, a person receives a patriarchal blessing once in their lifetime. The blessings are given when a recognized patriarch, ordained to the office by the church, places his hands on the recipient's head and announces the blessing. The church describes it this way on its website:

> Every worthy, baptized member is entitled to and should receive a patriarchal blessing, which provides inspired direction from the Lord. Patriarchal blessings include a declaration of a person's lineage in the house of Israel and personal counsel from the Lord . . . While a patriarchal blessing contains inspired counsel and promises, it should not be expected to answer all of the recipient's questions or to detail all that will happen in his or her life. If the blessing does not mention an important event, such as a full-time mission or marriage, the person should not assume that he or she will not receive that opportunity. Similarly, the recipient of the blessing should not assume that everything mentioned in it will be fulfilled in this life. A patriarchal blessing is eternal, and its promises may extend into the eternities. If one is worthy, all promises will be fulfilled in the Lord's due time. Those promises and blessings that are not realized in this life will be fulfilled in the next.[5]

Chad, who was not a church patriarch, nonetheless blessed Alex and recorded the ceremony. Lori's voice could be heard in the background; all three were crying and sniffling. Chad began by telling Alex he was a descendant of Joseph through the tribe of Ephraim. "Holi" is the past name Chad gave Alex's new wife, Zulema Pastenes. Chad even quoted one of his books in Alex's blessing.

In Alex's blessing, Chad said,

> I want to begin by opening up the portals of time, going back to your previous creations on which you've lived. I see you on the third creation as a valiant warrior fighting for truth and righteousness, always seeking to do what is right. Then you were selected by the Savior himself to be part of the fourth creation. Great warriors were needed in that creation. Powerful goddesses needed to be protected, and you were selected to protect your sister. You helped her in numerous probations as a defender. You have a special bond with her, even from the premortal world. You connected there, and as she grew in power, you were right there beside her, always with a humble heart. You both were so humble. After you had been exalted in the fourth creation, you could have gone on to exaltation with Holi as a resurrected being. However, you accepted the Savior's invitation to come to this mortal realm one more time in the fifth creation to condescend as a god to help us. You have already assisted in ways that can never be repaid, but you will continue to do so as you move forward in this life. You were born into a family that needed you desperately, with a set of parents who spoke the Gospel with their mouths but did not live it. Once again, you were reunited with your sister, who needed you . . . You will travel all over the world through portals, and you will begin to gather the souls that come unto Christ. I see you living in the New Jerusalem, but more importantly, I see you as a messenger of the Lord outside New Jerusalem where many people will gather who aren't

CHILDREN OF DARKNESS AND LIGHT

ready to enter into those heavenly terrestrial gates . . . With your companion, you will communicate with Mother Earth herself. You will know where to be before natural disasters happen so that you can be on location to protect key church leaders and to preserve those who should survive. I see you gathering little children in your arms, saving them from floodwaters. I see a collage of moments that await you in this life, rescuing the pure and innocent . . . After many years of service, as the second coming approaches, you will know when it is time to move to the other side of the veil. One day your spirit will leave your body that has served you well, and you will be greeted by the Savior Himself. After a day or two, you will be raised up and resurrected, so when the Savior does return, you will be right at the front of that amazing team of angels who sweep the Earth much like described in the book *The Renewed Earth*.

Once again, Chad had gone rogue and claimed authority he did not possess, just as he had done when he performed his own temple sealing to Lori.

On December 7, 2019, five days before his death, Alex drove to Mexico and bought medication. Authorities were never able to determine precisely what Alex bought. Also, about this time, Alex told Zulema that if anything happened to him, he had left a bag in the closet with some money. She told him not to think about it and that nothing would happen to him. She later found a bag of cash in a black gym bag that she estimates held between $5,000 and $7,000.

Alex texted Chad on December 10, 2019, asking for a blessing because he was having a "bad attack" and couldn't breathe. Members of the group often attributed physical ailments to being spiritually attacked by evil spirits and frequently asked Chad for blessings to ward them off. On December 11, 2019, Chad asked Alex how he was. Alex replied that he was winded every time he stood up and had a resting pulse of 100. Alex told Chad, "I feel like the poison from the spear in the heart has done some residual damage." Alex spoke of spiritual spears to explain his physical pain. Lori and Chad called Alex and Zulema that day to tell them the authorities were exhuming Tammy Daybell's body. Zulema was surprised at how calm Lori and Chad were about it, and it made her suspicious. Zulema knew that Lori and Chad would never admit they were involved, but she thought Alex might, so after their call, she confronted him. Alex denied involvement with Tammy's death but said he thought Lori and Chad might make him "their fall guy." Zulema was still concerned, but Alex settled back on the bed, then said, "Zulema, either I am a man of God, or I am not." He declined to elaborate further.

The following afternoon, Zulema received a frantic call from her adult son: Alex was very sick on their bathroom floor. Zulema's son called 911. On the 911 call, he told the operator that Alex was his mother's boyfriend; he didn't know Alex's last name or age. Zulema's children still did not know their mother had married Alex. Zulema dashed home and got there just behind the paramedics. Alex was unresponsive, and they rushed him to the hospital. Zulema and Alex had been married just two weeks when she paced the hospital waiting area, waiting for word. Finally, hospital staff came to Zulema and explained that Alex could not recover. Zulema spent a few minutes with him, then turned off his life support machines. Dazed, she left the hospital, supported by her daughter and son-in-law. Alex's brother, Adam, learned about his brother's death from Brandon Boudreaux. It would be another week before Alex's parents would hear of his death. When Alex died on December 12, 2019, less than six months after Charles's murder, Chad and Lori had been married for nearly a month and had already fled to Hawaii.

Zulema testified that Lori always said the numbers seven and eleven were lucky for her. When Charles died on July 11, 2019 (7/11/19), Lori said it confirmed that Charles's death was orchestrated by God, who had delivered Charles to her and Alex. Lori told Zulema the police had investigated and ruled Charles's death self-defense, clearing Alex, which was untrue. Lori said one of her missions was to clear the earth of evil spirits to open the way for Jesus Christ to return. Lori saw Charles's death as a step closer to ushering in that day. Lori also told Zulema that Tylee was possessed by a demon named Hillary. When Zulema visited Lori shortly after she moved to Rexburg, she asked Lori about Tylee. Lori said, "She had to be free." When Zulema pressed her, asking where Tylee was, Lori just put her palm in Zulema's face and said, "Don't ask."

Zulema explained that Chad and Lori's ideas about dark spirits developed in more detail as time passed. Lori told Zulema that when a person dies, there is a two-minute window before a new demon could inhabit the body. To prevent a new demon from entering the body, it must be destroyed by burning, binding, or taking the body apart. The jury, who had already heard in detail about the condition of Tylee's body, showed a variety of emotions, from tears to shock. Lori believed Tylee was her sister, Stacey, in a new probation. She also told Zulema she knew JJ would have a short life, but it was okay because he would be reborn as her son Colby's child.

Lori remained stoic while sitting at the counsel table, listening to her former friend testify against her. Like Melanie Gibb before her, Zulema avoided making eye contact with Lori. During cross-examination, when one of Lori's attorneys asked Zulema if she still believed Lori could cast out demons, Lori leaned forward in anticipation of the answer. When Zulema said, "No," Lori folded her arms across her chest and leaned back in her chair wearing an angry, tight half smile.

Many trial watchers hoped the jury would hear from Lori's niece, Melani Pawlowski. Melani had been closest to Lori and surely knew more than she had publicly revealed. When she appeared at trial, however, there was a problem. Before the trial began, Judge Boyce issued an exclusion order directing anyone subpoenaed to testify not to listen to or watch any news coverage, read any online information, or listen to any of the recordings of earlier trial days. The order was served to each witness along with their trial subpoena. Melani disregarded the judge's order and listened to the earlier testimony of her ex-husband, Brandon Boudreaux. She said it was because she wanted to know if there was anything in his testimony that could be useful in their ongoing child custody battle. Ultimately, the prosecution decided not to call her, and she returned home without testifying. Her new husband, Ian Pawlowski, did testify. He added to the conversation about

Lori's odd beliefs and testified that his suspicions eventually led him to contact law enforcement, suspecting Chad and Lori had something to do with Tylee and JJ's disappearance.

The testimony of Audrey Barattiero was some of the most explosive. Between the release of documents and Chad's earlier preliminary hearing, the public knew what to expect from much of the testimony. Not so, however, with Barattiero's story. The prosecutor walked the jury back through the days just before Charles Vallow was murdered and the months following, when Chad used Audrey to distract Lori.

According to Audrey, when Lori saw Chad for the second time in November 2018 at the PAP event in Mesa, Arizona, she also met Audrey Barattiero. About three months later, Chad called Audrey and asked her to befriend Lori. Chad said Lori needed a friend because he couldn't be with her or talk to her all the time. Audrey thought Chad was trying to keep Lori involved with his friends and PAP events to distract her while he tried to figure out what to do about Tammy.

As Audrey and Lori got to know one another, they frequently discussed spiritual things. Audrey saw Lori again in the early summer of 2019 at a conference near Salt Lake City, Utah. Just before the conference, as they spoke on the phone, Lori told Audrey about the new beliefs she was learning, that people could be possessed and that when an evil spirit takes over a body, the person becomes a zombie. This was the first Audrey had heard of Lori and Chad's theories about demonic possession and zombies. During that conference, Audrey spent time with Lori and her female friends. Near the end, Audrey and several other women visited Lori at her hotel. Lori said she wanted to "work on" getting the evil spirit out of her husband, Charles. The women held hands, and each took a turn calling down spiritual weapons such as knives and fire to drive the evil spirit out of Charles. Audrey, who had thought when the women joined hands they were beginning a prayer, was uncomfortable and didn't say anything. She didn't end their friendship, though; she continued to talk with Lori and Chad on the telephone.

Audrey met Tylee when she visited Lori in Arizona, so when Lori moved to Rexburg, Audrey often asked about Tylee and how she was adjusting to college. Lori's answers were vague until the fall of 2019 when Lori told her, "Tylee doesn't talk to me much these days." On an earlier visit to Rexburg, Audrey met Chad, Tammy, and their son, Garth, for dinner. She liked Tammy and Garth and said she enjoyed meeting them.

As Audrey got to know Chad better, he told her about his near-death experiences, his visions of the future, and his ability to ascertain who people had been during their earlier mortal probations. When Chad told people about their past lives, they were never beggars or shoemakers; they were always people of importance. Chad told Audrey that he had been Methuselah in a previous life and that in a later life, he had become James the Just, the brother of Jesus Christ. Audrey believed Chad when he told her she was special; then he told her she had been married to Jesus Christ. The idea that Jesus was married isn't novel; scholars of many faiths speculate Jesus had a wife. In fact, within LDS doctrine, where people must be married to ascend to the celestial kingdom, they believe both God and Jesus, who are two separate entities, have wives in the celestial kingdom. Chad told Audrey about his vision of Tammy's imminent death and assured her he had told Tammy about it.

Audrey moved to Missouri late in the summer of 2019, and Lori and her niece, Melani Boudreaux Pawlowski, visited her that October. Audrey took them to the Mormon historical sites around Missouri, including Adam-ondi-Ahman, where Mormons believe "Adam blessed his posterity after leaving the Garden of Eden."[6] When the three women returned to the hotel late in the evening, Melani and Lori suggested Audrey stay with them at the hotel rather than drive home. For months, Lori had told Audrey that Charles, Tylee, JJ, and Tammy were all possessed by dark spirits. Lori now said two of Melani's young children were also possessed. Lori said she and Melani needed Audrey's help to "work on Tammy" that night. Audrey took that to mean that they wanted to form a circle and cast the demon out of Tammy. Audrey resisted at first, but Lori pressed her. She called on their friendship and told her that Tammy's spirit was trapped and couldn't be freed as long as the evil spirit possessed her body. Audrey agreed to say a prayer, asking God to help Tammy with whatever she needed.

A few weeks later, Audrey joined Lori and Melani on a trip to Hawaii. Lori convinced her to come, telling her Melani was having a hard time since filing for divorce from her husband, Brandon, and could use a friend. Audrey was shocked when she got to Hawaii, and Lori told her Tammy Daybell had died in her sleep earlier in the week. At the time, Audrey took it as confirmation that Chad's visions were genuine. In Hawaii, Lori's moods swung from bubbly to agitated and snippy. After spending long periods on the phone with Chad, she abruptly announced she was going home to Rexburg. Melani and Audrey stayed in Hawaii for two more days, then flew to Rexburg themselves. Audrey said she went to Rexburg to support Melani and deliver her condolences to Chad and Garth in person. While Audrey was in Rexburg, she stayed at Lori's townhouse. She said Chad would come in late in the evening and stay the night with Lori. More and more, Audrey felt something wasn't right. She decided to leave immediately and end her friendship with Lori. The evening before she left Rexburg, she was going upstairs to pack when she had a terrifying conversation with Lori that reaffirmed her decision to cut ties.

Audrey sobbed on the witness stand at Lori's murder trial as she related the conversation:

> I asked her a question. 'Is there anything weird going on that I don't know about?' And she said, 'No, what do you mean?' And I said, 'I don't know . . . anything.' And she said no. So I took her at her word because I'm a trusting person. And as soon as I turned to start to go up the stairs, she started laughing the kind of laugh as if you're laughing at someone or think something is hilarious. And she said to me, 'You're so naive. I do trust you; you're like a little child. You'll believe anything anyone will tell you.' Then she said, 'You think the world is all unicorns and rainbows if you go around helping people, serving them. Well, I've got news for you, not everyone's a good person and not everyone can afford to be so nice and kind,' and then . . . she threatened to kill me . . . She said she would cut me up,

something about that she wasn't in the mental place to do that but that she would get herself in that place to be able to do it, that she didn't want to have to because it would be so messy because there would be so much blood, and then bleach, and something about trash bags, and that she would bury me where no one would ever find me.

The jury also heard evidence that some of Tammy Daybell's family members thought she had grown suspicious of what Chad was doing while he was away from home at his many conference appearances. Her suspicions were confirmed when Charles Vallow contacted her in late June 2019. It began just days before his death, after Charles discovered an email sent to Chad Daybell on June 29, 2019. The letter read:

Hello Chad,

I hope you are doing well. This is Charles Vallow from Arizona. We really enjoyed having you stay with us back in November when you came to the Preparing A People Conference. I appreciated you taking time to talk to me about the book I've been working on. Well, more than six months later I still haven't made much progress on it, but I feel an urgency to get it done. As the Managing Partner of RITE Planning Group I'm going to have the opportunity to speak at various conventions beginning in the fall, but everyone says I need to have a book available that summarizes my life and shares the principles I follow. So I will cut to the chase. I'm willing to pay you well to help me get this book into shape as my ghostwriter. I really liked your autobiography and the tone you took in sharing experiences without preaching. Is there any way you could come here for a couple of days and help me get the book underway? I feel talking in person would be much more valuable than a phone call or video chat, mainly because I would like you to read through some of my journals and explain to me how the publishing industry works. It would help me know whether I truly have a book in me, and whether you want to team up on it. I played minor league baseball and have plenty of stories that my audience could relate to, along with the knowledge I've gained running my own company. So I do feel the book would contain valuable information even beyond the convention circuit. I'm out of town until Saturday, but I would gladly fly you down here early next week before the holiday and cover your expenses. You could stay in our guest room like before, or in a hotel if you prefer. I hate to take you away from your family, but I know this book is vital to my speaking success. I understand if you don't want to take part in the project, but I would definitely make it worth your time.

With admiration,

Charles

Lori had created the fake email address, masquerading as Charles, to give Chad cover to visit Lori in Arizona. When Charles confronted Lori, he told her she needed to come clean about her relationship with Chad, or he would contact Chad's wife and tell her about the affair. Lori laughed at him, telling him Tammy was her friend and would never believe him. It would not be the last time Lori would claim friendship with Tammy. Charles told Lori he had Tammy's email and phone number. When Lori brushed him off, Charles sent emails to Tammy at her job as an elementary school librarian on June 29, 2019, and again on June 30, 2019. The second email's subject line read, "Your husband and my wife." The body of the email continued, "Are having an affair. Her name is Lori Vallow. I've got definitive proof if you care to see it. Contact me, and I'll share it with you. It's devastating, I know, but the truth needs to be shown." That same day, Chad Daybell Googled "when you surprise someone with accusations." Tammy's school email records show she received Charles's email, opened it, deleted it, and blocked him from sending her any more. Several family members testified that Chad and Tammy's relationship seemed strained during that time and later suspected Tammy was upset because she had learned of Chad's affair.

Nine days after Tammy's death, Chad posted an essay to the AVOW (Another Voice of Warning) website titled "Moving into the Second Half of My Life." The post reads in part:

My dear wife Tammy passed away in her sleep early Saturday, October 19. When I awoke at around 6 A.M., it was clear she had been gone for several hours. It came as a shock. I couldn't believe I hadn't been awakened somehow, but all indications are that her spirit simply slipped away during the night. Her face looked serene, with her eyes closed and a slight smile. It was devastating to discover her that way, but I'm grateful that her death was peaceful. Tammy really was the anchor of our family and our publishing business. We have worked side by side from the moment we were married in the Manti Temple in 1990. It is safe to say I never would have become an author without her faith in me and her constant encouragement. Tammy herself wasn't a visionary woman, but she believed what I told her and trusted my decisions. She often said she felt like Lehi's wife, Sariah, in the Book of Mormon, where her faith was often tested by the unexpected turns of our lives, but she was grateful when the Lord would fulfill the promises that had been made regarding our family. She had a brilliant mind, especially when it came to computers. She wore so many hats in our company, from being Chief Financial Officer, to operating our websites, to designing book covers. I'm still sorting out how I'm going to cope with this tremendous loss, but thankfully I have a son whose mind works like Tammy's, and we'll be able to muddle through the tasks, although not as efficiently as she did.

Ten days after Tammy's death, Alex Cox sent Zulema Pastenes a picture of Chad, Lori, and two other women at a restaurant. Chad and Lori are sitting beside each other, and Chad is no longer wearing his wedding ring. This is the message exchange:

> October 28, 2019 at 8:29 P.M. about the picture—Zulema to Alex: "He looks way too happy."

> October 28, 2019 at 8:33 P.M.—Alex to Zulema: "He escaped the warden, so it's all downhill from here."

> October 28, 2019 at 8:34 P.M.—Zulema to Alex: "Woohoo, He's a happy man Look at that smile!"

> October 28, 2019 at 8:43 P.M.—Alex to Zulema: "He is a little giddy."

> October 28, 2019 at 9:06 P.M.—Zulema to Alex: "That's so cute."

Medical examiner Dr. Erik Christensen explained a different version of Tammy's death to the jury. Tammy didn't simply slip away into a peaceful death wearing a slight smile; she was asphyxiated. He detailed his autopsy findings in his trial testimony. The pink, blood-tinged foam coming from her mouth and nose that first responders observed the morning of her death was the clue. Toxicology reports showed the only substance in Tammy's body was the antidepressant she had been taking for years. The doctor said Tammy had bruises on her arms and chest that had happened near the time of her death and were consistent with being restrained. From Dr. Christensen's description, it was easy to visualize what happened that early morning as someone pinned Tammy to the bed and covered her face with a pillow until she was dead. The question was who. The only people in the house that night were Tammy, Chad, and their son Garth, who was sleeping in the room across the hall. However, phone location records revealed that Alex Cox was nearby that night, parked in the church parking lot near Chad's home. Did Alex leave his phone in the car and walk the mile or two to Chad's house to commit the murder? Or was he there to provide backup in case Chad's nerve failed? It's a question that may never be answered because Alex Cox is dead, and Chad Daybell is not talking.

Ada County forensic pathologist Dr. Garth Warren, MD, was the other medical examiner to testify. He performed the autopsies on JJ and Tylee. He reported that JJ died of asphyxia from the plastic bag tied tightly over his head. He said JJ had scratches on his neck and a bruise under one fingernail, suggesting he fought back and tried to dislodge the bag that was wrapped over his face. Dr. Warren said that, like Tammy Daybell, JJ had symmetrical bruises on both of his upper arms, proof that he also had probably been restrained while being suffocated.

Chad's brother, Matt, and his wife, Heather, live in Rexburg. Heather, in particular, was dismayed when Chad announced he and Tammy were moving to Rexburg in 2015. Heather didn't want Chad to attend the same LDS ward she and her family attended for fear of being painted with the same broad brush as Chad. Church officials were dismissive when Heather reported her concerns about Chad's offbeat beliefs to church leadership. Even though Heather was the stake president of the Relief Society, Chad was a man with priesthood power, and Heather was only a woman. Tammy's sister, Samantha Gwilliam was surprised when, in September 2019, Tammy drove to Springville for a visit with her family. Samantha was surprised because Tammy didn't like driving long distances alone. Chad had pressed Tammy to go because he was convinced she would meet with a fatal car crash while driving. The prosecution called witness after witness to refute Chad's claims that Tammy had been in failing health. Friends from her clogging class and exercise group testified she was as healthy and energetic as ever. Samantha was one of the state's final witnesses. She testified about the void left in their family by Tammy's death.

Starting and finishing a trial with emotional testimony that humanizes victims is a good strategy because people absorb information more readily through a story. Annette Simmons's *The Story Factor* is often used in courses on trial practice:

People don't want more information. They are up to their eyeballs in information. They want faith—faith in you, your goals, your success, in the story you tell. It is faith that moves mountains, not facts. Facts do not give birth to faith. Faith needs a story to sustain it—a meaningful story that inspires belief in you and renews hope that your ideas indeed offer what you promise. Genuine influence goes deeper than getting people to do what you want them to do. It means people pick up where you left off because they believe. Faith can overcome any obstacle, achieve any goal. Money, power, authority, political advantage, and brute force have all, at one time or another, been overcome by faith.

A good story will never overcome bad facts. Still, masterful storytelling can make a case come alive for a jury and help them synthesize seemingly disparate facts into a compelling circumstantial chain.

After twenty-six days, the state rested. The gallery was abuzz with speculation about whether Lori would testify in her defense. Defendants have an absolute right not to testify, guaranteed by the Fifth Amendment of the US Constitution. Many thought Lori would take the stand, eager to be heard, while others thought she would take the advice of her attorneys and decline. The second camp was right; Lori did not testify. The burden of proving the case rests solely with the prosecution. A defendant is presumed innocent until proven guilty beyond a reasonable doubt, so the defense does not need to prove innocence or call a single witness. However, the defense often does call witnesses to refute prosecution testimony. Surprisingly, the defense in Lori's case rested without calling a single witness.

With the testimony finished, the court launched into closing arguments where, once again, the prosecution was methodical and measured, laying out the facts and the law and reminding the jury how the facts proved each element of the crimes. Rob Wood ended where Lindsey Blake had begun: money, power, and sex. Wood reminded the jury that Lori Vallow was the thread that tied all the events and people together.

When Jim Archibald began his closing, it was clear his strategy was to blame Chad Daybell. This was a novel approach because, throughout the case, Lori refused to bring up her mental illness or focus blame on either Alex or Chad. Lori's reaction was evident. She was seething as she listened to her attorney tell the jury that Lori had changed after meeting Chad, implying that none of this would have happened if it had not been for Chad. Archibald repeatedly called Chad's books and his blessings and castings and dark and light scales "crap." Lori sat, stone-faced, with her arms crossed tightly across her chest. Archibald choked up talking about the pain Lori's son Colby experienced in his recorded call with his mother. He said, "The religious aspect of this group is so intense that common sense has vanished." He choked up again while paraphrasing the Bible, "If someone wants your coat, give them your coat and your cloak. If someone wants you to walk a mile, walk two miles with them. However you can help someone, do that. Treat people like you want to be treated, judge people like you want to be judged. Since you're a sinner, be kind and forgiving to sinners. If someone has offended you, forgive them. That's the Jesus that we know; that's the Jesus Lori knew. That's the Jesus she taught her children about. That's the Jesus that Lori believed in until she met Chad Daybell." The gallery could practically feel the waves of fury coming from Lori as her lawyer tried a Hail Mary play aimed at preserving some hope for her of a life after prison. As Archibald sat down, there was no question of the toll the case had taken on him and his cocounsel. Lori had tied their hands and still expected a miracle.

As her attorneys stood by the next day, Lori was ushered into the courtroom by her security team, wearing all black. Although cameras had been banned from the trial, the judge permitted the reading of the verdict to be livestreamed on the court's YouTube channel. Jim Archibald and John Thomas looked weary. Although John Thomas's wife and son had visited the Boise courtroom for a few days, like everyone else, both attorneys had been away from home for weeks. Thomas was not as tall as Archibald; his hair was a sandy blond, just a shade darker than Lori's, and like Lori, he often wore reading glasses perched on his nose. The constant background of clacking keyboards that had accompanied the trial for days was silent as the jury foreperson handed the verdict forms to the bailiff, who walked them over to the judge. The judge reviewed the forms to ensure the jury had completed them correctly, then passed the verdict to the clerk to be read into the record.

Lori stood between her lawyers, who both wore blue neckties; John Thomas clasped his hands below his ample midsection, and Archibald looked down at Lori. The clerk began reading. "Count 1, conspiracy to murder Tylee Ryan, guilty. Count 2, murder of Tylee Ryan, guilty. Count 3, conspiracy to murder JJ Vallow, guilty. Count 4, murder of JJ Vallow, guilty. Count 5, conspiracy to murder Tammy Daybell, guilty. Count 7, grand theft, guilty." Kay Woodcock smiled with relief as the first guilty verdict was read and looked heavenward as the counts that applied to JJ were read. Larry Woodcock wiped away tears. As she had done on so many other occasions, Lori remained absolutely motionless as the clerk methodically read each count of the verdict. The lawyers and law enforcement displayed their own brand of practiced stoicism.

For the prosecutors and law enforcement, the guilty verdict was bitter-sweet. The prosecutors and detectives had spent much time with the family, getting to know and care about them. While the verdict felt like a reward for the thousands of hours spent collecting, analyzing, and studying every nuance and detail of the case, no verdict could ever compensate for what had been lost. Certainly, for everyone involved in the trial, there was a bone-deep feeling of weariness of both body and spirit, and the job was only half done. In less than a year, they would have to do it again when Chad Daybell went on trial.

15

ABSOLUTE POWER CORRUPTS

O ne of the themes that runs through this book is the importance of checks and balances in our democratic system and the need for transparency in our criminal justice system. We saw the death penalty dismissed in Lori Vallow's case because of a lack of transparency in the discovery process. Other cases have illustrated issues surrounding prosecutorial misconduct, judicial activism, and lack of transparency as this book was written, such as the Indiana case of Richard Allen and the YNW Melly case in Florida.

Our system is unique because our Founding Fathers understood the need to temper the government's power to protect our vision of a government of and by the people. In a system where the government has nearly unlimited resources, it's important to limit its official power. One of the many ways the power of the government is restrained is by assuring that every defendant has competent legal counsel. This is why the Sixth Amendment of the US Constitution guarantees that every criminal defendant is entitled to representation. In 1961, Clarence Earl Gideon appeared in court, accused of breaking and entering. He asked the judge to appoint an attorney because he was too poor to afford representation. The judge told Gideon that the only time he could appoint an attorney for a defendant was in a capital offense. Gideon appeared at trial representing himself and was convicted. From prison, he filed his own motions for appeal, handwritten in pencil. The US Supreme Court agreed with Gideon that the Sixth Amendment applied to state courts through the Fourteenth Amendment, and the universal right to counsel was born for any case that included a possible sanction of imprisonment.

The defense attorney is the protection against government overreach in criminal cases. Without a defense attorney to stand in the breach, calling the judge, prosecution, and law enforcement to account, the government's power would be nearly limitless. The defense attorney is responsible for putting the government's case to the test, demanding that only reliable evidence be presented and then testing whether the evidence proves what the government says it does. The defense assures that both sides of the story are presented to the judge or the jury. The press also plays a critical role in limiting government power. Defense attorneys might as well be shouting into the wind without the press informing the public. Whether the information is disseminated by a blogger or a national news organization, the effect is the same: public awareness of the inner workings of the criminal justice system.

Prosecutorial, judicial, and law enforcement misconduct is a common thread in some recent high-profile cases. It's difficult to say whether it is happening more or whether we are more attuned to it because of increased visibility, but in case after case, we hear about prosecutors who do not follow discovery rules, police who manipulate evidence, and judges who preside unfairly. The rules exist to check the excess of government officials. These aren't cases where reforms are needed; instead, they are cases where citizens need to be reminded of the vital role they play in public accountability.

The Indiana case of Richard Allen is a good example. The bodies of Liberty German, age fourteen, and Abby Williams, age thirteen, were found in a Delphi, Indiana, park in 2017 when they didn't return from an afternoon hike. For years, the murders went unsolved. Then, in a surprise move, Delphi resident Richard Allen was arrested in October 2022. Nearly a year later, his defense attorneys set off a firestorm when they filed a 139-page motion challenging the search warrants served on Allen's home and property. Officials even dug up the remains of Allen's family cat during the search. Allen's defense team claimed that law enforcement had failed to disclose to the court that alternate theories of the case existed that did not implicate Richard Allen.

The defense theory, while sounding far-fetched, was supported by some evidence. Defense counsel and some law enforcement investigators believe that Abby and Libby were murdered by members of a Norse cult known as Odinism. The lengthy defense motion revealed details of the crime scene that had long been withheld from the public. The girls' bodies were staged, with tree branches arranged over them in what appeared to be Norse symbols. The defense claims this alternate theory was suppressed because some of the correctional officers in the prison where Richard Allen was housed pretrial, and potentially other law enforcement members, practice Odinism. The defense said several prison guards wore patches that proclaimed, "In Odin We Trust." Those guards admitted they practice a form of the Norse religion, which believes in a pantheon of gods, but deny they had any connection to a group that murdered Abby and Libby. Of note is the fact that Odinism is a widespread religious practice in many prisons, particularly among white prisoners who also espouse white supremacist beliefs. Some prisons recognize Odinism as a religious organization and support regular Odinist worship services. When the prison guards were directed to remove the patches from their uniforms, one guard had the Norse rune representing Odin tattooed on his face. The defense continues to challenge the investigation's truthfulness and competence.[1] That filing and a defense evidence leak resulted in a firestorm.

In South Carolina, the trial of attorney Alex Murdaugh revealed a system rife with cronyism and deep corruption. Journalist Mandy Matney and her reporting partner, Liz Farrell, began investigating the South Carolina system years before the Murdaugh murder case drew widespread attention. They have routinely broken stories about lawyer and judicial misconduct in the high-stakes South Carolina system where judges are not elected but appointed by lawyer-lawmakers in a vicious circle of I'll-scratch-your-back-if-you-scratch-mine.[2] While Murdaugh was found guilty of murdering his wife, Maggie, and son, Paul, the legal wrangling continued as Alex Murdaugh's defense attorneys, who were also some of his oldest friends, sought to overturn the conviction alleging jury tampering. While the judge assigned to hear the defense motions for trial found no evidence of jury tampering, the appeals will continue for years to come.

The 2023 Florida case of YNW Melly is another good example. Melly's legal name is Jamell Maurice Demons. Melly, an emerging rap star, was charged in 2019 with the murder of two of his rapper associates. Melly claimed that the occupants of their vehicle were victims of a drive-by shooting, while prosecutors claimed Melly staged the murder to look like a drive-by. When the case was tried, the jury could not reach a verdict. Before the case could be retried, attorneys for the defense filed motions to dismiss the case because of prosecutorial and law enforcement mis-conduct. Defense attorneys claimed that the lead detective in the case illegally obtained evidence, and the prosecution, including the elected state attorney, covered up the illegal acts to protect illegally obtained evidence. The problem may have far-reaching ramifications because it calls into question every investigation done by that detective and every case prosecuted by those prosecutors. Public coverage of the government cover-up serves to disinfect our system. While the prosecutor in question was removed, at this writing, the case was indefinitely postponed while the prosecution appeals the judge's unrelated ruling about the suppression of a promotional video about the rapper's life.

Millions watched as video of the arrest of Chad Doerman played on news outlets and livestreams in June 2023. Readers may recall that Doerman stands accused of having executed his three young sons in a heinous act of family annihilation. Doerman quickly confessed to law enforcement. However, police were sloppy and failed to read Doerman his Miranda admonitions before his confession, leading a judge to rule that Doerman's rights had been violated and that his confession was inadmissible. There is ample other evidence, including eyewitnesses, in this case, and it is unlikely that Doerman will walk free. However, that is not always the case in every arrest. Rulings such as these serve as wakeup calls for law enforcement; they don't get a second chance to do things the right way.

The subject of governmental transparency continues to be an issue in the Vallow and Daybell cases. There remain many unanswered questions about what is contained in the scores of documents and hearings Judge Stephen Boyce sealed. Did the subject of those documents justify their sealing, or is this just another case of small-town cronyism or, worse, a case of LDS "brothers" protecting one another? It is a question this author is still intent on answering, because the misconduct of prosecutors and law enforcement taints credibility and distorts the criminal justice system, undermining the reliability of the outcomes for both the public and the victims. The criminal justice system and the public it serves have always relied on the honor and the professional ethics of judges, police, and prosecutors and assumed they could be self-policing. When that system breaks down, we sacrifice justice for the victims and risk that the guilty may go free or that the innocent may be convicted.

16

VISIONS OF GLORY AND THE BOUNDED CHOICE

Reading this book and watching the news, one may wonder if there are more incidents of family violence and murder in the LDS community or if we are just hearing about them more often. Some of the concern surrounds the tone deafness of the LDS community, particularly in Utah.

Early in 2023, Michael Haight, a Utah father of five, murdered his children, his wife, and his mother-in-law before turning the gun on himself. Haight had been investigated in 2020 on suspicion of child abuse, but local prosecutors decided not to criminally charge him despite reports from his eldest daughter of several incidents where her father choked her, including one where the girl said she was "very afraid he was going to keep her from breathing and kill her."[1] Despite Haight's heinous actions, his surviving family produced a tone-deaf obituary talking about his "life of service." The obituary listed his children's names, noting, "Each of these children were truly a cherished miracle to him. Michael made it a point to spend quality time with each and every one of his children. Michael enjoyed making memories with the family." No mention was made that this seemingly perfect Mormon father annihilated his entire family after forcing them to endure years of abuse.

Then there was Kouri Richens, the Utah mother who was accused of killing her husband, Eric, by lacing his evening Moscow Mule with fentanyl. Allegedly, she poisoned him after he refused to sign closing documents on a $2 million home she intended to purchase and flip. Kouri was widely lauded for the children's book she later wrote and published for her three young sons about grief and loss titled *Are You With Me?* At the time of this book's writing, Richens was being held without bail awaiting trial on murder charges.

Even in cases where victims are not murdered, the specter of LDS neo-fundamentalism rears its ugly head. The world met Jodi Hildebrandt and Ruby Franke in a collision of social media and criminal behavior. Ruby Franke was an LDS mommy-blogger with a popular YouTube channel called Eight Passengers. In her video blog, she documented her family life and the daily challenges of raising six children. She also took preparations and food storage very seriously. Her parenting approach was strict and punitive, raising concerns from both fans and family. When she and her husband, Kevin, hit a marital tough patch, they sought therapy with Jodi Hildebrandt, who was on a list of approved LDS therapists often recommended to parishioners by their bishops. Jodi's brand of therapy called for the couple to separate. She demanded Ruby's husband be isolated from the family until he "repented." Months later, Ruby Franke's twelve-year-old son knocked on the door of the house next to Jodi Hildebrandt's $5 million Ivins, Utah, home. The boy was emaciated, covered in bruises and scabs, and still wearing duct tape around his ankles and wrists; he said he was hungry and thirsty and asked the neighbor to call the police. He had managed to escape from Hildebrandt's home but reported that his nine-year-old sister was still a prisoner in the basement next door. Unbeknownst to Kevin, the children were living in Hildebrandt's home. Hildebrandt and Franke both pled guilty to child abuse charges and Kevin Franke filed for divorce. What makes this case even more disturbing is the connection Jodi Hildebrandt had to the neo-fundamentalist movement.

Jodi Hildebrandt was closely aligned with Thom Harrison, the "Spencer" of *Vision of Glory*. Harrison was one of Hildebrandt's professors, and they appeared on conference panels together.[2]

These cases illustrate the reach of the much larger conservative movement within the LDS Church that some call neo-fundamentalism, preppers, the Remnant Movement, or Snufferites. Since the 2012 publication of *Visions of Glory*, the movement has gained momentum, permeating the highest levels of the church. The book's author, John Pontius, died shortly after its publication. Pontius claimed he acted as a scribe, writing down Spencer's visions and near-death experiences. The book discusses themes that would later surface in Julie Rowe's and Chad Daybell's writings and teachings. Ironically, when Pontius initially proposed the book to his publisher, Cedar Fort Publishing, they were not sure there was a market for the subject matter.

After the book's publication, Thomas Jean Harrison, who goes by Thom, admitted he was Spencer. Harrison contends that Pontius took liberties with the story and did not apply Harrison's edits. Harrison is still a practicing and well-known LDS mental health professional. Right after *Visions of Glory* was published, Harrison held a few firesides—educational sessions for the LDS faithful—talking about his visions. He soon drew the attention of church leadership, and in March 2014, he released a statement addressed "To Whom It May Concern." He decided to write the letter after meeting with his stake president. He states, "Under no circumstances did John or I ever mean or [sic] conspire, deceive or acquire gain from these sacred things. Our hope was to lift, bless, and bring people to Christ. I am sorry for any offence [sic] this has caused any member." The letter also said, "At this time of my life, I wished I would have kept it all to myself. That, *Visions of Glory* the book was just those experiences one man had and that no one else had ever read this account. It has caused me great grief, despair, family discord, public ill treatment, derision, and criticism. I have learned that when we undertake to cast sacred things before the masses that they turn and rend you and that the rending is very severe." Harrison pointed out that the publication rights belonged to John Pontius's family and that

Harrison would no longer make any comments about the book.[3] Then, in an apparent quid pro quo, shortly after the letter was published, Harrison was rewarded for his compliance and future silence by being made a bishop.

Nonetheless, Thom Harrison's silence could not put the *Visions of Glory* genie back in the bottle. Throughout LDS circles, people were sharing and studying the book and claiming their own near-death experiences and their own visions of the end times. Although Cedar Fort Publishing had been unsure of the book's appeal, by the time the fifth-anniversary edition was published in 2017, the cover included a banner that claimed "Over 100,000 copies sold."

Thom Harrison and *Visions of Glory* also figured into the recent fall from grace of Tim Ballard, a popular LDS author and purported foe of human trafficking. Ballard founded Operation Underground Railroad (OUR), an organization that sent teams into countries where human trafficking is rampant, to aid those being trafficked. Ballard asked Harrison to provide trauma therapy to victims after their rescue. Ballard was the subject of the movie *The Sound of Freedom*, a heavily fictionalized version of Ballard's exploits. Women who had been volunteers in Ballard's organization, many of whom participated in the foreign operations, began coming forward to report that they had been sexually abused and harassed by Ballard. He was removed as the head of OUR and has been sued in civil actions by several of the alleged victims. Reminiscent of Chad Daybell, some of Ballard's alleged victims claim Ballard excused his overtures by claiming he and the victim had been married in previous probations. Followers say Ballard relied on psychics to direct his rescue operations and took the drug ketamine to induce psychedelic experiences about his past lives. Ballard, who once enjoyed the friendship and support of Utah Attorney General Sean Reyes and senior LDS apostle M. Russell Ballard, who was not related to Tim Ballard, has been excommunicated by The Church of Jesus Christ of Latter-day Saints. Still an active member of the church, Thom Harrison continues to flirt with neo-fundamentalism. He organized the Eternal Core conference on mental health in March 2019 and invited both Jodi Hildebrandt and Tim Ballard to speak. Also on the dais were Bruce Hafen, former president of Brigham Young University's Idaho campus, and his wife, Marie. The conference, subtitled "Exploring God-Centric Mental Health," featured many speakers who talked about chakras, vibration, and energy work. Jodi Hildebrandt spoke to the group about bringing God into mental health treatment.[4] Despite the outcry from social media, the church scrupulously ignores these outliers until they become headline news.

Mormonism is a high-demand religion, defined as "a faith community that requires obedience; discourages its members from questioning its rules, principles, and practices; expects subservience and loyalty; discourages trusting relationships outside the group; perpetuates the notion that those within the group are right and superior to those outside of it; promotes extreme or polarizing beliefs; and expects its members to suppress their authentic selves in exchange for the sense of belonging and security the group offers."[5]

Some experts have called Mormonism a cult. Dr. Steven Hassan is an expert in cults; at age nineteen, he was recruited into the Unification Church, also sometimes called the Moonies, after their founder, Reverend Sun Myung Moon. Dr. Hassan was a member for twenty-seven months before injuries from a serious car accident required him to seek medical care. After two weeks in the hospital and surgery to repair his shattered leg, he sought permission from the Moon organization, where he had become a trusted leader, to convalesce at his sister's home. Hassan said his visit to his sister was the first time he'd had enough food or sleep since he joined Moon's organization. Like many cults, the Unification Church kept its members frenetically busy, leaving them chronically hungry and short on sleep. His convalescence was the first time Hassan was able to reflect on his choices. His parents hired counselors to work with him, promising that if, after five days, Hassan still wanted to return to the Moonies, they would drive him. The rest, as they say, is history. Hassan began to see the irrationality of his devotion to the Unification Church and devoted his life's work to studying and understanding cults and helping others leave them.

There is debate about whether the Mormon Movement is a cult. In his book *Combating Cult Mind Control*,[6] Hassan describes a cult as an organization that controls behavior, information, thought, and emotions. He says that cognitive dissonance theory predicts if any of the components of a belief system change, members will shift their beliefs to relieve the tension of the dissonance. Hassan uses the example of a Wisconsin flying saucer cult who believed they would be picked up by spaceships before a massive flood destroyed the world. They sold all their belongings and waited all through a long night for the aliens to arrive. When morning dawned, the aliens had not materialized, and the flood had not occurred; rather than becoming disillusioned with their prophet, they became even more committed to the leader, who told them the aliens had seen the devotion of their vigil and decided to spare the Earth. We saw this same sort of mental gymnastics from Lori Vallow when the tribulation did not begin on July 21, 2020, as she believed it would. While there can be debate over whether The Church of Jesus Christ of Latter-day Saints is a cult or a high-demand religion, there can be little doubt that Chad's tiny organization was a developing cult. It was, like nesting Russian dolls, a cult in its infancy within the larger neo-fundamental movement, all within the LDS Church.

The social media platform AVOW (Another Voice of Warning) became a gathering place for like-minded neo-fundamentalists like Chad Daybell and Julie Rowe. The title is a reference to the book *A Voice of Warning*, written in 1837 by Parley Pratt, who was an ardent follower of Joseph Smith Jr. According to the church website, Pratt's book was "the most important of all Mormon missionary tracts of the 19th century."[7] Even then, they were preparing for the callout. Doctrine and Covenants 113:10-12, 14 reads, "Prepare yourselves for the great day of the Lord. Watch, therefore, for ye know neither the day nor the hour. Let them, therefore, who are among the Gentiles flee unto Zion. . . . Go ye out from among the nations, even from Babylon, from the midst of wickedness, which is spiritual Babylon." The church interprets this passage by saying, "Like Alma, we too have been *called out* of Babylon to find shelter by gathering with the Saints of God. In order to do so, we may need to leave what is comfortable and familiar to dwell under the gospel's tent. No matter how enticing the world might appear, it was never intended to be our home. Nor does it provide the true happiness available to those faithful to the Lord. We, like Alma's people, can trust that the Lord will enable us to bear our burdens with ease."[8] According to the neo-fundamentalists, the callout will be when church leadership directs those who have prepared to bring their hoarded supplies to their stake, where they will be loaded on trucks and taken to remote camps in the mountains where the faithful can wait out the tribulation. Those Saints who have not prepared will be left behind with the Gentiles to fend for themselves.

Christopher Parrett owned the AVOW (Another Voice of Warning) website, which provided a platform for like-minded individuals to gather and exchange ideas about preparing for the end times. The site requires that users pay for a subscription, screening participants behind a paywall. Many of the neo-fundamentalist movement's most vocal adherents were active AVOW members, and many still are. Parrett wrote, "As time has gone on, I have had many dreams which speak of economic collapse not just in our country, but around the world. America's great power, both economic and military, has been eroded to the point where America is just one poor nation among many."[9] The essay contains Parrett's predictions of the collapse of Western Europe and recounts how church members will hide in camps around the country as they wait out the tribulation. According to information that has now been taken off the AVOW website, Chad Daybell wrote ten books for AVOW, including a three-book series about the United States being invaded by United Nations peacekeepers after a natural disaster.

The Southern Poverty Law Center lists AVOW as an Antigovernment Group, which they define as groups that are "part of the antidemocratic hard-right movement. They believe the federal government is tyrannical, and they traffic in conspiracy theories about an illegitimate government of leftist elites seeking a 'New World Order.' In addition to groups that generally espouse these ideas, the movement comprises sovereign citizens, militias, overt conspiracy propagandists, and constitutional sheriff groups. In the past, this movement was referred to as the 'Patriot' movement by adherents and critics."[10] Chad Daybell and many other neo-fundamentalists were active in the chatroom on the AVOW site. Chad Daybell contributed to Christopher Parrett's book *Dreams, Visions and Testimonies III*, a collection of end-time dreams and visions members posted on the AVOW site. The dreams and visions have similar themes: tent cities, war, natural disasters, and atrocities. Some feared children might be taken to "FEMA reeducation camps" and predicted China and Russia would attack the United States, much like the 1984 movie *Red Dawn*.

Chad Daybell's infant cult nests within this neo-fundamentalism movement, which is, in turn, contained within the high-demand Church of Jesus Christ of Latter-day Saints. Dr. Steven Hassan developed the model he calls **BITE** to better define cults and cultlike organizations.[11] A cult is an organization that controls Behavior, Information, Thought, and Emotions. Using that definition, it's clear Chad Daybell was developing a cult within the larger neo-fundamentalism movement. It's uncertain whether, if left unchecked, his cult would have caught on to become the predominant group in the movement or whether it would have been just another stunted branch on the Church of the Firstborn's ever-growing tree.

Nonetheless, the BITE model defines Chad's group. In their developing cult, Chad and Lori used religious beliefs to control the physical reality of their adherents and each other. Lori controlled her behavior and the behavior of her niece Melani and her other followers, Melanie Gibb and Zulema Pastenes, by spending hours in the LDS temple every day and encouraging them to be there with her to share the transcendent experience. Chad directed each of his followers to move to Rexburg, ID, and directed couples to marry. Cults are usually authoritarian, with a clear leadership structure that encourages the down-rank people to strive for the approval of the leaders above them, who receive public praise and criticism. The group saw Chad as their leader. They also typically deferred to Lori as the communication conduit to Chad. Cults tend to have their own set of ritual behaviors that give outward proof of their specialness. In the case of Lori and Chad, the castings and temple attendance were the heart of those rituals. Dr. Hassan explains that obedience to the leader is the peak lesson because a cult leader learns that while they can't control a person's inner thoughts, if they control behavior, the heart and mind will follow.

Information control is the next component of the BITE model. When the cult is the source of all information, the person receiving the information can easily be manipulated. The LDS Church has long controlled the information that Saints are allowed, and those raised in the church are accustomed to deferring to the church for which information they can and cannot have. The advent of the internet makes it harder for the church to control the message. Still, the faithful are cautioned against relying on outside sources, lest Satan influence them. Once the cult controls a person's behavior and the information they consume, it's easy to manipulate their thoughts. When a person is thoroughly indoctrinated and has internalized the doctrine as truth, the members manipulate their thought process to stop outside ideas from intruding into their consciousness. In LDS culture, anytime a Saint has a question about their faith or receives conflicting information, they are encouraged to "put their questions on the shelf" because their faith is not mature enough to understand them. The message is that the fault is not with the church doctrine; the believer's lack of faith or spiritual immaturity is the problem. The LDS Church not only revises its history but then denies it ever made the revisions, thereby altering and redefining reality for its members.

We must wonder how this affected Lori's and Chad's grasp of reality. Like cults, the LDS Church employs particular coded language that helps the believer feel special and sets them apart from the general public—the Gentiles, as the LDS Church refers to any non-member. Members are trained from birth to treat any criticism of the church as a lie perpetrated by Satan. They see criticism of the church as confirmation that church ideas are true, reasoning that Satan would not be trying so hard to infiltrate their thinking if their doctrine was false. In time, the believer simply stops registering information that doesn't comport with their LDS worldview. Members are taught thought-stopping techniques to avoid negative thoughts or opposing views. Often, these are daily activities that the believer will practice to the extreme, such as prayer, singing, meditation, or scripture reading. In Lori Vallow Daybell's case, she spent hours each day dancing, praying in the LDS temple, or studying LDS scripture, short-circuiting her ability to test reality. When coupled with her diagnosed personality disorder and religious delusional disorder, the combination was potent.

The last layer of control in the BITE model is emotional control. The organization attempts to narrow the range of emotions from the extremes of euphoria at being chosen or pleasing the leader to guilt and brokenness when the leader is disappointed. Many groups use complex and shifting expectations to keep the believer off balance, including dictating when and how the believer can engage in interpersonal relationships. That manifests in extremes, from demanding celibacy to dictating whom the believer will marry or when and with whom the believer can engage in sex. Confessions of past misdeeds often become mechanisms by which the organization controls the believer. The mainstream LDS Church demands sexual purity before marriage. Young people who are candidates for mission service or ready for their temple endowment are routinely grilled in minute detail about even the most innocent dating behavior. Any suspected transgressions, including masturbation, are met with swift action. Young people are singled out publicly and forced to sit out church sacraments as a sign of their unworthiness because of their sexual behavior. The punishment is initiated when a youth is called into the bishop's office for "counseling," which consists of insisting the young person fully confess every intimate detail. Church leadership thinks nothing of requiring a teenage girl to attend a private meeting with her bishop, an unrelated older man, to confess every intimate detail of every sexual encounter she has ever had.

Cult control often includes altering the believer's identity, beginning with their name. In the LDS Church, each young person must undergo a temple endowment ceremony designed to affirm the covenants made at baptism. They are given a new name in that ceremony, which no one else can know. If the believer is a woman, only her husband can know her temple name. Her name must be known to her eternal husband so he can call her through the veil and into the celestial kingdom. In the case of Lori and Chad, they consistently called one another by alternate names. They were more than just pet names; they were designed to identify them as special, exalted beings selected by God to lead His chosen people. Chad claimed that he and Lori were reincarnations of James the Just, the brother of Jesus, and his wife, Elena. When he called Lori Elena, he identified her as a being with special powers and purpose.

Chad called on Mormon traditions to normalize claims that he was a prophet. He used the familiar history of Joseph Smith Jr. to draw parallels with his own teachings. He used an owl necklace he found while cleaning his Rexburg, Idaho, ward as a pendulum. Much the way Joseph Smith Jr. believed he could divine answers by use of a seer stone in a hat, Chad believed he could divine answers by dangling the necklace over the person. Using the pendulum, he divined information about past lives and his subject's place in the scale of darkness and light. Melanie Gibb told police that at a prayer circle meeting at Lori's home shortly after Charles Vallow's death, Chad produced what he claimed was a seer stone for use in the ceremony. Lori and Chad often likened themselves to biblical and Book of Mormon heroes or claimed they had been those heroes in previous lives. When police asked Melanie Gibb about Lori and Chad comparing themselves to Nephi and Laban, Melanie said she knew it meant Charles's life needed to be sacrificed. She wasn't overly concerned, though, because, according to LDS scripture as amplified by *Visions of Glory*, Charles was already gone, and Alex was doing Charles a favor, killing the body to rid it of the evil spirit and free him.

One thing that perplexes those interested in the Vallow and Daybell cases is how Lori and Chad could be so delusional and yet so functional. This seeming contradiction has led many to doubt Lori's mental health diagnosis and suspect instead that she was malingering. On the one hand, Lori appeared to believe completely that she was a translated being and an exalted goddess. Yet she could still navigate daily demands, like putting gasoline in the car and making travel arrangements. On some level, she understood the need to hide her actions and disguise her true intentions. She traveled and rented a storage unit using the last name Ryan rather than her legally married name of Vallow. She appeared to have deleted text messages, used telephone calls rather than texts to discuss plans, and taken many other steps that showed awareness and planning and reflected her consciousness of her guilt.

The question becomes, can someone be deep into religious delusions and still express some consciousness of guilt in the things they do? Further, can a person be that delusional and still intentional in the way they manipulate others into following their delusions? Zulema Pastenes said Chad and Lori were master manipulators full of lies and deceit. She said that unless you've experienced it, you cannot fathom that someone could be so evil. Zulema said she would never be the same after her experience with Chad and Lori. Surprisingly, many who met Chad Daybell were shocked that anyone could find him charismatic. He was odd, awkward, and soft-spoken. Not so with Lori; her cousin, Braxton Southwick, said Lori was the kind of person who made people feel special. People were drawn to her good looks and her effusive personality. When Lori turned her attention to you, it was like being caught in a shaft of sunlight. Zulema Pastenes said while Lori was outgoing and in your face, Chad was reserved and calculating.

Dr. Janja Lalich is an author, researcher, and educator. She has studied cults and other social movements for years. Her "bounded choice" theory is especially helpful in understanding cults and other high-demand organizations. Once we understand her thesis, it's easy to see how Chad, Lori, and their followers fell into this carefully choreographed dance. In Chad and Lori's case, they were born into it. Many mainstream members of the LDS Church are quick to point out that what Lori and Chad believed was not the mainstream doctrine of The Church of Jesus Christ of Latter-day Saints, but there is no question that their deep inculcation into the faith informed their later actions.

Dr. Lalich studied the Heaven's Gate cult in particular and drew some crucial generalizations about cults and high-demand organizations from its specifics. The applications are relevant to the Vallow Daybell case. Dr. Lalich begins by explaining the structure of the bounded choice model, which she describes as having four interlocking dimensions. First, a charismatic authority must create an emotional bond between leaders and followers. As Dr. Lalich describes it, "The relational aspect of charisma is the hook that links a devotee to a leader and/or his or her ideas."[12] Many would dispute the charisma of Chad Daybell. Still, Lori used her considerable charm to convince people of their shared ideas. Arguably, there was also something compelling about Chad, as a soft-spoken, self-deprecating prophet that people responded to.

Second, there must be a transcendent belief system—"an overarching ideology that binds adherents to the group and keeps them behaving according to the group's rules and norms." Chad made his followers feel special. They were never shoemakers or slaves in past lives; instead, they had always been people of influence and power, called upon for special callings.

Third, the organization needs a system of control—in other words, an acknowledged method by which members' behavior is managed and manipulated. One of the ways Chad and Lori manipulated people was by controlling information and dispensing it in small bits. The other was to make their constant counsel indispensable and then to disappear, leaving their followers floundering for days as a way to keep them off balance and needy.

Finally, Dr. Lalich says there must be a system of influence. This is how the members interact with the group culture and where they learn to conform their ideas, thoughts, and attitudes to the group and its beliefs. Lori and Chad Daybell and their followers were uniquely groomed for their leap into a doomsday cult by their lifelong inculcation in The Church of Jesus Christ of Latter-day Saints. This high-demand organization expects its members to make a bounded choice to join or continue membership.

First, the LDS Church encourages the elevation of larger-than-life leaders, beginning with the founder, Joseph Smith Jr., who is seen as a holy man whose spiritual gifts are akin to Jesus Christ. Smith's successors were all given the titles of prophet, seer, and revelator. They are also men who are larger than life. These men teach and perpetuate a transcendent belief system that thoroughly explains the past, present, and future. It gives followers an exact methodology to achieve personal transformation: be baptized; attend church regularly; if male, receive the Aaronic and Melchizedek priesthoods and perform a mission; remain chaste until marriage; receive a temple endowment and marry a partner in the temple for time and eternity; have as many children as possible; do church work aimed at bringing relatives, both living and dead, into the church; participate in baptisms and marriages for the dead; tithe; answer calls to leadership willingly and cheerfully; educate children and youth into the system; hold your fellow brothers and sisters accountable; and finally, defend and protect the message of the church.

Next, the church most certainly exerts control over its members. Members' behavior is explicitly and expressly circumscribed: from whom and when they marry, when they can have sex, what they wear, what they can drink, whether they can smoke or use drugs, how they raise their children, where they work, how much they contribute to the church, and thousands of other rules both large and small. By doing so, the church creates a system of influence where threats work and blame reversal is the norm. It's not the religion that has failed you; it is you who have failed the religion. It is a culture where members are entirely dependent on the church for their social interactions and where they learn to conform their thoughts and actions to the organization's expectations or risk expulsion. High demand? No question.

Lori and Chad were born into this culture and experienced a lifelong campaign of indoctrination; Lori believed angels woke her up at night to give her temple work to do. Chad believed he could see beyond the veil and received visions from his dead ancestors. Their beliefs made them feel special within the pale, homogenized LDS culture, where sameness is valued. They attached to ideas rooted in their church but just a tick off center, embracing ideas the church abandoned and no longer talks about. The church controls so much of the message members hear that it's no wonder most church members won't believe Lori and Chad are true Mormons. To the contrary, Chad and Lori would argue that their teachings are the original ideas in their purest form from the prophet Joseph Smith Jr. and the disciples who knew him. So how do two faithful members of a religion that values conformity and rule following take their beliefs to the point of murder?

The answer is in Dr. Lalich's bounded choice theory because, as she says, "The interrelated and interlocking nature of the four dimensions form a self-sealing system . . . Now a dedicated adherent becomes a true 'true believer' in the sense of being a deployable agent for the group or leader . . . The member's life and choices are constrained not only by the system but also, perhaps even more powerfully, by the close-mindedness of the individual him- or herself, who is functioning in alliance with that system. Now, the dedicated adherent has entered a social-psychological state of being that I am calling bounded choice: in essence, life outside the cult has become impossible to imagine."[13] A vital part of the transcendence dimension is the appeal of the message of transformation, the moral imperative, and the sense of urgency and freedom. In the Heaven's Gate cult, members were encouraged to evolve into a genderless ideal. For Chad and Lori, the transformation was from humans to gods endowed with the power to banish evil. Some of the Heaven's Gate cult members castrated themselves to achieve the genderless ideal. Lori and Chad were willing to end the lives of people they loved as they exercised their power to scourge the evil spirits they believed lurked within.

17

ECHOES OF NARCISSUS

M ental illness played a significant role in most of Lori Vallow Daybell's life. Still, until she was indicted for murder, no one knew how
deeply she was impacted by it. This is because her particular diagnosis does
not limit her day-to-day functioning to the extent other illnesses often do.
For one, Lori was diagnosed with a personality disorder with narcissistic
features. The layperson expects someone with a narcissistic personality disorder (NPD) to be grandiose and have an exaggerated sense of superiority.
However, recent developments in brain science suggest that vulnerability
may also be deeply rooted in the condition, and it seems that there is more
than one type of NPD. Dr. Jay Searle, PhD believes what appears to be
constant on both ends of the spectrum is the narcissist's extreme preoccupation with themselves. [1] The grandiose type believes they are the most
intelligent, most beautiful, most magnetic person in the room. They have
an exaggerated sense of self-importance, a preoccupation with unlimited
success and power, an excessive need for admiration, and a lack of empathy.
But people who have those characteristics also often have phases of vulnerability. In fact, vulnerability and grandiosity appear to form a dynamic
relationship and may wax and wane depending on circumstances and the
person's stage of development.

Many people, including members of Lori's family, believe that Charles, Tylee, JJ, and Tammy would all be alive today if Chad and Lori had not met in October 2018. Family members and media analysts have called Lori and Chad's meeting the "perfect storm." It appears that their individual narcissistic personalities meshed uniquely and destructively. They fed each other's grandiosity while assuaging the other's doubts and vulnerabilities. They knew they were marked for greatness. Chad believed he was a prophet with visionary abilities; Lori believed she was a powerful goddess. God personally and individually elected them to lead the peak moment in history.

At Chad's trial, the prosecutor pointed out instances where Lori and Chad each manipulated the other. One of the clearest examples was a text exchange that began in early August 2019. Charles Vallow had died several weeks earlier, and Lori was ready to move to the next stage with Chad. She told Chad she and Melani Boudreaux were planning a trip to Rexburg. Chad told Lori the dates she planned wouldn't work because he had a family trip planned with his wife, Tammy. Lori promptly cut off contact with Chad for more than twenty-four hours. Chad was frantic. After Lori didn't respond to several professions of love, Chad wrote: "Grandpa Keith is here. (Referring to the spirit of a deceased relative.) I am supposed to warn you that you are unprotected. The angels are angry that you are ignoring me. I told him to go back, but he says he wasn't allowed to. I'm honestly not trying to manipulate you to respond. I understand that you need your space. But they say you have cut me off, and the protection I built around your house is gone. I love you and don't want you getting attacked. They said that if you at least give me a (emoji) it will restore our connection enough to give some protection." A few minutes later, Lori responds, "I love you." Followed by kissing and heart emojis. Two days later, Lori sends Chad a photograph of herself on a beach in a low-cut yellow swimsuit with the caption, "Surprises are waiting!!" followed by a fire emoji. The next day, Chad texts, "But I will leave you alone, as excruciating as that will be, until I hear from you." Lori answers, "U can't say to me nothing else matters. Because everything is before me. It That's what the Lord wants them I'm.

I just need to do something ekes [*sic*] so I can pull myself out of this deep despair. It's not like me to be this way. It's been way too much for way too long." Chad answers, "The pain is unbearable."

At Lori's sentencing, Judge Boyce made public her complete diagnosis: "delusional disorder mixed type with bizarre content and hyper-religiosity and a continuous and unspecified personality disorder with histrionic and narcissistic features." The two conditions feed off of each other. Lori refused to cooperate with any screenings during her presentence investigation. Her cooperation could have given the judge more information about her mental health. Lori's attorneys attempted to mitigate the deficiency by submitting hundreds of pages of mental health records to the court, but the judge refused to consider all but a few of those pages. It was also suggested Lori was provisionally diagnosed with late-onset schizophrenia.

Generally, medical and mental health records are confidential. Lori's mental illness only became public because she was found incompetent to aid and assist in her defense, delaying her case for more than ten months while she received treatment. There is no information available on any mental health screenings Chad Daybell may have had since his arrest on June 9, 2021. We can, however, draw some conclusions from Chad's writings. Chad Daybell published two memoirs. The first, *One Foot in the Grave*, records his memories of being a cemetery sexton. The second, *Living on the Edge of Heaven*, is his account of his near-death experiences. There are clues to his personality in the books. In one case, he recalls an experience as a boy when he came upon a patch of clover busy with bees. Chad began stomping on the bees, counting how many he killed. When he reached 120, he heard a voice tell him to stop. Rather than attributing the voice to his conscience, he credited an angel, fed up with him killing God's innocent creatures. "That incident helped me realize how pathetic I had become, and I decided to start making some better choices."[2] By age fourteen, Chad was deeply immersed in the study of his LDS faith. He said he was inspired to get his patriarchal blessing then, rather than wait until he was sixteen, as most young men did. "Admittedly, the song 'Only the Good Die Young' by Billy Joel had strangely affected me, and I started wondering if I was going to die young because I was doing my best to live the gospel." Later, he says, "Deep down, I knew the book [of Mormon] was true and felt good when I read it, but I suppose I expected something along the lines of a heavenly messenger appearing to me."[3] These passages reflect Chad's growing sense of grandiosity, but he also felt alone and vulnerable. In his mind, he would have to die young because he was so good. Chad was the oldest of five children. His position in the birth order meant his parents' attention was often taken up by his younger siblings, and he rarely felt special or even seen. He talks about how alone he felt as a freshman at BYU.

People with NPD lash back when their superiority is challenged. Consider Lori's recorded jail telephone calls with her son Colby Ryan and her sister Summer Shiflet. In the call with Colby, Lori repeatedly said she did nothing wrong. She said Colby didn't understand the truth and had no right to judge. He demanded that his mother tell him that what she had done was God's will. "Tell me that this is God's will, for my whole family, including my stepfather, to be dead . . . that you can tell me that Jesus Christ, the savior of the world, is on your side." Lori's answer: "I can tell you that." Lori had absolute confidence in her delusions, to the point of unshakable belief that the deaths of her victims were God's will. On the phone with Colby, she said, "One day, you will know what actually happened." When Colby accused Lori of blasphemy, she laughed a spontaneous and childlike giggle. She assured him that Tylee and JJ were fine and they still loved her and knew the truth about what happened.

In her call with her sister, Summer sobbed while Lori sounded defiant. She told Summer she couldn't talk about what had happened and to ask the Lord for answers. Lori told her sister, "Nobody knows what I've been through, those are *my* children, that I love more than anything . . . *mine*." When Summer confronted her about dancing on the beach while her children were dead, Lori explained, "That was months later," and said that she was trying to find some happiness. She asked, "Do you think I wanted to be alone?" When Summer urged Lori to consider that she'd been deceived, Lori became defensive. The grandiosity, the preoccupation with herself, and her belief that she was the victim all scream narcissistic personality disorder.

One hallmark of NPD is the person's inability to accurately read a room. On the advice of her lawyers, Lori remained silent throughout nearly all of her case, limiting her answers to yes or no. When she finally had the chance to speak her truth, her allocution before sentencing was stunning in its tone deafness and lack of accountability or even self-awareness. Clearly, Lori believed that, finally, this was her opportunity to make the world see her truth. But, as with most people with NPD, it was a skewed and fabricated truth. A truth made crooked by her uncompromising belief that she is divine. The public would finally glimpse the depth of those delusions when she spoke. Throughout the sentencing hearing, Lori sat slumped between her much larger attorneys as if she were hiding. Still, when it was her turn to speak, she sat up straight, adjusted the microphone, crossed her ankles under the table in a relaxed pose, and spoke confidently.

> I would like to start by quoting John from the New Testament in the Bible. In John 8:7, Jesus said, "He that is without sin among you, let him first cast a stone at her." Then, in verse 15, Jesus says, "Ye judge after the flesh, I judge no man, and yet if I judge, my judgment is true." Jesus knows me, and Jesus understands me. I mourn with all of you who mourn my children and Tammy. Jesus Christ knows the truth of what happened here. Jesus Christ knows that no one was murdered in this case. Accidental deaths happen; suicides happen; fatal side effects from medications happen. I have a different perspective in life because in 2002 when I was pregnant with Tylee, I died in the hospital while in labor with her. They tried to stop my labor, they put me on the table, they put something in my IV, and I felt my spirit falling to the floor. I was standing near my pregnant body, watching doctors try to revive me, which took them a few minutes. In that time, my sister Stacey was standing to my left; I turned to hug her and was surprised that her spirit was as tangible as a physical body because I knew I was in spirit and she was in spirit. She said she needed to show

me some things, and we went to heaven. I later returned to my body. Because of this experience, I have access to heaven and the spirit world. Since then, I have had many communications from people now living in heaven. Including my children, Tylee Ashlyn and Joshua Jackson, my sisters, Stacey and Lolly, my aunts and my uncles, and my grandparents. I have had many communications with Jesus Christ, the savior of this world, and our heavenly parents. I've had many angelic visitors who have come and communicated with me and even manifested themselves to me. Because of these communications, I know for a fact that my children are happy and busy in the spirit world. Because of my communications with my friend Tammy Daybell, I know that she is also very happy and extremely busy. I have always mourned the loss of my loved ones, and I have lost many in the mortal world. However, I know more than most people; I know where they are now and what they're doing. I know how wonderful heaven is, and I'm homesick for it every single day. I know we all lived in heaven before we were born on Earth, and we were all adult spirits in the heavenly realm. We chose to come to Earth as mortals. Heaven is more wonderful than you can possibly imagine. I do not fear death, but I look forward to it. I did not want to return to my body when I was out of it, even though my son Colby, who I adored more than anything, was only six years old at the time, and I was about to give birth to this new baby girl that I wanted so badly. I was a young mother, and you would think I wouldn't want to leave my children, but as I stood in heaven, I did not want to go back. I thought that they would be fine without me because I was peaceful and I was happy, and I was home. But then I was told by Jesus that I needed to go back and complete things that I have covenanted or promised to do before I was born. This caused me a lot of distress because I knew heaven was my real home, and I only wanted to be there. I was free from pain, emotional and physical, and then I was shown how I would help my children and others in the future, so ultimately, I did agree to go back to my body. Tylee has visited me. She is happy and very busy. Tylee is free now from all the pains of her life. Tylee suffered horrible physical pain her whole life. I sat with Tylee in the hospital year after year after year while she screamed in pain when the morphine wasn't even enough to take away the pain of her pancreatitis. I sat there while she cried and held back her hair while she threw up, and I'm the only person on this Earth who knows how much Tylee suffered in her life. She had pain every single day. She never felt good. Her body did not work right, and I don't know if that was from complications from me dying while she was being born or something else, but she had a very difficult life. She was sexually abused by her own biological father since she was three years old, and she was forced by family court to go visit him for ten years against her will. I fought for her in court. I protected her. I tried to protect her with my whole life. I tried to protect her. I worried about her every single day. Tylee had to get her GED because she couldn't go to school every day because she never felt good. She felt sick. Nobody knows this because Tylee, like myself, tries to put on a good front, tries to be a happy person, tries to have hope in life, tries to know that she's here for a purpose and that she has an eternal purpose to be on this Earth. But I never stopped worrying about her. One of the times that Tylee came to me as a spirit after she died, she said, she commanded me, and she said to me, "Stop worrying, Mom, we are fine." She knows how I worry and how I miss her. The first time JJ visited me after he passed away, he put his arm around me, and he said to me, you didn't do anything wrong, Mom. I love you, and I know you loved me every minute of my life." JJ, Joshua Jackson, was an adult spirit, and he was very tall, and he put his arm about me; he is busy, he is engaged, he has jobs that he does there, and he is happy there. His life was short, but JJ's life was meaningful. JJ was a wonderful person and touched the lives of everyone, and I adored him every minute of his life. My eternal friend Tammy Daybell has visited me on several occasions. She came to bring me peace and comfort, and I know she is extremely busy helping her family, especially her children, and grandchildren, and I have a great love for Tammy. My beautiful children, Tylee Ashlyn and Joshua Jackson, rest safely this day in the arms of Jesus. My wonderful friend Tammy Daybell rests safely this day in the arms of Jesus, and I look forward to the day when we are all reunited, and I, too, will rest with them in the arms of *my* Jesus.

While Lori had claimed for years that she had seen Jesus, the Holy Spirit, and Moroni and that angels visited her to do her geneological computer work or that she recalled talking to Jesus in the premortality, this was the first time anyone, including her family, had heard about Lori's near-death experience. By telling the story, she put herself in the company of Chad Daybell and Julie Rowe. She, too, was a visionary who had been given special access to heaven. She, too, had visions of glory. Another hallmark of NPD is their inability to accept responsibility. She blamed the near-death experience for Tylee's lifelong struggle with pancreatitis because it couldn't just be bad luck. She claimed that the deaths she was accused of were the result of suicide, accident, and a fatal drug interaction.

Lori's diagnosis of delusional disorder, mixed type with bizarre content and hyper-religiosity, presents an interesting question. How can someone who seems so out of touch with reality also be so functional? In part, it's because delusional disorder is sometimes referred to as "partial psychosis," meaning that aside from her specific delusions, her cognitive organization and reality testing were otherwise intact. This makes her mental illness hard to distinguish from malingering. The uninformed look at her ability to function in the world and to take steps to avoid detection as an indication that she was faking her mental illness. Instead, it is one of the key distinctions between delusional disorder and other psychotic disorders;

despite the delusions, the person retains most psychosocial and reality-testing abilities. The description fits what we know about Lori. It is why so many people close to her described her as a good mother and a faithful sister in the church and were shocked to learn of her crimes.

One question that looms over this case is, when does religious belief become religious delusion? Mental health experts say, "To be classified as a religious delusion, the belief must be idiosyncratic rather than accepted within a particular culture or subculture. Strongly held beliefs that are shared within an existing religious or spiritual context would not, therefore, be considered to be religious delusions, irrespective of co-occurring psychosis. For example, believing oneself to be able to hear the voice of Jesus is not uncommon in a Christian society and thus would not in itself be classified as a religious delusion. In contrast, believing oneself to be inhabited by the warring spirits of multiple interspatial deities would be considered to be a religious delusion."[4] So, how can the layperson understand the distinction? Most would say that a great deal of the doctrine of The Church of Jesus Christ of Latter-Day Saints is idiosyncratic. The belief that after his crucifixion and ascent, Jesus Christ appeared to the Native Americans and taught them the gospel and the belief that Joseph Smith Jr. received the Book of Mormon on gold plates that he translated with the use of a seer stone are idiosyncratic to most Judeo-Christian understandings of faith. They are, however, firmly held beliefs within the LDS subculture. The Christian Bible defines faith as "the assurance of things hoped for, the conviction of things not seen."[5] Faith, by definition, requires confidence or certainty in things one can't prove. Further complicating the analysis, psychological experts also say that religious beliefs can play an essential part in the treatment of some mental illnesses.[6] This puzzle is what makes understanding and treating religious delusions so tricky. To decide whether someone is suffering from religious delusions requires that we first determine what "normal" religious beliefs are. For example, the Christian, the Hindi, and the agnostic all have vastly different ideas of what constitutes normal. This makes understanding the doctrine of The Church of Jesus Christ of Latter-Day Saints in the context of Lori's delusions critical and why this book spent so much time describing it. It also makes her treatment problematic. If, as experts suggest, religious beliefs can play an essential role in her treatment, how do clinicians encourage her reliance on faith while disabusing her of her delusions? It is one of the reasons religious delusions are one of the most difficult conditions to treat.

It is often hard to determine when a small religious division becomes a subculture, and as we've seen, definitions matter. Clearly, the Fundamental Church of Jesus Christ of Latter-Day Saints (FLDS), with their prairie dresses and their polygamous families, is a subculture of the Mormon movement. But had Chad Daybell's group also become a subculture with their belief in dark and light spirits, multiple mortal probations, and their visions of the coming tribulation? Many have classified this group as a cult, and perhaps they meet that definition too, but there is a good argument that they are a subculture of the mainstream LDS Church. While a cult suggests a certain level of organization, a subculture is more diffuse. We've seen that people who ascribe to beliefs similar to Lori and Chad's hide in plain sight among the Sunday worshippers at any LDS ward, and the neo-fundamentalist beliefs are more widespread and diffuse than the mainstream church cares to admit.

When she met Chad, Lori was looking for a less conditional kind of love within the LDS Church's highly conditional, high-demand construct. She found it in Chad and in the people who became their followers. Psychologists define religious delusions as idiosyncratic beliefs that are not accepted within a particular culture or subculture, so strongly held beliefs that are shared within an existing religious or spiritual context are not delusions.[7] In Lori's case, believing that she could receive revelations from God was not unusual in the Mormon faith. However, believing that both Jesus Christ and the angel Moroni in their physical bodies attended her sealing and gave her to Chad is likely delusional, as is believing you can control light, fire, and earthquakes.

That leaves the experts to ask, is Lori experiencing religious delusions, or does she have a firmly held religious belief and a co-occurring delusional condition? It's a question that is more than just academics estimating angels on the head of a pin because culturally acceptable religious beliefs are often seen as an essential coping strategy for people with schizophrenia. Religious beliefs can help lower the severity of a schizophrenic's symptoms, but religious delusions are linked to poor prognosis for people with psychotic disorders.[8] Experts point to something called reasoning bias. The delusions arise from and are maintained by biases and errors in evidence-based reasoning. A person reaches conclusions based on limited data and has difficulty adjusting their beliefs in response to contradictory evidence. That person has trouble considering the possibility of being mistaken and has difficulty identifying plausible alternative explanations. Those with religious delusions cannot recognize the occurrence of coincidence and tend to make causal connections where none exist.

As it did with Zulema, if a person believes they can create earthquakes, and an earthquake occurs somewhere in the world, they must have caused it. Zulema believed it because her prophet confirmed that a coincidental earthquake was her doing. Suppose the person also ascribes to a doctrine that teaches that their belief system is the only true faith, within which there is no room for question or deviation. In that case, it is easy to see how their religious delusions could become so deeply entrenched as to become untreatable. However, studies show that those with religious delusions have attitudes and levels of engagement similar to those with other delusional conditions, and the modes of treatment are the same.[9] In other words, a person can be delusional about their deeply held beliefs but can still put gas in their car and get their children off to school. It remains to be seen whether Lori's religious delusions will lessen over time, allowing her to really test her beliefs. For the moment, it appears Lori is firmly entrenched in her belief system. She believes she is a goddess and that God will deliver her so she and Chad can be together eternally and complete their mission.

18

ALL RISE REPRISE— CHAD DAYBELL'S TRIAL

It was spring again in Boise, Idaho, when the trial began for Chad Guy Daybell. It was nearly a year to the day after the start of his wife's trial on the same charges. Unlike Lori Vallow, Chad faced the death penalty. Chad's attorney, John Prior, approached the case zealously, making Chad's trial much different from Lori's. Where Lori's trial had seemed like a slow and agonizing march to a guilty verdict, John Prior planned and executed a vigorous defense.

Also different from the year before, spring came early to Boise, treating the waiting spectators to chilly but sunny days as the ornamental trees lining Front Street burst into lacey white billows of flowers. There was less buzz outside the Ada County Courthouse, fewer television cameras, and fewer people milling around. Unlike Lori's trial, Chad's proceedings were livestreamed. The court rebuffed offers from Court TV and East Idaho News to provide a camera pool and opted to use their own system, raising many public complaints about the lack of quality images and sound. Still, so many trial watchers opted to observe the case from home that by the start of the third week of the anticipated eight-to-ten-week trial, the court did away with the cumbersome registration system and admitted trial watchers to the courtroom on a first-come, first-served basis.

The feeling inside the courtroom was different, too. The atmosphere felt less tense and more matter-of-fact. It was more like a run-of-the-mill trial and less like a trial of the century. The jurors in Chad's trial seemed less emotional than Lori's. There were few tears as photographs of the victims were displayed, and no piercing looks of shock or disgust directed at Chad as the details of the case unfolded. Instead, the jurors remained mostly stoic as they paid close attention and took notes.

The prosecution team had also changed since Lori Vallow's trial. Fremont County prosecutor Lindsey Blake still led the team, with Madison County prosecutor Rob Wood appearing as a special prosecutor. Missouri attorney and paid consultant Rachel Smith left the case, and Assistant Attorney General Ingrid Batey joined just before the trial began. Rocky Wixom from Lindsey Blake's office rounded out the team.

John Prior, whose office is in Meridian, Idaho, a Boise suburb, appeared in Rexburg with Chad for the first time on June 12, 2020, three days after Chad was arrested; Chad had privately retained Prior. The court entered a non-dissemination order, restricting what the attorneys could say in public, but it became clear from Prior's filings and comments during hearings that he believed in Chad. Prior regularly made the three-hundred-mile drive from Meridian to Rexburg to meet with his client, spending hours reviewing thousands of pages of discovery with Chad. As interest in the Daybell case exploded in the media, it took over Prior's practice, sharply curtailing his ability to accept other cases.

Death penalty cases are expensive. The cost of legal fees, investigation, and experts can run into the millions. When an attorney is retained, the payment method is private between client and lawyer. With all of his and Lori's legal fees, Chad's available cash was soon expended. His only remaining asset was his home, and in May 2021, he transferred ownership of the property to John Prior in lieu of attorney fees. It's unclear whether Daybell got financial support from other sources, such as followers or family.

Then, after nearly four years as Chad's attorney and just weeks before the start of the trial, Prior filed a motion asking the court to permit him to withdraw from Chad's case so public defenders could be appointed. The move shocked both court watchers and the judge. During a hearing on the motion, Prior pointed out that a year earlier, during a sealed proceeding, the judge had declared Chad indigent and authorized the appointment of a death penalty qualified state public defender at the state's expense if John Prior could find one. As discussed in earlier chapters, there was a shortage of available public defenders, especially highly skilled ones. The chronic underfunding and underpayment of lawyers who do public defense led experienced lawyers to leave the field and new lawyers to spurn it in favor of better-paying opportunities. The result was that a year later, John Prior was still unable to find a death penalty qualified attorney willing or able to join his team. Prior said he hoped if he withdrew entirely, the state would be forced to appoint two death penalty qualified attorneys for Chad. Of course, appointing new attorneys might delay Chad's trial by as much as two more years.

During this hearing, John Prior attempted to thread a legal needle. He wanted to use the fact that he was no longer being paid as justification to withdraw—not because he needed the money but because he felt that, alone, he couldn't do a proper job for Chad. Prior said, "I don't desire to get off this case; regardless of Mr. Daybell's financial situation, I want to stay on this case. I could care less about the money. Mr. Daybell wants me to stay on this case."

Judge Boyce responded, "That's not really what your motion says, though, Mr. Prior. Your motion says you want off the case because it's going to cost too much for you to work . . . the work it's going to take for you to get it through trial without compensation."

"That's correct, Judge."

"This is an important issue for me today. Are you wanting to withdraw because you think you deserve to be paid for the work you do, which I understand, but when I'm considering the standards under rule 44.1, which is discretionary under part (a) on a leave to withdraw, I may allow you to withdraw for good cause and what I'm trying to determine is, do you want to withdraw because you're not being paid enough to continue through trial or are you seeking to withdraw because you're not going to be prepared and ready for trial?"

"Judge, the situation is this, when I say to the court, and I'm saying this in all sincerity, I don't need to get paid for this case. The concern is this, at least at this perspective, Judge, I'm going to be doing this by myself, and it's going to expend a lot of resources and a lot of time that I'm not going to be able to commit to other projects or other situations. Obviously I'm not taking on other obligations because of the case. Do I want to get paid? Everybody wants to get paid for what they do. Am I making that the only reason to withdraw? Well, it's twofold. Do I want to get paid for the work I've done in this case? I do. I'd like to get compensated for the next two and a half months and the two months of the trial. I do want to get paid, and Mr. Daybell and I had a discussion about this. Mr. Daybell expressed to me that he doesn't feel comfortable with me continuing in this case if I'm not getting compensated for the work. And I advised him and told him I don't need to get paid, I'm willing to do that. If I'm not being clear, judge, I'm willing to do it . . . but it's twofold Judge. The only way that Mr. Daybell is going to . . . or the only way the court can order Mr. Daybell additional counsel is if I withdraw, and that's the only situation that would cause the court to say Mr. Prior is granted leave to withdraw because he's not being paid . . . If the court denies the motion, I want to make it clear that I'm prepared to go forward and push this case to the end." Prior stressed that while he wanted to be compensated, he acknowledged that it had been his choice not to become death penalty certified by the state of Idaho and that he would not harbor any resentment against Chad Daybell if the judge ordered him to remain on the case.

Prior tripped himself up in his own tangled argument so much that by the end of the hearing, Judge Stephen Boyce declined to permit Prior to withdraw. The judge confirmed his order that if Prior could find help, the state would pay for it, but the trial started on April 1, 2024, without co-counsel. Chad appeared to be helping keep track of trial exhibits.

As the trial began, Detective (now Lieutenant) Ray Hermosillo was the prosecution's first law enforcement witness, as he had been twice before.

Hermosillo provided the jury with an overview of the case. During the weeks of testimony, the jury heard from Melanie Gibb and her estranged husband, David Warwick, Lori's adult son, Colby Ryan, Zulema Pastenes, Melani and Ian Pawlowski, Emma and Joe Murray, Garth Daybell, Brandon Boudreaux, a local realtor, and the funeral director that took care of Tammy Daybell's arrangements, in addition to a stream of law enforcement officers and other experts. Both Brandon and Colby choked up as they talked about Tylee and JJ. Chad Daybell's mother, Sheila, and his sister-in-law, Heather, were also called by the prosecution.

As he had in Lori's trial, Hermosillo recounted the story of the morning the children's bodies were found. The first witness to provide previously unheard evidence was Detective Eric Wheeler. Wheeler had been a patrol cop in a marked car on the morning of June 9, 2020. He'd been positioned outside Chad's home and had heard two messages over the radio that were so close in time they nearly ran together. First was the message that human remains had been found on Chad's property, followed nearly immediately by a direction to stop Chad Daybell as he sped away from his daughter Emma's home across the street. When Wheeler stopped Chad, they were still in view of the backyard where the search operation was underway. Wheeler placed Chad in the back of his police cruiser, hands cuffed in front of him. Seconds later, Emma arrived and was told she could talk to her father. A camera in the car recorded their interaction. A tearful Emma told Chad she followed him because she didn't want him to be alone. Chad gave Emma his wallet, and they discussed what she needed to do to handle his financial obligations. He told her which accounts had money and where to find $9,000 in cash he had stored in the house. He told her he wanted her to keep putting money on Lori's commissary account and pointed out his Telemate card. Emma told him she had her own Telemate account because she had already been talking to Lori in jail. Telemate is the phone system the Madison County Jail uses for inmates. Twice during the conversation, he told Emma he didn't think he would be coming home. He was right.

As they had done in Lori's trial, the prosecution painted a vivid picture of Lori and Chad's affair through text messages. On August 11, 2019, exactly a month after Charles Vallow was murdered in Lori's mirrored living room, she sent a text to Chad: "I'm so alone without you!! It is devastating!"

Chad replied: "I feel so alone, too. We are surrounded by telestial relatives that are simply obstacles. I'm so sick of it!"

Lori said: "Me too!! What is it that you really want?"

Chad's response: "I want to be with you. That is my greatest hope and dream. I would happily join you tomorrow if it felt like heaven would not strike us down." The jury had to be wondering about a God that would strike them down for being together while Chad was married but turn a blind eye to murder.

Law enforcement noted how Lori and Chad manipulated each other and how that mutual manipulation spurred them to act to remove the obstacles they complained about. FBI Special Agent Doug Hart analyzed thousands of messages from Lori's iCloud accounts. Her original account, Lori4style, went back years. A newer account, Lollytime, was named for her sister who died in infancy. Just four days after Charles Vallow was murdered, on July 15, 2019, Chad sent Lori a text: "You are my wonderful best friend that I can't live without."

Lori's response: "And yet you are. So sad."

A few days later, on July 22, 2019, Chad said, "Going with Garth in an hour to see The Other Side of Heaven 2 . . ."

Lori said, "U will enjoy the scenery . . . looks like Kauai a lot." Then she texted, "Hopefully, we will be there someday soon together."

Chad replied, "That is the plan." As law enforcement sifted through message after message, a clear picture emerged. Lori and Chad had a plan; it was a plan that didn't include spouses, a difficult teenager, or caring for a special needs child.

When Lori told Chad she and her niece Melani wanted to visit Rexburg in August 2019, Chad told her he couldn't see her because he had a family trip with Tammy planned for the same weekend. The disagreement resulted in Lori and Chad's first fight. Lori went silent for a full day until a desperate Chad told her that the angels were so angry with her silence that he couldn't guarantee the spiritual protections he put in place around her wouldn't be disrupted. Once Lori responded that she loved him, he promised to restore her spiritual shields. Lori then sent him a selfie wearing a low-cut yellow swimsuit. On August 11, 2019, Chad responded, "I can't take much more. So trapped."

Lori's answer: "R we supposed to wait forever?"

Chad's case was different from Lori's in another way; while Lori Vallow was only charged with conspiring to murder Tammy, Chad was also charged with her murder. Only Chad knows for sure what happened in the Daybell home that night, so the prosecution had to dive deeply into the circumstances surrounding Tammy's death. Witness after witness came forward to testify that Tammy was a healthy, vibrant woman of forty-nine who took high-intensity exercise classes. Friends and colleagues remembered her fondly as someone always ready to help them. No one except Chad and his children said Tammy had been sick.

Several witnesses recounted what Chad had told them about Tammy's death, and each story was slightly different, depending on who Chad told. To some, Chad insisted he'd awakened early when he felt Tammy roll off their bed, but that wasn't his only version. In all of the renditions, Tammy had been coughing and had vomited at least once, despite the report from both the coroner and the medical examiner that Tammy had undigested food in her stomach. In one version, Chad was working in his office when Tammy came in at about 10:00 P.M. and said she was feeling better and going to bed. In that version, Chad worked until about 1:00 A.M., and when he came to bed, he found Tammy half off the bed and cold to the touch. In another version, he left his office and came to bed when Tammy came to tell him she was feeling better because he was worried about her, then woke in the morning to find her dead. It was clear his explanation changed depending on the listener and his whim.

Steve Schultz had known the Daybell family all his life. Like Chad, he grew up in Springville, Utah. He and Chad had been neighbors and friends with much in common as adults. Chad was the sexton of the Evergreen Cemetery in Springville, and Steve was the funeral director at the local mortuary. When Chad lived in Springville, he and Steve saw each other frequently and sometimes had long conversations while they waited for funerals to finish at the cemetery. Steve was shocked to learn of Tammy's death, but he wasn't surprised when Chad called on him a few hours after Tammy's passing to ask if he would help with her final arrangements. Steve also knew Tammy's family, and asked her brother-in-law, Jason Gwilliam, to ride along with him as he made the four-hour drive to Rexburg to help Chad with the arrangements and pick up Tammy's body. When he arrived on Sunday, October 20, 2019, Tammy's body had already been picked up by the local mortuary in Rexburg and embalmed. Steve sat with Chad at his home to work out the arrangements. He was caught off guard by the speed at which Chad wanted Tammy buried. Chad asked for the burial to take place the following day in Springville. Steve cautioned Chad that he wasn't sure they could make everything happen so quickly, but Chad was adamant that he "didn't want to drag it out." They settled on having Tammy's viewing the next day and her burial on Tuesday morning. Chad and his children traveled to Springville for the funeral and were back in Rexburg before sundown.

When Central Elementary School principal Richard Garner found out their beloved school librarian had died, he asked her husband when the memorial would be. He was dismayed to learn that nothing was planned in Rexburg to honor and remember Tammy. When Garner proposed having a memorial, Chad was resistant; the funeral was in Springville, Utah, and he didn't want anyone to be inconvenienced by a memorial in Rexburg. Garner took it upon himself to organize the event to remember Tammy. He obtained permission from the school district to close his small kindergarten through third grade school so that students, parents, and colleagues could have time to honor Tammy. Garner remembered Tammy as someone who always did the extras. He said when Tammy noticed the children in the computer lab were being distracted by their peers, she made curtains for the windows. While Tammy's Rexburg memorial was going on, Lori Vallow waited in her apartment, searching Amazon for beach wedding dresses.

Craig Huff, another of Chad's friends from the Rexburg ward of The Church of Jesus Christ of Latter-day Saints, testified that Chad told him about a minor miracle that had happened recently. Tammy had always managed the Daybell household, including their finances. She had also been in charge of the business end of Chad's now-defunct Spring Creek Books publishing company. Chad told Huff that he had miraculously managed to get all the usernames and passwords for their accounts just a week before.

Even with four years to prepare and Lori Vallow's trial already behind them, there were still legal surprises in the trial. Most laypersons don't fully understand what a mistrial is or how one can be caused. Mistrials are rare and occur when either side makes an error after the jury has been seated that can't be fixed by the judge giving the jury a curative instruction. Two incidents occurred that made both sides nervous. The first was when John Prior mistakenly projected a document on the screen in the courtroom. The document appeared to be some of his notes. The print was small, and it was unclear whether the jurors could even read it. Nonetheless, it prompted the judge to give the jury an instruction to disregard whatever they may have seen and led to the court clerk taking control of the courtroom screen. Each time Prior wanted to display an image, he would have to ask the clerk to put the document on the screen. As the trial went on, Prior's annoyance at the restriction became evident.

The second occurrence came when John Prior was cross-examining Ron Arnold. Arnold was a Rexburg real estate agent. He testified about being asked by Chad to help with subdividing the Daybell property. He explained that the property could not be subdivided, but an additional dwelling could be located on the property. He said he and Chad had discussed the possibility of putting a mobile home on the Daybell property for Chad and Lori to live in. The prosecution suggested Chad's intent was that the site preparation would disguise or destroy any evidence located in the yard. On cross-examination, John Prior asked Arnold about the size of the property. As Arnold became more annoyed with Prior, he clapped back, "You own it; how many acres is it?" Prior tried to appear unruffled as he asked for a sidebar conference, but the cameras caught Prosecutor Rob Wood openly smirking at Prior's embarrassment. Once again, the judge instructed the jury to disregard the information.

On April 26, 2024, during a weekend break from Chad's trial, people from all over gathered in Idaho Falls, Idaho, to honor Tylee and JJ at a memorial. JJ's pawpaw, Larry Woodcock, said, "My insides tremble with both sadness and joy." Large photographs of each child flanked the podium, each encircled with fresh pink and purple spring flowers. Hundreds attended in person, while thousands watched a live stream of the program. Friends had said Tylee wanted to be famous—but not like this. Lori Vallow's cousin, Megan Connor, sang several songs during the ceremony. Lori's uncle, Rex Connor, and her brother, Adam Cox, were also in attendance. It was a welcome break from the unremitting seriousness of the trial. At the event, in a venue filled with flowers, Tylee and JJ were remembered with fond and sometimes funny stories while a looped slideshow of photographs ran in the background. For several years, Tylee's and JJ's bodies had remained in limbo. The attorneys could not agree on the release of the children's remains, and they were held in storage as evidence. Then, in October 2023, the lawyers stipulated to the release of JJ's body. In December 2023, they followed suit and released Tylee's remains. For many, it felt as if the past four years were one long winter, but finally, spring had come, and both Larry and Kay Woodcock seemed lighter after the memorial event.

As the trial unfolded, there was no one in the courtroom to support Chad. His children had been subpoenaed by John Prior but could have attended because, as Tammy's immediate family, they weren't subject to the witness exclusion order. Chad seemed surprised when his brother, Matt, appeared in the courtroom on the fifteenth day of the trial. Matt made it clear he was only there to encourage his wife, Heather, during her testimony and to support Kay and Larry Woodcock and Tammy's sister, Samantha Gwilliam.

The prosecution called Chad's mother, Sheila Daybell, to testify. It is hard to imagine what a mother must feel when called upon to testify against her own son in a murder trial. She told the jury that she had seen Tammy just six days before her death when she and her husband, Jack, were in Rexburg for a family baby blessing. She said Tammy seemed healthy and fine when she saw her, which is why Tammy's death a few days later came as such a shock. She also told the story of how she met Lori Vallow. In mid-November, just a month after Tammy Daybell's death, Sheila and her husband, Jack, met Chad for dinner at a restaurant in Idaho Falls. It was there that they first met Lori. Sheila said Chad didn't say much about their relationship, but Lori had a lot to say about it. Sheila noticed Lori and Chad were wearing matching rings and asked them if they were engaged. No, Chad said, they were married. Sheila and Jack were stunned by the speed at which they had married. Lori told them she had been married before and that her husband had recently died of a heart attack. As Tylee and JJ decomposed in Chad's backyard, Lori said she'd also had a daughter who had died. There was no mention of a young, autistic son.

On cross-examination, John Prior continued to portray Lori Vallow as the driving force in the relationship. Prior got Sheila to say that Chad was an introvert and that Tammy was similar, while Lori, in contrast, was outgoing and persuasive. Sheila agreed that Chad "was not a man of the world." Sheila also said Chad seemed genuinely upset on the day Tammy died.

Heather Daybell, Chad's sister-in-law, was one of the most anticipated witnesses against Chad. Heather and Matt had lived in Rexburg most of their married life when Chad announced he was moving his family from Springville to Rexburg. His intent made Heather nervous. Chad was predicting the end times as early as 2015. Chad said the worst of the destruction from earthquakes and natural disasters would occur in Salt Lake City, forcing the locus of the church to shift to Rexburg. He began telling them about his visions that Heather and Matt's beautiful riverside home and property would become a haven for displaced Saints, and that their home would become a temple. In a move that Chad would repeat in other situations, he appeared to assume that if God wanted their property, Chad would be free to take it.

Heather was concerned that Chad would be moving into their neighborhood and, consequently, their LDS ward, and that he would openly discuss his strange brand of Mormonism. For over fifteen years, Heather and Matt had built a life in Rexburg, a life that included Matt's thriving occupational therapy practice and Heather's church calling as the stake president of the relief society. They each had reputations as community leaders. Even with Matt and Heather's direct request that they not move into their ward, Chad and Tammy bought a house just a half mile away and began attending church with Heather and Matt.

Before long, Chad was speaking openly around Rexburg about his visions and predictions that the end times were imminent. Heather tried to raise the alarm, both to her church leaders and to Tammy. Case agent Lieutenant Vince Kaaiakamanu testified about text messages he found in Chad's chats and Tammy's emails. Kaaiakamanu believed the messages proved that "Tammy, along with Mark, Emma, Garth, Seth, and Leah, have knowledge of the belief of light and dark people that Chad talked about and believed." When Mark's camera didn't work on a Zoom call from South Africa, Tammy replied in a message that Mark's camera was cursed, but Dad was removing it. In an email, Mark asked if anything notable had been found when they "body coded" him. Body coding is a form of energy work often associated with the work of Dr. Bradley Nelson and his book *The Emotion Code*. Body coding is the highest level of training offered by Dr. Nelson's company, Discover Healing. Tammy replied, "You has [*sic*] a lot of weapons, negative cords, and curses, plus trapped emotions. We cleared out quite a bit, will do that more regularly for you."

In a thread that Emma was part of, Chad wrote, "Mom and I taught 12-year-old Sunday school yesterday. Canyon Scott's actions confirmed he is a 4.2 dark."

Emma answered, "I like Canyon, though."

Chad replied, "I will enjoy watching his growth to world terror and domination."

The emails begin to explain why Chad's children continued their loyalty to him, even after the murder of their mother. Heather testified that she became even more concerned when Chad began trying to recruit Heather and Matt's children. Still, when Heather tried to alert their church leadership to Chad's unsettling beliefs, the bishop and stake president discounted her concerns. Chad's father called Heather a "pot stirrer."

There were other stories about Chad's control over his wife and children. Chad openly talked about how, when he thought Tammy was playing video games too much, he told her he'd received a message from her dead grandmother telling her to stop wasting her time on the computer and focus on her church work. When Chad made the decision to move to Rexburg, although she was initially resistant, Tammy said she prayed about it and received confirmation from God that the move was right.

Heather testified about Tammy's funeral. She and Matt had been at a work conference in Las Vegas. When Chad told them about Tammy's death and that the funeral would be in two days, they asked if he could wait until they and one of Chad's other brothers, who was also traveling, could return. Chad said no, that he wanted to get it done. When Heather asked if there would be an autopsy, Chad said no, because the coroner had already determined that Tammy died when she vomited and aspirated in her sleep. This would be only one of several causes of death Chad Daybell claimed. Heather and Matt left the conference early and headed for Rexburg. Heather said the funeral program was odd. A lifelong church member and leader, she'd never heard an LDS funeral begin with a hymn called "Put Your Shoulder to the Wheel." The chorus, "Put your shoulder to the wheel; push along, Do your duty with a heart full of song, We all have work; let no one shirk. Put your shoulder to the wheel,"[1] seemed a strange sentiment to remember a beloved wife and mother.

A month later, Heather heard from Tammy's friend, Alice Gilbert, that Chad had remarried and that his children were struggling with his decision. Heather reached out to her nieces and nephews, assuring them she was there for them. Chad called Heather and angrily told her she had been a problem for him his entire life. When she again asked during that call what had happened to Tammy, Chad told Heather Tammy's death was the result of a pulmonary embolism because she had gained forty pounds. In Chad and Lori's later recorded call with Melanie Gibb, Chad was quick to blame a sister-in-law for raising suspicion about how Tammy had died. He could have been talking about either Heather or Tammy's sister, Samantha Gwilliam. Chad had already announced that not only was Samantha a 3D, but the demon occupying her body was a multiple creation.

When John Prior took over cross-examination, his approach to Heather Daybell was uncharacteristically cautious. Prior asked Heather about the time she reported Chad for using the church property as a place to write during the week, trying to make her appear spiteful. Heather replied that the church did not permit its property to be used for commercial purposes.

As they had done in Lori Vallow's trial, both Alice and Todd Gilbert testified. They told the jury how close Alice had been to Tammy Daybell and how, just a few weeks after Tammy's death, Chad had introduced them to Lori and shown them photos of their white beach wedding in Kauai. They told Alice Lori was a widow whose husband had died of a heart attack. They also said Lori had a daughter who had recently died. Alice told the jury that when Chad returned from Hawaii after Lori's arrest, he asked them to pledge their property to secure Lori Vallow's million-dollar bail. Of course, Alice and Todd had heard that Lori's children were missing and called Chad to ask about them. Chad confirmed that the missing children were Lori's but assured her that they were fine; it was a custody dispute that would soon be cleared up. When Alice asked about Lori's daughter, he denied he had ever told Alice that Lori's daughter had died. Alice pressed him, asking how a young woman at the start of her life could simply disappear. Chad answered, "She didn't like people and didn't like me." His use of the past tense was hard to miss.

As it had at Lori's trial, the locations of Lori, Chad, and Alex Cox's electronic devices were of interest in Chad's trial. The information, while crucial, was also often dry and highly technical. FBI agents Ricky Wright and Nick Balance were the prosecution's experts who presented the results of the Cellular Analysis Survey Team's (CAST) findings. On September 9, 2019, the day after Tylee Ryan was last seen, there were several unusual device readings. Alex was at Lori's between 2:42 A.M. and 3:37 A.M. After that, he returned to his own apartment. It was the only time they found evidence of Alex being at Lori's apartment in the middle of the night. The following morning, between 7:20 A.M. and 8:03 A.M. there was a flurry of text messages and a phone call from Chad's phone located on his property to Lori at her apartment. Chad also called Alex at 8:11 A.M. At 8:49 A.M., Alex's device indicated he was at his apartment, but by 9:15 A.M., he was located at Chad's property. From then until 11:46 A.M., Alex's device was in Chad's backyard near the area where Tylee's remains were later found. While Chad and Alex were in the yard, Chad sent several text messages and had one voice call with Lori, whose phone indicated she was in her apartment. The text messages themselves were not recoverable. After Alex left Chad's house, presumably after helping dismember and burn Tylee's body, he stopped at Del Taco to pick up lunch.

Likewise, the location of cellular devices on September 23, 2019, the day after the last known sighting of JJ Vallow, was of interest. Between 3:55 A.M. and 8:35 A.M., Lori and Chad exchanged many text messages. Then, at 9:25 A.M., Chad called Alex, likely telling him Tammy had gone to work. At 9:45 A.M., Alex began driving toward Chad's property. His device was located on Chad's property between 9:55 A.M. and 10:20 A.M. near where JJ's body was discovered. The timing suggests Chad was the one who prepared JJ's grave and that Alex delivered JJ's body and helped fill in the burial place.

After seven weeks, the prosecution rested, and the defense began their case in chief. John Prior's first witness was Emma Daybell. Like Melani Pawlowski and Zulema Pastenes, Emma had radically changed her looks. Melani Pawlowski, like Lori and Melanie Gibb, had been blond when the case began, but Melanie appeared at Chad's trial with long dark hair and wearing heavy-framed white glasses. On the other hand, Zulema had lightened her hair since Lori's trial the year before, going from a dark reddish-brown to blond. Emma's transformation was the most troubling. When Chad was arrested, Emma's hair was short and dark, and she, among Chad's five children, most resembled her mother. When she appeared to testify on Chad's behalf, her hair was long and very light blond. Sadly, she looked more like Lori Vallow than her mother, Tammy.

John Prior asked Emma many questions about Tammy's health, fitness, and use of natural supplements. Emma said Tammy took colloidal silver.

She said her mother added it to water, making it taste metallic. The Mayo Clinic reports that silver is not an essential mineral for the human body, and the claims that it cures everything from cancer to HIV and COVID-19 are unsubstantiated. They report that, in general, colloidal silver does not cause health problems, but if it builds up in the body tissues, it may cause the skin, whites of the eyes, and gums to turn a blue-gray. In very rare cases, it can cause kidney damage and seizures.[2] If you recall, extensive toxicology testing was done on Tammy's remains, including for metals. Neither of the medical examiners who participated in Tammy's autopsy reported any overall discoloration of Tammy's skin, eyes, or gums. The only notable skin changes were due to bruising and postmortem lividity. Emma also said her mother bruised easily and used arnica gel. Arnica is a plant claimed to help with osteoarthritis and muscle pain. Medical experts dispute its efficacy. The primary side effect of using arnica topically is skin irritation. Consuming arnica orally may cause gastric symptoms, including diarrhea and vomiting. There is no indication Tammy took arnica orally.

Emma disputed that Tammy was physically fit, saying Tammy did not train for a 5K road race but was a race volunteer who may have walked across the finish line to encourage some lagging participants. She also disputed that Tammy had been participating in fitness classes for the past year and said she and Tammy usually stayed in the back of the room, where they would not be noticed if they stopped participating. She reported that Tammy was often short of breath and had fainting spells.

We also gained insight into Chad and Tammy's relationship and their brand of Mormonism from the testimony of Emma and her brother, Garth. Emma said Chad and Tammy's views were more fundamentalist than hers and that she thought her mother leaned even more fundamentalist than her father. Emma also admitted that she sometimes believed in her parents' teachings and relied on their ability to do energy work, muscle testing, and castings. Emma testified that Tammy tried to help Emma with her anxiety. She said she had suffered from anxiety most of her life and that she told her parents she felt like there was a being with her, an actual person trying to control her. She said her father cast it out using his priesthood power, and she instantly felt better. John Prior attempted to introduce *The Emotion Code*, but the judge did not allow its admission. But he allowed Prior to question Emma about Tammy's energy work, which Prior bootstrapped into the necessary questions. Emma said her mother learned about muscle testing and reflexology from Tammy's parents and through later classes. Emma said Tammy was more skilled at using the tools learned in the book *The Emotion Code* by Bradley Nelson, an LDS chiropractor who has made a fortune offering a three-tier system of classes through his company, Discover Healing. Body coding is the second-highest tier of training offered by Dr. Nelson. To become a certified Body Code practitioner, you must have completed the prerequisite first-tier Emotion Code training for $997, then complete the Body Code Practitioner training for $1497, and subscribe to the Body Code System computer application. Anyone who has read *Educated* by Tara Westover will see the parallels. Emma said her mother also rated people as dark or light and assigned them numerical dark or light ratings.

In one of the most stunning statements, Emma contended that it was she who searched the computer in her parents' home for wind direction and speed on September 9, 2019, the day Tylee Ryan's body was burned in her father's backyard. "I saw a rainstorm. We were planning an outdoor event, and I wanted to know if those clouds were coming our way . . . The weather forecast for where we live in Rexburg is sometimes inaccurate because we don't live in Rexburg, so I was trying to be an amateur meteorologist, and the wind, the weather app said it was coming from the south-southwest, and I didn't know if that meant it was coming or going from the south-southwest, so I did a Google search on the desktop computer that my parents kept in the living room. That would have been typical at that time. I was late to getting a smart phone." September 9, 2019, was a Monday. The Sugar City school district typically begins classes in late August, so that day was a workday for Emma. She didn't explain why she was at her parents' home during that time.

John Prior then steered his direct examination of Emma to the day Tammy died. He told Emma to let him know if she needed a break to compose herself or to get a tissue. Emma was entirely collected during her testimony; her answers were emotionless and robotic. Emma was ironically stoic when she described her father as emotionally "out of control" on the morning of her mother's death. "He may not have had the same romantic relationship with my mother," Emma said, "but I know he valued her as a person, and to see her die was very traumatic." Chad had never claimed he saw Tammy die, only that he found her dead. Many trial watchers wondered if the jury would pick up on the apparent contradiction.

Emma's testimony about when she learned of Chad's affair with Lori conflicted with itself. At one point, she said she only learned of Chad's affair with Lori Vallow after he was arrested, but on June 9, 2020, the day of Chad's arrest, he and Lori were already married, and Emma said she already had a Telemate account so she could talk to Lori in jail. Emma also said during a 2021 news interview that she knew her father had an emotional affair with Lori. In her trial testimony, she said that she didn't learn her father's affair was physical until after 2021.

Chad's son, Garth, was the next witness for the defense. He testified that Tammy sometimes became short of breath and experienced occasional dizziness when she had been kneeling for a while. He said that on the night of her death, he came home from his job as an eighth-grade science teacher. He said his mother said she didn't feel well, and he drove into Rexburg and bought McDonald's for Tammy, Chad, and himself so Tammy wouldn't need to cook dinner. Later in the evening, Garth says he left for his seasonal job as a scare character at the Haunted Mill. He testified that he got home a little after 1:00 A.M., walked past his parents' open bedroom door, saw their forms in the bed, and heard his father snoring. He said he got on his computer and watched YouTube videos until about 3:30 A.M. He awoke around 6:00 A.M. when he thought he might have heard a thump, and then his father calling his name and saying he needed help. Garth rushed into the room, where he found his mother half off the bed with her feet still tangled in the sheets. When he picked her up and put her back on the bed, she was cold and pale, and her lips were blue.

Garth also said that on September 9, 2019, the day Tylee Ryan's body was burned and buried, he came home from work in the late afternoon and found his dad in work clothes. Chad told him he'd shot a big raccoon and showed him where he had buried it behind the silver shed. Garth said he'd never seen raccoons during the day, only at night, and that every time they killed a raccoon, it was buried behind the silver shed, never in the pet cemetery.

John Prior asked Garth about his experience with the grand jury. The grand jury was convened for a second session nearly a year after Chad and Lori's indictment. Because of the secret nature of grand juries, the public had never been informed of the purpose for the second grand jury session, but we found out at trial. Garth said he was called before the second grand jury and pressured to change his story about what happened the night Tammy died. He claimed he was threatened with perjury if he didn't change his story, but he also said his story didn't change. The prosecution called rebuttal witnesses who revealed Garth told more than one story about that night. He told his then-girlfriend, now wife, Kara Briggs Daybell, that he found Tammy on the couch but claimed later at trial that information was misconstrued, that he actually saw her on the couch earlier in the evening as he left for work. There was also testimony that less than a week after her death, Garth told his friend Mackay Abegglen that he found his mother in bed dead, and his father was gone. Garth said he did not know his father had designated his mother as a dark entity named Viola until later.

John Prior called Emma's husband, Joseph Murray. Joe became somewhat prickly with the prosecutor when cross-examined. He appeared especially disdainful of law enforcement and said he believed one of the officers was intentionally inaccurate in reporting the incident with the paintball gun. He insisted he and Emma were there when Tammy pulled up a picture of a paintball gun on the computer and showed it to the officer. The officer denied he ever got past the front entry of the Daybell home that night and denied he was ever shown a picture. Joe complained that Detective Hermosillo drove by the property frequently. He said he didn't see any reason for Hermosillo to be still driving by the property after the bodies were found. The prosecutor asked, "You're not a law enforcement officer, are you?"

To which Murry retorted, "Absolutely not. I'd rather choose any other profession." Joe Murray resisted any suggestion that the family had made mistakes in their reports to the sheriff.

Emma testified about an incident where she was at the same gym as Hermosillo and thought he was eavesdropping on her conversation with a friend. Emma later refused to meet with law enforcement when they tried to inform her of the results of Tammy's autopsy because she feared the meeting would be used to elicit information from her. Emma insisted on receiving a copy of the autopsy, which law enforcement declined to release for fear it would be made public and jeopardize the case. It was evident from their testimony that Emma, Garth, and Joe were all suspicious of law enforcement and suspected they were trying to entrap them, which seems an unusual reaction from victims with nothing to hide.

John Prior presented several expert witnesses, none of whom gave Prior his Perry Mason moment. Dr. Kathy Raven is a forensic pathologist from the San Francisco Bay Area. She concluded from a review of Tammy Daybell's autopsy that there was no anatomical or toxicological reason for Tammy's death. She went on to say the bruising on Tammy's body was "nonspecific" and that the cause of death should not have been homicide. Instead, Dr. Raven opined that the cause should have been listed as "undetermined." Dr. Raven didn't even mention the foamy pink sputum that was the central reason for Dr. Eric Christensen's autopsy conclusion that Tammy had been asphyxiated. The state did not cross-examine Dr. Raven on the subject of the foam; rather, they decided to hold it for rebuttal and closing argument. During their rebuttal case, the prosecution recalled Dr. Eric Christensen, the Utah medical examiner who completed Tammy's autopsy. He testified about the thoroughness of the autopsy, all the collateral sources he reviewed, and the significance of the bloody sputum he observed, essentially negating Dr. Raven's analysis of his work. Several of Prior's witnesses were more fizzle than bang, including Reegan Price, who lived across from Chad and Tammy and next door to Emma and Joe. She reported that she heard a gunshot from the direction of Chad's property but, on the stand, could not recall when she'd heard it.

The defense offered testimony from Patrick Eller, a forensic data analyst and examiner who is the CEO of Metadata Forensics. Eller reviewed both the geofencing information and the location data from all the seized phones. Geofencing is the gathering of information about what devices were in a particular location during a specific time. Law enforcement sends a warrant to Google, which returns the information anonymously, identifying the users by a user code assigned by Google. Once law enforcement reviews the data, they send Google a warrant for the specific user information for devices that meet their refined search criteria. The September 9, 2019, geofence warrant returned nineteen devices near the Daybell property that morning. When Eller asked law enforcement why they didn't request user information for all the devices, he was told that Google limits the number of users they would identify, but Eller said he had not heard of Google doing that before. Alex Cox's device was caught in the geofence, but nothing in the geofence evidence from September 19, 2019, returned Chad Daybell's device as being near his property. Lori's geolocation data proved she was in Hawaii. John Prior went painstakingly through the location data on all the various devices to establish Lori, Chad, and Alex's locations on each critical day. Eller said that on the day of Tammy's death and the days the children's bodies were buried, Chad Daybell's telephone was not on the Daybell property; however, it was significant that Chad's phone also didn't locate him anywhere else during the relevant time. Officer David Stubbs would explain during the prosecution's rebuttal case.

The data on the night Tammy died was enlightening.

Time range (all P.M.)	Sender/Receiver	No. of Messages/calls
6:13–8:24	Between Chad and Lori	6 texts
6:56–8:24	Between Lori and Alex	6 texts
8:44	To Alex from Chad	1 text
8:47–9:04	Between Lori and Alex	12 texts
8:52	To Lori from Chad	1 text
9:35	To Chad from Alex	1 text
9:59–11:12	Between Lori and Zulema	11 texts

10:07	Alex arrives at the LDS church 2.6 miles from Chad's home	
10:12–10:28	Between Chad and Alex	4 texts
10:22	Tammy is playing games on her phone	
10:23–10:54	Between Chad and Alex	10 texts
11:28	A single image is deleted from Tammy's phone	
11:34–11:35	Between Chad and Alex	2 texts
11:46	Alex Cox leaves the church and drives to a hotel in Idaho Falls (about thirty minutes away)	
11:53–12:09	Alex calls Lori	
12:10	Lori to Zulema	1 text
12:35	Chad to Lori	1 text

The critical time was while Alex's phone was at the church near Chad's house. It appeared Alex left his phone in his car and walked the 2.6 miles to Chad's house. Between 10:54 P.M. and 11:34 P.M., everyone's phones go quiet. We can surmise that by 11:28 P.M., Tammy is dead, and someone else deleted an image from her phone. At 11:34 P.M., Chad and Alex text again. How does this square with the testimony we heard on rebuttal from Garth's friend and coworker Mackay Abegglen? He said Garth told him that on the night Tammy died, he came home and found her hanging off the bed. Her skin was pale, and her lips were blue, and he didn't know where Chad was. Mackay said that work at the haunted house usually ended between 12:30 P.M. and 1:00 A.M. but sometimes ended earlier if there weren't many visitors. It was early in the Halloween season, so the haunted house may not have been very busy that night. Is it possible that Chad was driving Alex back to his car when Garth came home? Or was

Chad working on a plan to dispose of Tammy's body that Garth foiled by coming home too early?

Detective David Stubbs's testimony provided the bombshell. While working for the Rexburg Police Department, he served a warrant on Google for Chad Daybell's phone. The warrant return revealed that on January 3, 2019, Chad looked up how to turn off location services on an iPhone. Stubbs testified that the Google warrant returned no location data for Chad's device. He also said that on August 14, 2019, Chad requested his entire location history be deleted. On August 24, 2019, Google complied and deleted Chad's complete location history. This information sealed the prosecution's argument that Chad was involved in the conspiracy and showed his consciousness of guilt. It also explained why Chad's device did not appear on his property on any of the relevant dates.

After eight weeks, both the prosecution and defense rested. The attorneys' exhaustion was evident. John Prior, who did an excellent job of handling the complex case alone, looked weary, and even the four-person prosecution team walked slower as they moved to the podium to question the final witnesses. There was a palpable air of relief when the judge decided to adjourn court on Thursday afternoon and not reconvene until the Tuesday after the Memorial Day holiday. After two final rebuttal witnesses, on Tuesday, the prosecution rested, and the attorneys and the judge began the jury instruction and exhibit conference. At the close of evidence, both sides met with the judge to settle on which jury instructions would be given to the jury. They also reviewed all the exhibits to ensure they were numbered correctly and admitted so that when the jury began their deliberation, they would be sure all the information was correct. Closing arguments were scheduled for Wednesday, May 29, 2024.

Fremont County prosecutor Lindsey Blake gave the closing argument for the state. She masterfully walked through the evidence, reinforcing and reviewing each point, illustrated by a PowerPoint presentation of photos, documents, and video clips. She talked about Chad's need for money, sex, and power. She emphasized all the information that showed how Chad was the one who directed and planned as he shared his visions. During much of the trial, including the state's closing, Chad sat very still, his hands under the table, but his chin tipped up, to lift his nose. Body language experts say that pose indicates disdain. Blake pointed to the lack of remorse or grief from Chad, Lori, or Alex. Over and over, she pointed to the evidence that Chad and Lori wanted everyone out of their way. Over and over, the jury saw that Chad had a plan that didn't include the telestials, Tammy, Tylee, JJ, or Charles.

John Prior promised his closing wouldn't take too much time, but it took longer than he anticipated. He talked about the fact that Chad was not charged in the death of Charles Vallow or the conspiracy to shoot Brandon Boudreaux. Prior said Lori Vallow was entirely to blame for everything. He suggested Chad was Lori's next target. During his defense, he insisted the gun that had shot at Tammy was a paintball gun. Yet in his closing, he insisted that on October 9, 2019, when Alex Cox fired a gun, his target had been Chad and not Tammy. He suggested Lori was after Chad's life insurance but never presented evidence that Chad even had life insurance. Prior complained that Dr. Christensen, who performed Tammy's autopsy, was looking for support for his preconceived theory, claiming confirmation bias. Prior accused Melanie Gibb and David Warwick of being complicit in JJ's death. He insisted Chad was not present when either Tylee's or JJ's bodies were buried, ignoring the fact that Chad had asked that his location data be deleted. He also said the police failed in their investigation. It was a classic shotgun defense, attempting to raise reasonable doubt.

It took just six hours for the jury to return a verdict of guilty.

―――

In all death penalty cases, once there is a guilty verdict, the jury must then decide whether to impose the death penalty. Usually, the defense presents information to the jury to prove the defendant is worth saving from the death penalty. In this case, Chad Daybell shocked everyone by waiving his opportunity to plead for leniency and waiving his opportunity to present a statement or allocution. Instead, John Prior made an opening statement, saying that people and circumstances don't change unless some event changes their trajectory. For Chad, that was meeting Lori Vallow. He called Lori Vallow the bomb that went off in Chad's life. He painted Lori as a four-time married worldly woman who enthralled a naive man. He reminded the jury that he'd asked them during jury selection about the phrase "not all that glitters is gold." He said Lori was a glittering thing, but not gold. Prior urged the jury to evaluate Chad on how he lived his life, not on the choices he made after meeting Lori.

JJ's grandmother, Kay Woodcock, gave a victim impact statement. She talked about bringing JJ home from the hospital. She talked about the hole that was left in her heart and her family. Colby Ryan, Lori's son, also gave a statement, which he ended by saying, "I stand here today, motherless, fatherless, sisterless, and brotherless." Tammy's brothers, Ron, Matthew, Michael, and Benjamin; Ben's wife, Kylee; and sister Samantha Gwilliam all gave statements, as did Tammy's father, Ron Douglas. Tammy's family talked about how much they missed Tammy, and about the Tammy Douglas Daybell Foundation that they started to support children's literacy, a cause that was close to Tammy's heart. The symbol of the foundation is a duck wearing glasses, to remember Tammy's love of reading and raising ducks (https://www.tammydaybellfoundation.com). Annie Cushing, Tylee's aunt, read a statement. She said she reconnected with Tylee in 2018. Annie said Tylee was exacting; accuracy mattered, and she didn't suffer fools. She found Lori's extreme beliefs troubling and didn't want any more to do with Lori but had hoped to develop an adult relationship once Tylee turned eighteen. Chad's children were conspicuously absent from the courtroom.

After the victim impact statements, the jury retired to deliberate. They were sequestered and continued their deliberations into the weekend. On Saturday, June 1, 2024, the jury signaled they had a verdict. The clerk of the court read the lengthy verdict form. Ultimately the jury found the aggravating circumstances necessary to impose the death penalty. For each of the six counts of murder and conspiracy to commit murder, the verdict read, "The aggravating circumstances, when weighed against the mitigating circumstances do not make the imposition of the death penalty unjust." Unlike in Lori's sentencing, Judge Boyce did not address the defendant. He said the victim impact statements had already said it all. He sentenced Chad to death and imposed an additional fifteen-year sentence on each of the insurance fraud cases and ordered that they run concurrent with each other and concurrent with Chad's death sentence. He said he would consider restitution to the insurance companies if presented to him in a later hearing, but that Chad being indigent and sentenced to death made him hesitant to impose financial obligations. The judge advised Chad and his lawyer of the deadlines for post-conviction review. The imposition of the death penalty triggers a mandatory appeal to the Idaho Supreme Court. The judge gaveled court closed.

It is customary for security to be heightened after the verdict is rendered and sentence is imposed, particularly in violent crimes. In the early days of Lori's trial, her feet were shackled to a ring in the floor. Security measures for Lori were relaxed as the trial went on without incident. As the court concluded for the final time and the bailiff intoned, "All rise," much was made online of Chad's failure to stand for the jury and the judge. Many were outraged and accused Chad of disrespect. In truth, John Prior shook Chad's hand, and as Chad tried to stand, it was clear he was restricted by his shackles under the table, probably locked to the same ring in the floor that had held his wife the year before. It was the last day Chad Daybell would wear street clothes or enjoy any measure of freedom.

19

THE NEW JERUSALEM

They exist in the shadows. They talk privately in the hallways of their LDS wards and during meetings in private homes. They attend church regularly but whisper with friends about the coming latter days. They buy guns, food storage, tents, and survival gear. They pack seventy-two-hour bugout bags. They are the ones who will be ready for the callout. They prowl websites like AVOW and treat books like *Visions of Glory* as scripture. Among them are many who believe the early church made a mistake when it abandoned hope for their own theocratic state and tossed their lot in with the United States of America. These are the Deseret Nationalists, yet another subset of neo-fundamentalists like Chad Daybell and Christopher Parrett of AVOW. While Chad Daybell was excommunicated after the bodies of his stepchildren were found buried in his backyard, most neo-fundamentalists are still active members of the church, and many hold influential leadership callings.

Members of The Church of Jesus Christ of Latter-day Saints are, for the most part, kind and faithful. They make good neighbors, and they vehemently deny that their church would ever condone the sort of alt-right behavior the neo-fundamentalists support. But, as we've seen, mainstream LDS doctrine is not that far from where their conservative brethren come down. If mainstream doctrine can be represented by the hands of a clock firmly set at midnight, the neo-fundamentalists are just a tick away at 12:01. The Deseret Nationalists want to undo every social advance the church has made since 1831 and return to the racism and misogyny of Joseph Smith Jr., by force if necessary, and they are gaining ground.

Church leadership often supports these zealots by proxy. Apostles and bishops continue to recommend and endorse Thom Harrison as a popular mental health provider, ignoring his shadow authorship of *Visions of Glory*. The church still employs Avraham Gileadi as a professor at Brigham Young University. Gileadi was a Jewish rabbinical student who converted to the LDS Church in 1972. His area of study was the Old Testament Book of Isaiah. His book *The Last Days: Types and Shadows from the Bible and the Book of Mormon* received criticism from the church because of his analysis of the scripture events leading up to the second coming of Jesus Christ. Gileadi's work studies the prophecies in the biblical Book of Isaiah, finding parallels with the Book of Mormon. He operates a website and an organization called The Isaiah Institute.[1] Like the scholars and preachers in the era that gave rise to Joseph Smith Jr., his teaching and writing are profoundly postmillennial. Gileadi was excommunicated in 1993 for apostasy. In 1996, the church rebaptized him, and he remains a member in good standing.

One of the prophecies from the Book of Isaiah that Gileadi focused on is that of the Davidic Servant. Some scholars say the term refers to Jesus Christ when he returns to rule in the new millennium after the second coming. Others believe the Davidic Servant will be a mortal man serving the church in the end times. Like Thom Harrison, Gileadi has been influential in the neo-fundamentalist Mormon movement. Like the One Mighty and Strong, many have been called the Davidic Servant, including some church presidents.

In October 2023, Spring Thibaudeau and her brother, Brook Hale, fled to Alaska with Spring's son, Blaze Thibaudeau, age sixteen, and her adult daughter, Abigail Snarr, because she believed her son was the Davidic Servant. The party was detained at the Alaska-Canada border, and Spring and Brook were arrested for custodial interference. Spring had become deeply interested in apocalyptic beliefs, especially those of Thom Harrison and *Visions of Glory*. She had recently purchased thousands of dollars' worth of survival gear. Spring's daughter, Abigail, was raised with Spring's increasingly radical ideas. The morning the family absconded, Abigail called her husband, Brayden, claiming she needed to go to the hospital. When he rushed home, he discovered she was packing; she announced that she wanted him to go with them as they fled into the mountains to await the second coming of Jesus Christ. Like the many members of AVOW, Abigail's mother, Spring, was having dreams she interpreted as prophecies. Spring and her husband, Ben, Blaze's father, were estranged. Ben reported Blaze missing and said he feared for his son's safety. He was worried that if Blaze expressed any skepticism or resisted going with them, they might hurt him. The case has many parallels to the Vallow case, and Ben's fear for his son was understandable. Like Lori Vallow, Spring's brother was involved.

Again, we're forced to ask, are these incidents more common, or has it simply become more difficult for the church to control the information? News feeds are filled with stories of the latest LDS scandal, from Hildebrandt and Ballard to the latest sex abuse scandal. In 2023, a jury awarded a Riverside, California, woman $2.28 billion in a sex abuse case that involved her stepfather, who abused her from age five to fourteen, often on LDS Church property. The church was named in the suit and settled their portion for $1 million. The case is one of many. The website Floodlit[2] lists fifty-one confirmed cases; many perpetrators were bishops, elders, or scout leaders. Only three of the perpetrators were female. A religion that is decidedly patriarchal and claims that men are superior to women and controls sexuality with an iron fist seems to breed these offenders. The site acknowledges that these cases are merely the tip of the iceberg because most victims never disclose their abuse, and of those that do, most incidents are never reported to authorities.

Additionally, church leaders are protected from mandatory reporting laws if the information comes to them in their capacity as clergy, which has been very liberally interpreted, particularly in Utah. The LDS Church has no ordained or professionally trained clergy; all LDS Church leaders are laypersons selected from their congregations. A newly appointed bishop is handed a guidebook and nearly unlimited power. Many victims of sexual abuse refuse to report for fear of the stigma attached, particularly if they are young, unmarried women who are required to remain chaste until marriage. In communities like Rexburg, Idaho, where most of the population, including prosecutors and judges, are church members, crimes may be under-prosecuted. There is a temptation to refer the matter to the church for discipline rather than subject a brother or sister to criminal prosecution and public scrutiny.

In response to the modern pressures of twenty-four-hour news cycles and podcasts that offer broad access to viewpoints critical of the church, the church leadership continues trying to control the message as it did before the internet. While many may see it as a laughable attempt to staunch a firehose of information, some don't feel the church is doing enough to keep the faithful on the straight and narrow. These brethren urge the faithful to focus on the end times in part to distract them from their questions about church leaders and motivate them to stay safely in the fold. Because they are useful, the church leadership does not distance themselves from the Christopher Parretts, Thom Harrisons, and Avraham Gileadis of the faith, and it's only when their misbehavior becomes public that they excommunicate the Jodi Hildebrandts, Tim Ballards, and Chad Daybells. Church discipline, including excommunication, is supposed to remain confidential. Chad Daybell's and Tim Ballard's excommunications were leaked to the media. While it's been reported that Lori Vallow was also excommunicated, that information is unconfirmed.

It remains to be seen who will win the battle for the soul of The Church of Jesus Christ of Latter-day Saints. Will the church find a way to outrun its questionable history and modernize, or will the Deseret Nationalists pull the church back into the darkness of its murky history? In the past, such impasses have led to divisions and spin-off denominations. While the church denies it, there is ample evidence that the faithful are leaving the mainstream church in droves. The church can only offset their dwindling numbers by proselytizing heavily in third-world countries. Some leave the church because they can no longer participate in a faith that minimizes the lives of women, the LGBTQ community, and people of color. But many others leave because the church is not orthodox enough. These people present an existential threat to the rest of the world. These are the preppers, the Deseret Nationalists, who stockpile guns and ammunition, believe in blood atonement, and will kill for their beliefs. It's up to the mainstream church leadership to claim their legacy, but so far, they've tried to have it both ways. The church has attempted to walk a tightrope, hoping to appease both sides. So long as they continue to walk that line, people like Chad Daybell and Lori Vallow will rush in to fill the vacuum created by their lack of true leadership.

20

ARIZONA WANTS ME

As Lori Vallow Daybell awaited trial in Idaho, the wheels continued to spin in Arizona. Law enforcement there had never given up seeking justice for Charles Vallow and Brandon Boudreaux. Lori was indicted on June 24, 2021, on conspiracy to commit murder for her part in Charles Vallow's death. On February 24, 2022, she was indicted on charges of conspiring to murder Brandon Boudreaux. The indictment involving Brandon Boudreaux was sealed until after Vallow's Idaho trial. Unlike in Idaho, in Arizona, conspiracy to commit murder does not carry the possibility of the death penalty.

After her July 31, 2023, sentencing, Lori was transferred to the Idaho Department of Corrections Women's Prison in Pocatello, Idaho. The State of Arizona requested she be extradited to answer the charges involving Charles and Brandon. Authorities from Arizona drove to Idaho and picked Lori up. They made the two-day trip back to Arizona in a caravan of two sheriff's SUVs. They reported that as Lori watched the winter landscape roll by and the highway spooled out behind her, she was cheery and talkative.

Lori made her first appearance in Arizona on November 30, 2023. The Maricopa County court granted the prosecutor's request to designate the cases as complex, allowing them extra time to bring Lori to trial. Lori is represented by a public defender and has not waived her right to a speedy trial, and her trial is scheduled for September 1, 2024.

EPILOGUE
GUILTY

LORI VALLOW DAYBELL IS GUILTY

The world did not end in July 2020, and God did not send an earthquake to break her chains and topple the walls of her prison. Instead, Lori will spend the rest of her life behind bars and inside walls. She is guilty of murdering her wild, beautiful, imperfect daughter, Tylee. Guilty of silencing Tylee's songs, her laughter, and her sarcasm. Guilty of stealing Tylee's young adulthood, her college days, her first love, her own opportunities and dreams. Tylee, who was like a second mother to her little brother, will never raise children of her own. Lori stole Tylee's future when she took her life and denied the world all Tylee could have offered.

Lori is guilty of snuffing out the promise of her bright, precious, ebullient, imperfect son, JJ Vallow. Guilty of robbing those who loved him of the right to see him grow up and shine. She is guilty of murdering Tammy Daybell, of denying Tammy's children and grandchildren a beloved mother and grandmother who loved her ducklings to the moon and back. Lori is also accused of stealing Charles Vallow's life and denying a father to Zach, Cole, and Colby, the young men who called him Dad.

Lori will live the remainder of her life amid the fear, chaos, and scarcity of prison, and that is as it should be. There will not be a day when she won't hear the clang of metal gates and barred doors. There will never be silence or comfort. She will dance her life away in her cell to music only she can hear and live in a fantasy where she is a goddess. Her actions did not exalt her. In her strange, twisted reasoning, she robbed the world of warm, vital, and imperfect humans in an attempt to prove she was perfect.

CHAD DAYBELL IS GUILTY.

He deprived his five adult children and their children of their North Star when he murdered their mother. He buried the broken and desecrated bodies of other men's children in his own backyard, then looked out over their graves for months. He, too, will live every day with the cacophony, fear, and stink of prison until the day the state of Idaho issues his death warrant. The process is lengthy and Chad Daybell may very well die in prison before his sentence is carried out. The state of Idaho recently reinstituted death by firing squad, so it is possible that when his death day comes, Chad Daybell may face a firing squad and receive what he did not give when he had Alex Cox do his dirty work; he may get the chance to look his killer in the eye.

None of the deaths Chad and Lori caused will "be a blessing" to the dead, "because they could no longer add additional inequity to their divine ledger,"[1] as Thom Harrison claimed in *Visions of Glory*.

After a long career as a small-town public defender, it is rare that I consider a defendant irredeemable; perhaps it's because I've seen a few surprising success stories in my time. Still, even I can't see how Chad or Lori redeem themselves in this world, or in the next.

All of the might-have-beens amount to this: Lori Vallow and Chad Daybell made choices for others they had no right to make. They were not special, and they were not exalted, and they took from each of their victims their one wild, precious, and imperfect life.

If there is one lesson from this case, it is the resilience of the human heart. It is spring once again in Rexburg, Idaho, and in the backyard of 202 N 1900 E., a shaggy outlier tree bears witness and begins to bud.

ACKNOWLEDGMENTS

W here to begin?

Writing a book is a paradoxical experience. It's a solitary activity that also takes a village, which means I have many people to thank.

First, thanks to my family—the one I was born into and those I've chosen along the way. None of this would have been possible without Carl, my husband of nearly forty years. His steadfast support of all my harebrained ideas is a testament to his love and his resilience. Thanks to my daughter, KJ, who grew up to be a remarkable woman who I think still likes me. I think I have done a few worthy things in life, but giving her to the world is my proudest accomplishment. Thanks also to her husband, Ryan, and the Patterson family for becoming my family, too. Thanks to my chosen sister, AK, and my Gaussoin family, who kept me close and loved and believed in me, even when I didn't.

I also must thank every client I ever represented and every colleague I ever worked with for teaching me daily about life, the law, and myself. This book would not have been possible without every one of you.

Thanks to my agent, Max Sinsheimer, for taking a chance on me, and to Pegasus Books and Jessica Case for your support and patience as we made this book together. Thanks to Lisa Gilliam for her thoughtful copy editing and Julia Romero for letting the world know about the book.

Finally, thanks to everyone in the remarkable True Crime community for caring for the families of the victims who were thrown into this community without choice. Thanks to my early readers, Jayne, Bruce, Aimee, and Julie, to everyone who followed my early newsletters and those who discovered and joined me along the way. Thanks also to the many generous online creators for your encouragement. You've proven the tent is big enough for all of us.

NOTES

1: The Scattered Tribes

1   Fawn Brodie, *No Man Knows My History* (Knopf, 1945), chapter V.

2   Fawn Brodie, *No Man Knows My History* (Knopf, 1945).

3   https://www.churchofjesuschrist.org.

4   https://www.churchofjesuschrist.org.

5   https://www.ldsdiscussions.com/abraham-translation.

6   New Living Translation Bible (Tyndale Publishers, 2008).

7   Doctrine and Covenants 132:34-35, 37a.

8   Doctrine and Covenants 132.

9   Hamilton Gardner, "Communism Among the Mormons," *The Quarterly Journal of Economics* 37, no. 1 (1922).

10   Brigham Young General Conference speech, April 9, 1852.

11   https://www.fairlatterdaysaints.org/answers/Mormonism_and_doctrine/Repudiated_concepts/Adam-God_theory.

12   Joseph Fielding Smith, *Doctrines of Salvation*, 3 vols., ed. Bruce R. McConkie (Salt Lake City: Bookcraft, 1954-56), 1:133-138.

13   *Deseret News,* February 18, 1857.

14   *Utah Historical Quarterly*, January 1958, page 62, footnote 39.

15   https://www.churchofjesuschrist.org.

16   President Lorenzo Snow, 1843.

17   Leon D'Souza, "Room for Reincarnation in LDS Theology?," *The Salt Lake Tribune*, July 30, 2005.

18   George Orwell, *1984* (Harcourt, 1949).

19   https://www.churchofjesuschrist.org/study/manual/gospel-topics-essays/essays?lang=eng.

20   Book of Mormon, 2 Nephi 5.:21.

21   *Times and Seasons*, John Taylor.

2: Somewhere Cold

1   Denver Snuffer, *The Second Comforter: Conversing with the Lord Through the Veil* (Mill Creek Press, 2006).

2   Ibid.

3   Colby and Kelsee Ryan, *The God Over Odds* (independently published, 2022).

4   Ibid.

5   "All men should uphold their governments and owe respect and deference to the law." D&C 134

3: I Can't Get in Touch with My Kids

1   Rex Conner and Adam Cox, *Lori's Lies and Family Ties: Healing from the Tylee and JJ Tragedy* (Many Realms Media, 2023).
2   https://podcasts.apple.com/us/podcast/zion-part-1-translation/id1470764844?i =1000591850392.
3   https://www.churchofjesuchrist.org.
4   April's comment refers to the 1978 Jonestown Massacre in Guyana, where 908 followers of American cult leader Jim Jones drank cyanide-laced Kool-Aid in a mass suicide. Some investigators suggest that not all of the deaths were voluntary, and some followers may have either been injected with poison or forced to drink the mixture.

5: I Shot My Brother-in-Law

1   https://www.eastidahonews.com/2021/10/listen-ex-wife-details-bizarre -relationship-between-alex-cox-and-lori-vallow-daybell/.
2   https://www.newsnationnow.com/crime/jill-kimmel-alex-cox-asked-me-where -to-buy-a-gun/.
3   https://www.churchofjesuschrist.org/.

7: "Lori, where are your children?"

1   *Sins of Our Mother*, Netflix, 2022.

8: Social Media Just Isn't That Social

1   Louis Brandeis, *Other People's Money and How the Bankers Use It* (New York: Frederick A. Stokes Company, 1914), 92.
2   Anne and Doug Bremner, *Justice in the Age of Judgement* (Skyhorse Publishing, 2022).

9: He Can Pierce the Veil

1   Holy Bible, New Living Translation, Matthew 24:36.
2   Chad Daybell, *Living on the Edge of Heaven* (Spring Creek Book Company, 2017), 66, Kindle.
3   Chad Daybell, *Living on the Edge of Heaven* (Spring Creek Book Company, 2017), 185, Kindle.
4   Chad Daybell, *Living on the Edge of Heaven* (Spring Creek Book Company, 2017), 71, Kindle.
5   Chad Daybell, *Living on the Edge of Heaven* (Spring Creek Book Company, 2017), 76, Kindle.
6   Chad Daybell, *Living on the Edge of Heaven* (Spring Creek Book Company, 2017), 185, Kindle.
7   *Desert News*, September 26, 2015.
8   Holy Bible, New Living Translation, Hebrews 12:23.
9   Bruce R. McConkie, *The Promised Messiah* (Desert Books, 1978).
10   Bruce R. McConkie, *A New Witness for the Articles of Faith* (Desert Books, 2985).
11   N. B. Lundwall, *Temples of the Most High* (1941).
12   Journal of Discourses, 7:239.
13   https://docplayer.net/63938125-Possession-by-devils-and-unclean-spirits-by -scott-gillespie-and-kylie-gillespie.html

14   Christopher J. Blythe, blog post: "Dating Chad and Lori's Apocalypse," July 22, 2020.

15   Holy Bible, New Living Translation, Acts 16:25-26.

10: Your Young Men Will See Visions

1   Eric R. Smith and Gregory Christensen, *Multiple Probations—a Lost Doctrine Remembered,* edited by Julie Rowe (independently published, 2020).

2   Interview with *Hidden True Crime* podcast dated August 20, 2021.

3   Eric Smith and Gregory Christensen, *The Church of the Firstborn: Unraveling the Mystery of the Tree* (independently published, 2020), 9.

4   Eric Smith and Gregory Christensen, *The Church of the Firstborn: Unraveling the Mystery of the Tree* (independently published, 2020), 94.

5   Sara M. Patterson, *The September Six and the Struggle for the Soul of Mormonism* (Signature Books, 2023). Quoting David Wright's journals.

6   Sara M. Patterson, *The September Six and the Struggle for the Soul of Mormonism* (Signature Books, 2023).

7   Ibid.

8   Jean B. Bingham, "Endowed with Power" (Brigham Young University Women's Conference, May 2019).

9   Ryan T. Cragun, Bethany Gull and Rick Phillips, *Journal of Religion and Demography* 10 (2023): 162-184.

10   David P. Wright, "Exile to Reconstruction," May 6, 1994.

11   Eric Smith and Gregory Christensen, *The Church of the Firstborn: Unraveling the Mystery of the Tree* (independently published, 2020), 172.

12   Ibid.

13   *Sunstone Magazine,* "Reincarnation in Mormonism," January 1, 2006.

14   Ibid.

15   Journal of Discourses, 6:63.

16   Journal of Discourses, 4:329.

17   Lorenzo Snow, MS 56:49-53; Collected Discourses 3:364-65.

18   Carol Lynn Pearson, *The Ghost of Eternal Polygamy: Haunting the Hearts and Heaven of Mormon Men and Women* (Pivot Point Books, 2016).

19   Sara M. Patterson, *The September Six and the Struggle for the Soul of Mormonism* (Signature Books, 2023).

11: You Will Be Held Accountable for Your Knowledge

1   History of the Church at 4:588.

2   Denver Snuffer, *The Second Comforter: Conversing with the Lord Through the Veil* (Mill Creek Press, 2006).

3   Denver Snuffer, *The Second Comforter: Conversing with the Lord Through the Veil* (Mill Creek Press, 2006), 44.

4   Hidden True Crime YouTube interview https://youtu.be/An85UC7JUIM?si =IqI-LsKBdjHL6HHk.

13: The Long Run-up

1   Idaho Criminal Rule 12(b).

2   ICAR 32.

14: All Rise (Lori's trial) (9016)

1   *State v. Payne*, 199 P.3d 150 (2008).
2   Idaho Rules of Evidence Rule 404 (b)(1).
3   Idaho Rules of Evidence Rule 404 (b)(2).
4   Fawn Brodie, *No Man Knows My History* (Knopf, 1945).
5   https://www.Churchofjesuschrist.org.
6   https://www.Churchofjesuschrist.org.

15: Absolute Power Corrupts

1   Memorandum in Support of Defendant's Motion for Franks Hearing, *Indiana v. Richard Allen*, CAUSE NO. 08C01-2210-MR-0001.
2   https://lunasharkmedia.com/truesunlight.

16: The Visions of Glory and the Bounded Choice

1   Sam Metz, "Utah Man who Killed Family Faced 2020 Abuse Investigation," *AP News*, January 18, 2023.
2   Mormon Civil War, https://www.youtube.com/watch?v=EIkO563Wprk&t=4707s
3   https://www.reddit.com/r/exmormon/comments/17hqwrp/lds_bishop_thom _harrisons_apology_letter_that/.
4   Mormon Civil War podcast https://www.youtube.com/watch?v=EIkO563Wprk.
5   Psychotherapy Networker, https://www.psychotherapynetworker.org/article /leaving-high-demand-high-control-religion January/February 2023.
6   Steven Hassan, *Combating Cult Mind Control* (Freedom of Mind Press, 1988).
7   https://history.churchofjesuschrist.org/media/a-voice-o-warning-by-parly-p -pratt-1837?lang=eng#1.
8   https://www.churchofjesuschrist.org/study/ensign/2012/07/take-your-tents -and-flee?lang=eng.
9   *Dreams, Visions and Testimonies II*, Compiled and edited by Christopher M. Parrett (LDS-AVOW, 2014).
10   https://www.splcenter.org/fighting-hate/extremist-files/ideology/antigovernment -general.
11   Steven Hassan, *Combating Cult Mind Control* (Freedom of Mind Press, 1988).
12   Janja Lalich, "Using the Bounded Choice Model as an Analytical Tool: A Case Study of Heaven's Gate," *Cultic Studies Review* 3, No. 3 (2004).
13   Ibid.

17: Echoes of Narcissus

1   https://www.verywellmind.com/signs-of-a-vulnerable-narcissist-7369901.
2   Chad Daybell, *Living on the Edge of Heaven* (Spring Creek Book Company, 2017), 45, Kindle.
3   Chad Daybell, *Living on the Edge of Heaven* (Spring Creek Book Company, 2017), 51, Kindle.
4   Iyassu, R., Jolley, S., Bebbington, P. et al, "Psychological characteristics of religious delusions," *Social Psychiatry and Psychiatric Epidemiology* 49, 1051–1061 (2014). https://doi.org/10.1007/s00127-013-0811-y.
5   Holy Bible, New Living Translation, Hebrews 11:1.

6   Iyassu, R., Jolley, S., Bebbington, P. et al, "Psychological characteristics of
        religious delusions," *Social Psychiatry and Psychiatric Epidemiology* 49, 1051–1061
        (2014). https://doi.org/10.1007/s00127-013-0811-y.
7   Ibid.
8   Ibid.
9   Ibid.

18: All Rise—Reprise
1   https://www.churchofjesuschrist.org/study/manual/hymns/put-your-shoulder
        -to-the-wheel?lang=eng.
2   https://www.mayoclinic.org/healthy-lifestyle/consumer-health/expert-answers
        /colloidal-silver/faq-20058061.

19: The New Jerusalem
1   https://isaiahinstitute.com/about-us/.
2   https://floodlit.org/accused/.

Epilogue: Guilty
1   John Pontius, *Visions of Glory* (independently published, 2017).

WORKS CITED

Books

1984, George Orwell, Harcourt, 1949.

A Greater Tomorrow, Julie Rowe, Spring Creek Books, 2015.

An Errand for Emma, Chad Daybell, Cedar Fort Publishing, 1999.

An Insider's View of Mormon Origins, Grant H. Palmer, Signature Books, 2002.

CES Letter, Jeremy T. Runnells, CES Foundation, 2012.

Child Victims of Homicide, Christine Alder and Ken Polk, Cambridge University Press, 2001.

Cult Insanity, Irene Spencer, Hachette Book Group, 2009.

Doug's Dilemma, Chad Daybell, Cedar Fort Publishing, 2000.

Dreams, Visions and Testimonies III, Compiled and edited by Christopher M. Parrett, 2014.

Early Mormonism and the Magic World View, D. Michael Quinn, Signature Books, 1998.

Educated, Tara Westover, Random House, 2018.

Escape to Zion, Chad Daybell, Cedar Fort Publishing, 2000.

Feel the Fire, Melanie Gibb, Gibb Publishing, 2019.

God Over Odds, Colby Ryan, 2022.

Handbook of Idaho Criminal and Traffic Laws, Pocket Press, 2021.

I Walked Through Fire to Get Here, Megan Connor, Beyond Publishing 2023.

Justice in the Age of Judgment, Anne Bremner and Doug Bremner, Skyhorse Publishing, 2022.

Leaving Mormonism, Corey Miller, Lynn K. Wilder, Vince Eccles and Latayne C. Scott, Kregel Publications, 2017.

Lighthouse, Jerald and Sandra Tanner, Ronald V. Huggins, Signature Books, 2022.

Living on the Edge of Heaven, Chad Daybell, Spring Creek Book Company, 2017.

Lori's Lies and Family Ties, Rex Connor and Adam Cox, Many Realms Media, 2023.

Mothers Who Kill Their Children, Cheryl L. Meyer and Michelle Oberman, New York University Press, 2001.

Multiple Probations, Eric J. Smith and Gregory P. Christiansen, 2020.

No Man Knows My History, Fawn M. Brodie, Knopf, 1945.

One Foot in the Grave, Chad Daybell, Cedar Fort Publishing, 2001.

Saints, The Standard of Truth, 1815 – 1846, The Church of Jesus Christ of Latter-day Saints, 2018.

Shattered Dreams, Irene Spencer, Hachette Book Group, 2007.
Strangers in Paradox, Margaret and Paul Toscano, Signature Books, 1990.
The Church of the Firstborn, Gregory P. Christiansen and Eric J. Smith, 2020.
The Ghost of Eternal Polygamy, Carol Lynn Pearson, Pivot Point Books, 2016.
The Great Gathering, Chad Daybell, Spring Creek Book Company, 2007.
The Mormon Mirage, Latayne C. Scott, Zondervan, 2009.
The Second Comforter, Denver Snuffer Jr., Mill Creek Press, 2006.
The Sociopath Next Door, Martha Stout Phd., Three Rivers Press, 2005.
Under the Banner of Heaven, Jon Krakauer, Random House, 2004.
Visions of Glory, John Pontius, Cedar Fort Press, 2012.
When the Moon Turns to Blood, Leah Sottile, Twelve, 2022.
Without Conscience, Robert D. Hare, PhD., The Guilford Press, 1993.

YouTube/Podcasts
Defense Diaries
Hidden True Crime
Law and Crime Network
The Lawyer You Know
Mommy Doomsday, Dateline NBC
Mormon Civil War
Mormon Discussions
Mormon Stories
NuanceHoe
Pretty Lies and Alibis
Radio Free Mormon
Silver Linings Podcast